I0821506

ISLAND PASSAGES

THE UNIVERSITY OF GEORGIA PRESS ATHENS

ISLAND PASSAGES

AN ILLUSTRATED HISTORY OF Jekyll Island, Georgia

Jingle Davis PHOTOGRAPHS BY BENJAMIN GALLAND

Publication of this work was made possible, in part, by a generous gift from the University of Georgia Press Friends Fund and by Fran and Richard Lane in memory of his father, Tom Lee Lane.

Unless otherwise noted, all photographs in the book were taken by Benjamin Galland.

Athens, Georgia 30602
www.ugapress.org

Designed by Erin Kirk New
Set in Adobe Garamond Pro
Printed and bound by Four Colour Print Group
The paper in this book meets the guidelines for permanence and durability of the Committee on Production Guidelines for Book Longevity of the Council on Library Resources.

Most University of Georgia Press titles are available from popular e-book vendors.

Printed in China
20 19 18 17 16 C 5 4 3 2 1

Library of Congress Cataloging-in-Publication Data

Names: Davis, Jingle. | Galland, Benjamin.
Title: Island passages : an illustrated history of Jekyll Island, Georgia / Jingle Davis ; photographs by Benjamin Galland.
Description: Athens : The University of Georgia Press, 2016. | Includes bibliographical references and index.
Identifiers: LCCN 2015044562 | ISBN 9780820348698 (hardcover : alkaline paper)
Subjects: LCSH: Jekyll Island (Ga.)—History. | Jekyll Island (Ga.)—History—Pictorial works.
Classification: LCC F292.G58 D375 2016 | DDC 975.8/742—dc23 LC record available at http://lccn.loc.gov/2015044562

To my family, always, and to my friend and favorite wingwoman, Linda White Wood

Contents

Preface

MY BROTHER Jaxon Hice and I grew up on the south end of St. Simons Island in the 1940s and 1950s, just across the mile-wide sound from Jekyll Island. From our bedroom windows, we could see the trunks of individual trees lining Jekyll's beach and, once in a while, an ant-sized person strolling along the strand. When we were small, Jekyll seemed a long way away, although it was closer to our house than St. Simons Elementary, the school we walked back and forth to almost every day.

We got our first close-up look at the island from Jekyll Creek. Jekyll had no causeway at the time, so we went with our parents in their small boat. We anchored in the creek, where everybody else aboard fished for speckled trout. While they watched their corks, I stood on tiptoe on the boat's bow, trying to see as much of the island's interior as I could. The five-story Victorian clubhouse rose among giant live oaks and magnolias like a fairy-tale castle. It had been built in the late 1800s by a group of northern millionaires who belonged to the beyond-exclusive Jekyll Island Club and wintered on the island for more than fifty years. Scattered around the grounds were mansion-sized cottages built by some of the club members. The buildings had been shuttered for most of the 1940s by the time we saw them from the creek. Dad told us stories about some of the millionaires who had vacationed on the island. His favorite was the well-known and possibly apocryphal tale about banker-financier J. Pierpont Morgan, who owned a series of ever-larger yachts that he brought to Jekyll every winter. Another club member once asked Morgan what one of his yachts cost. Dad always chuckled at the arrogance of Morgan's reputed answer: "If you have to ask, you can't afford it."

When they first moved to St. Simons in the 1930s, our parents often fished in Jekyll Creek in winter, when the fish were biting and the millionaires were in residence. Mother remembered seeing exotic French pheasants perched in trees along the shore. The club imported them as game birds, but none adapted to the island's sultry climate. Our parents saw club members riding horses or racing along the beach in little open-air vehicles called Red Bugs. The club's riding stable is now the Jekyll Island Museum, but visitors can still ride horseback on the beach, just as the world's wealthiest people did more than half a century ago. The Red Bugs, at least the motorized variety, were sold to a St. Simons entrepreneur, Brantley O'Quinn, when the club closed, but tiny red mites called red bugs are still ubiquitous on the island, especially in clumps of Spanish moss.

After the state bought Jekyll in 1947, the island opened briefly to the public and then closed for about four years while state convicts cleared overgrown roads, dug drainage ditches, cut brush, and helped prepare Jekyll for more development and visitors. Former governor Herman Talmadge, who opposed the state's purchase of the island, at least in part for political reasons, established Jekyll's convict camp in the early 1950s, which Jaxon and I thought was exciting but which upset our grandmother Bessie, who lived with us. "They'll swim across that sound and steal everything we own," Bessie predicted. She had begun visiting the Georgia sea islands as a child in the late 1800s and was always fascinated by Jekyll, especially its plantation-era history. One of Bessie's aunts married a du Bignon, a member of the aristocratic French family that owned the island for almost a century and grew sea island cotton with slave labor. Today, a memorial on Jekyll honors the hundreds of African captives who were smuggled to Jekyll by two du Bignon brothers in what was probably the last major illegal importation of slaves to the United States.

As a teenager, I dreamed of swimming from St. Simons to Jekyll, something the male beach guards did at the start of the summer season. I wanted to lifeguard on the beach, too, but girls were not considered strong enough to pull drowning swimmers from the ocean. I never swam to Jekyll or worked as a beach guard, but did land a summer job lifeguarding at the clubhouse pool. A state senator rented the clubhouse and ran it as a hotel for a few years. Almost every day at lunchtime, I would explore the fairy-tale castle I had fantasized about as a little girl. The state had replaced a handmade wooden staircase with concrete stairs and metal-pipe handrails, which seemed out of place even to a teenager. There were empty guestrooms and a library full of mildewed books left by club members, whose famous names were scrawled on some of the bookplates. One or two of the cottages were in use, but most, with their dirty, spider-webbed windows and sagging roofs, were vacant. Designed by top architects of their day, the fine old buildings were slowly melting in the humid, salty air. Then and for many years afterward, the state had neither the money nor inclination to restore the historic structures. At one time, members of the state authority appointed to oversee Jekyll considered having the properties condemned, and some of the buildings were razed. Attitudes and economics changed eventually, starting with the complete restoration of the clubhouse by a private partnership that turned it into the elegant Jekyll Island Club Hotel in the late 1980s. A number of the millionaires' cottages, servants' quarters, and other outbuildings have also been restored, and more work is planned. Collectively, they are now the crown jewels of Jekyll's spectacular National Historic Landmark District.

Dad was hired to publicize the state park in the late 1950s. He photographed draglines and bulldozers as they leveled Jekyll's forty-foot-high sand dunes. Photos show Georgia secretary of state Ben Fortson looking on proudly from his wheelchair as work progressed. Fortson, by virtue of his elective office, was a member of the Jekyll Island State Park Authority for many years. In Fortson's era, few people realized that sand dunes were vital to the health of the sea islands.

Dad had big plans for publicizing Jekyll on a small budget. To save money, he recruited me and four teenage girlfriends to line up on Jekyll's freshly bulldozed beachfront, each of us holding the flag of one of the five nations that had claimed the island. I carried the U.S. flag and envied the other girls who got to dress up in the colorful costumes of the countries their flags represented: Spain, France, Great Britain, and the Confederate States of America. When survivors of a highly publicized Canadian mine disaster were invited to spend a week on Jekyll, courtesy of the state, we Flagettes greeted most of them as they got off the buses that brought them to the island. For one of Dad's brochures, he took pictures of my beautiful cousin Carole Langston and me picnicking on Jekyll's beach with our boyfriends. The wind happened to be blowing hard that day, as it often does on Jekyll, and we couldn't eat our sandwiches, because they were filled with more sand than tuna salad. Dad also snapped pictures of us putting on a Jekyll golf green, admiring airplanes at the island's small grass strip, posing on the historic wharf, and sightseeing at other locales on the island. Between the paid lifeguard job and the unpaid modeling gig, I spent a lot of time on Jekyll during my teenage years. In addition, once the causeway to the island opened in 1954, Jekyll became a favorite hangout for area young people. During summer nights on the beach, we built driftwood fires that burned with purple and green flames because phosphorous-laden seawater had soaked into the wood. We walked the beach at night with flashlights, ostensibly searching for loggerhead turtles but really looking for private places to make out with our dates. When we stumbled across a turtle crawl (tracks in the sand), we would follow it to the edge of the dunes to watch a giant loggerhead dig her nest. Loggerhead eggs were a favorite of coastal cooks, who claimed they made wonderful cakes because the whites never hardened, which kept the cakes moist. Loggerheads, along with other rare sea turtles, are now the focus of a major rescue and education program on Jekyll. The turtles still nest on the island's beaches on summer nights, and visitors are invited to accompany center personnel to scout for them.

A group of us teenage girls once held a weekend house party at the Crane Cottage, an Italian Renaissance mansion with seventeen bathrooms. It had been built for Richard Teller Crane Jr., who made his fortune in plumbing fixtures. Even unrestored, the building was beautiful, with whitewashed walls, arched loggias, and rooms that opened onto a central courtyard with a fountain. I won't say we trashed the place—house parties were chaperoned in those days—but every teenager we knew came to party with us. Scores of hyperactive teens milled around the place, spilling food and drinks, leaving wet beach towels on the furniture, and committing other crimes against property. Now, having lunch in the dining room of the beautifully restored Crane Cottage, I cringe at how carelessly we treated the historic building.

Later in life, as a reporter for the *Atlanta Journal and Constitution*, I covered meetings of the Jekyll Island State Park Authority, the board that oversees the island and maps its future. All authority members at the time were elected state officials. Now, all the voting members are appointed by the governor, as they were during the early years of state ownership. There is no doubt that politics played a major role in decision making about Jekyll. It still does. Because authority members are sometimes at odds with island residents, conservation organizations, and others over a variety of issues involving the state park, several watchdog organizations have formed in recent years to monitor ongoing operations on Jekyll and to challenge what they consider unwise decisions. Public oversight of any government entity is always a good thing. Fewer people live full-time on Jekyll now, and many of them are getting older. Younger Georgians need to get involved and take up the slack.

Jekyll is unique among Georgia sea islands. Only four, including the gated and private Sea Island, have causeways. Access to government-owned islands without causeways is limited; the two privately owned sea islands—Little Cumberland and St. Catherines—are not open to the public at all. Jekyll is open to everyone year-round for the modest price of a daily parking fee. The state park attracts millions of annual visitors from Georgia, the rest of the United States, and the world. No matter where they hail from, people who discover Jekyll's natural beauty and rich history tend to return again and again. I know I do. The windows of my home on south St. Simons still offer views of Jekyll, reminding me every day of how lucky we state residents are to own the lush little sea island often called "Georgia's Jewel."

Acknowledgments

THE FOLLOWING PEOPLE provided a variety of help with the book, including scholars who offered information and helped make it understandable, who suggested other experts to consult and topics to explore, and who read and commented on the manuscript or portions thereof. Others told great stories about Jekyll; provided bed, board, good company, and encouragement; and helped in a thousand other ways. They include, in no particular order: my editor, Patrick Allen, and all the staff at the University of Georgia Press; the Hargrett Rare Book and Manuscript Library at the University of Georgia; OCEARCH.com; Wynn Baker, retired flight instructor, Darien; Leslie Faulkenberry, St. Simons; Gretchen Greminger, head archivist, Jekyll Archives; Ben Carswell, conservation director, Jekyll Island State Park Authority; Fred Marland, former chief, Marshlands Protection Division, Georgia Department of Natural Resources, and his wife, Sarita; Steve Engerrand, deputy director, and Kayla Barrett, librarian, Georgia Archives; Mary Jane Reed, owner, G. J. Ford Bookshop, St. Simons Island; Patricia Cofer Barefoot, historian and author, St. Simons and Quarantine Islands; Buddy Sullivan, coastal Georgia historian and author; Sharon E. Mozley-Standridge, Estelle Nuckels, Ed Wallace, and the undergraduate students Lani Green, Brittany Davis, Marissa Barron, and Miranda Anderson, Middle Georgia State College; Zachary Standridge, whose online photograph introduced me to magnetotactic bacteria; Erv Davis, artist, Darien; Hal and Marie Sigman, St. Simons; Larry McDonough Sr., longtime Jekyll resident; Terry Dickson, chief, South Georgia Bureau, *Florida Times-Union*; Larry Evans, architect, Brunswick; Hans Neuhauser, director, Georgia Land Conservation Center; Jim and Pat Bentley, Jekyll;

David Egan, cofounder of the Initiative to Protect Jekyll Island; June Hall McCash, writer, scholar, and Jekyll authority; Dan Chapman, reporter, *Atlanta Journal-Constitution*; Clark Alexander, coastal geologist, Skidaway Institute of Oceanography; Tim Chowns, geologist, University of West Georgia; Chester Jackson, coastal geologist, Georgia Southern University; Mimi Rogers, curator, Coastal Georgia Historical Society; David Dallmeyer, geologist emeritus, University of Georgia; Tim Keyes, wildlife biologist, Coastal Division, Georgia Department of Natural Resources; Jerry Milanich, Timucua expert and former archaeology curator at the Florida Museum of Natural History, University of Florida; Anthony Martin, paleontologist and geologist, Emory University; Ken Sassaman, archaeologist, anthropologist, and Native American pottery expert, University of Florida; John Griffin and Mimi Skelton, friends, St. Simons; Kathie Shinholser, friend and dance aerobics instructor, YWCO, Athens, as well as all the members of her class; Susan Murphy, aerial dance instructor, Meridian, and my former classmates at Susan's studio; my son Ervin, who read every draft of the manuscript and offered suggestions; my son Karl, a historian, who provided research ideas and interpretations; David K. Secrest, Frank Swisher, and, finally, Glenda and Ransom, the rescue dogs.

ISLAND PASSAGES

CHAPTER 1 The Nature of Jekyll

[from c. 50,000 years ago]

JEKYLL ISLAND is geologically unique among the sandy sea islands of the world. Like the larger Golden Isles of coastal Georgia, Jekyll is a composite island, its core dating back fifty thousand to twenty-five thousand years ago to the late Pleistocene epoch. Its beaches, sand dunes, and salt marshes are much younger, washed into existence during the modern Holocene epoch, which began about twelve thousand years ago and continues today. The Holocene parts of Jekyll began forming around five thousand years ago; most are much younger, including the bulk of the island south of the causeway bridge.

The Pleistocene began almost two million years ago. Dinosaurs were long gone, but many large mammals roamed Georgia's coastal plain: giant ground sloths, mammoths, mastodons, prehistoric horses and camels, and other creatures now extinct. Their fossilized teeth and bones are often dredged up in sediments during the deepening of the Brunswick ship channel or are found where sediments have been pumped up to make way for pilings or to build roads.

Ice ages were the chief characteristic of the Pleistocene, a time when the planet cycled through periods of extreme warming and cooling. In the cold times, called glacials, snow falling at higher latitudes did not melt but became compressed into huge polar ice caps. Massive ice sheets covered as much as 30 percent of the earth's surface, locking up vast amounts of water and lowering sea levels worldwide. In warmer times, called interglacials, the ice melted, releasing enormous volumes of water and lifting sea levels again.

The Laurentide Glacier, an ice sheet that appeared about ninety-five thousand years ago, covered more than five million square miles of North America. In parts of Canada, the ice was two miles thick. Its crushing weight carved many of the continent's most distinctive geological features. Laurentide ice reshaped the Great Lakes, dug the track of the Missouri River, and scoured out deep midwestern valleys. The piles of rock and rubble it pushed along, called moraines, built Massachusetts's Cape Cod and New York's Long Island.

Some researchers say forests might have grown on top of the ice, the trees rooted in thick layers of dirt blown onto the glacier over thousands of years by harsh glacial winds. As the great Laurentide moved and fractured, deep crevasses opened, exposing glittering walls of pale blue ice and perhaps plunging mature trees into frigid darkness. Relics of the Laurentide ice sheet still exist as the Barnes Ice Cap in the Arctic Archipelago.

Even during its glory days, the glacier never came close to Jekyll. Its southern limits were the present-day locales of New York and Chicago. Still, the ice sheet played

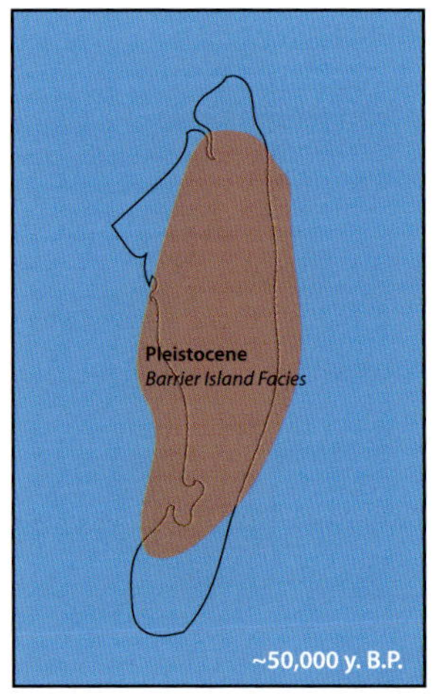

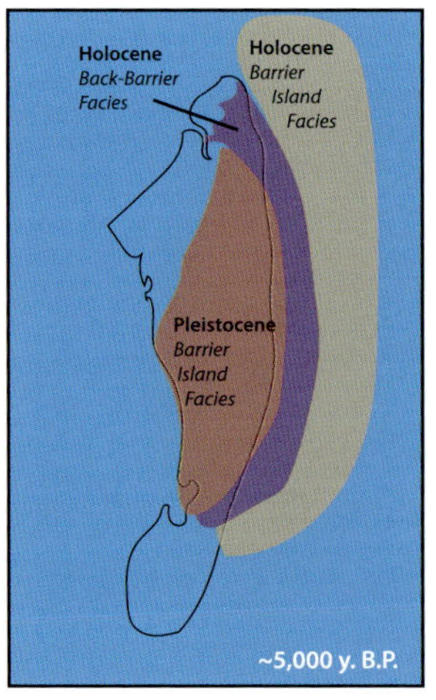

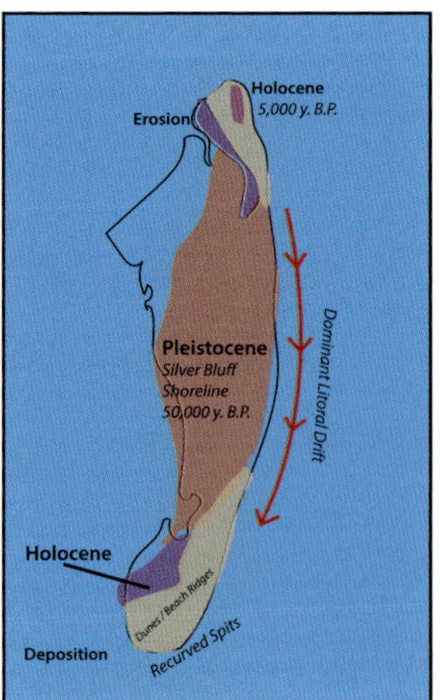

Images of Jekyll showing erosion in geologic time over thousands of years.

a leading role in the configuration of Georgia's modern coast. When the Laurentide locked up masses of water during cold periods, the shoreline of today's Georgia advanced as far as the edge of the continental shelf, about eighty miles east of the present coastline. During warm periods, when the Laurentide melted, the shoreline wandered some sixty-five miles inland from today's coast.

During past interglacials, when sea levels rose slowly or paused in one place for a few thousand years, islands formed at the edge of the ocean. During the 1960s, researchers at the University of Georgia's Marine Institute on Sapelo Island discovered that the sand hills of the lower coastal plain, which extends inland about sixty-five miles, were once sea islands. They were stranded on the mainland when the sea retreated. The oldest and highest documented Pleistocene shoreline in Georgia is the Wicomico (We-COM-e-co). It included an island much longer than any of today's Golden Isles. The island stretched 130 miles from northern Florida to the Altamaha River, eventually blocking the entrance to a 700-square-mile ocean bay. Over time, the saltwater bay became the Okefenokee Swamp, the largest freshwater wetland in the United States. The remains of the giant island, now called Trail Ridge, flank the Okefenokee's eastern side. The Wicomico shoreline is about ninety-five feet higher than the coast today. From the Wicomico, successively younger, lower shorelines parallel the coast, descending toward the Atlantic Ocean like giant stair steps leading to the sea.

The Princess Anne and Silver Bluff shorelines were the last two formed during the Pleistocene. Like their older counterparts, the Princess Anne sand hills now rise gently above Georgia's low-lying coastal plain. The sand hills served for many years as game trails, and prehistoric Indians built villages on their high, dry ground. Modern builders also favor the old shorelines. A Princess Anne island underlies the coastal city of Brunswick as well as a stretch of Interstate 95 between Glynn and McIntosh Counties. The Silver Bluff shoreline, which forms the core of some Georgia sea islands today, is the youngest one formed during the Pleistocene. Jekyll is the smallest Georgia sea island with a Silver Bluff core. The other small Golden Isles—Little Cumberland, Sea Island, Little St. Simons, Blackbeard, Wolf, Wassaw, Tybee, and Little Tybee—are all newer, Holocene islands with no Pleistocene components.

The bulk of Jekyll Island, from half a mile north of the causeway bridge, is Silver Bluff vintage, formed sometime between fifty thousand and twenty-five thousand years ago. When the Laurentide ice sheet reached its glacial maximum, or greatest extent, about twenty thousand years ago, it locked up so much water that the shoreline

Unidentified tabby ruins on the site of the historic Horton House.

dropped to the edge of the continental shelf, about 450 feet lower and about 80 miles east of the coast today. Jekyll and the other Silver Bluff islands were left behind on the mainland, where they remained stranded for several thousand years.

As the massive ice sheet melted, sea levels began rising again. New sea islands formed and rolled inland as storms washed across them, tumbling them backward over themselves. About five thousand years ago, during the Holocene, sea-level rise slowed almost to a standstill just east of, and five or six feet lower than, the old Silver Bluff shoreline. Tidewaters crept up around the Silver Bluff sand hills, including Jekyll's, re-creating them as sea islands. New Holocene land began forming, shaped by wind, tide, and currents. Some attached itself to the older islands.

Tony Martin, the director of environmental science at Emory University, recently discovered a population of freshwater crayfish on Jekyll. Martin said the crayfish could not have crossed miles of tidal marshes and rivers after a group of Silver Bluff sand hills was reborn as Jekyll, since the species cannot tolerate salt water. Martin's theory is that

Mature trees felled by erosion and washed into the marsh by high tides.

the crayfish are descendants of a mainland population that colonized Jekyll thousands of years ago during its sand-hill phase and were later trapped on the island by rising sea levels. Martin, a scientist with a sense of whimsy, imagines the ancestors of the Jekyll crayfish waving good-bye to their mainland counterparts as Jekyll rose once again from the sea. The crayfish on the island have adapted well to their environment. They avoid the salty beach, living instead in woods near freshwater ponds.

Jekyll has undergone radical geological changes in fairly recent times. Clam Creek, which enters the island behind the fishing pier on the north end and angles southeast for about a mile, peters out behind a narrow stretch of beach and low-lying dunes. The area now occupied by the creek once accommodated a much larger waterway, according to Tim Chowns, a geologist at the University of West Georgia. In recent years, Chowns and a team of scientists took core samples on and around Jekyll. They found evidence that the Mackay and Frederica Rivers, large tidal waterways west of St. Simons, once entered the Atlantic by way of an inlet that followed the path of Clam Creek. The inlet, which predated St. Simons Sound, was at least a mile wide

Clam Creek.

and more than twenty feet deep. A long sandspit stretched south from St. Simons to the north side of the inlet that then separated the two islands. The Brunswick River followed a different route then, too. It flowed down the western shore of Jekyll, where Jekyll Creek runs today, and emptied into the Atlantic between Jekyll and Cumberland about half a mile north of Jekyll's present-day causeway. Jekyll's south end had not yet formed; no prehistoric archaeological sites have been found on Jekyll south of the causeway.

About 1,500 years ago, everything changed. Rising sea levels, possibly with help from a major storm, prompted the Brunswick River to break through the sandspit between Jekyll and St. Simons and follow a more direct route to the sea. The river destroyed the sandspit; its sand probably washed south to form the Driftwood Dunes ridge on Jekyll's northeastern end. The Clam Creek area silted up, leaving only the meandering creek and a wedge of marsh to mark its glory days as a full-fledged coastal sound.

After the Brunswick River changed course, a series of comma-shaped dune ridges that today form the south end of Jekyll began building up. All the land south of the Historic District and Captain Wylie Road is a Holocene sandspit backed by Man of War Marsh, which formed in the lee of the spit. Chowns said other inlets along the state's coast adjusted similarly to elevated sea levels and the buildup of new Holocene land, which scientists call the Holocene transgression.

Because Holocene land on Georgia's coast is often five or six feet lower than Silver Bluff, it is generally more vulnerable to erosion than the older, Pleistocene formations. Ironically, Holocene property constitutes some of Georgia's priciest real estate. On Jekyll, the new $50 million convention center and Great Dunes Park are located on the south end, on land that did not exist as recently as

Downed trees on Jekyll's north end, picturesque markers of severe erosion in the area.

1,500 years ago. Exclusive and gated Sea Island, where even modest houses sell for millions of dollars, is a narrow Holocene island that fronts directly on the Atlantic Ocean. Million-dollar houses also line the oceanfront on East Beach, an upscale St. Simons subdivision built on a narrow Holocene fragment. At the moment, Jekyll's south end is the only part of the island still growing, but it is neither as high nor as stable as land formed during the Silver Bluff period. Some of the houses built on south Jekyll since the 1950s were once beachfront; now they are separated from the hard-packed sand beach by more than half a mile, their ocean views blocked by new sand dunes and vegetation.

Although sea-level rise has been fairly slow and constant in recent centuries, studies published in 2013 indicate that global warming is accelerating the rate of rise much faster than scientists had predicted earlier. Some researchers say sea levels will rise about six feet by 2050, enough to inundate low-lying coastal areas worldwide. Carbon dioxide from burning fossil fuels is the main greenhouse gas blamed for global warming, but methane, which is even more effective at trapping heat than CO_2, is another

Jekyll's new convention center, which offers beachfront views.

serious offender. It is produced in part by livestock such as cows, goats, sheep, and other ruminants whose digestive processes generate up to 100 million tons a year of methane gas. This is not the first time ruminants have contributed to global warming. Recent studies indicate that farting dinosaurs similarly affected Earth's climate with their gaseous emissions 150 million years ago.

Like the other Golden Isles, Jekyll has natural advantages that help protect it from hurricanes, tropical storms, and big, beach-eroding waves. A high-pressure weather feature called the Bermuda High forms every summer and deflects tropical systems away from the Georgia coast. Large waves are born far out to sea, but by the time they reach the Golden Isles, they splash onto the beaches as gentle surf. The waves spend much of their energy in crossing the wide, shallow waters of the Georgia Bight, the deep incurve of the continent between Cape Hatteras, North Carolina, and Cape Canaveral, Florida.

The tree canopy on Jekyll's ocean side, sculpted by strong winds and salt air.

Jekyll and its near neighbors are tucked into the westernmost curve of the bight, their longitude close to that of the midwestern city of Cleveland, Ohio. The location puts Jekyll farther away from the Gulf Stream than anyplace else on the Atlantic coast. The stream, a fifty-mile-wide, fast-moving oceanic river, flows around the tip of Florida and follows the edge of the continental shelf to North Carolina, where it bends northeast toward the British Isles and Norway. Hurricanes and other tropical systems that draw energy from warm water tend to track the turquoise stream north, usually passing Jekyll far offshore. The last major hurricane, defined as at least a category 3 storm (wind speeds of 111–129 miles an hour), hit the Georgia coast in 1898. There were no

Two or Three Jekylls

AS ON THE rest of the sea islands, erosion continues to nibble away at parts of Jekyll even as accretion builds up other parts. Experts predict that a hurricane, tropical storm, or even a sustained nor'easter could divide Jekyll into two, or perhaps even three, islands. Researchers say that storm tides could breach the narrow strip of beach and low dunes separating the ocean from the end of Clam Creek, reopening the old inlet and severing the northeastern part of the island from the rest of Jekyll. The island could be breached at other low-lying points, including its narrow waist, where new Holocene land joins the old Pleistocene core. Jekyll's waist was where the Brunswick River once cut through to the ocean—and it is home to the new convention center.

Chester Jackson, a coastal geologist at Georgia Southern University, said new cuts through the island might refill with sand—perhaps rapidly, perhaps over time, perhaps never—but in the meantime, modern developments, historic sites, natural areas, and trails for hiking, biking, and horseback riding could be damaged or destroyed.

The island may have already lost significant sites to the course change of the Brunswick River and ongoing erosion. Destructive though it is, erosion on north Jekyll has created one of the island's most picturesque, poignant, and popular features: the driftwood, or boneyard, beach. Salt water is undercutting a maritime forest on the north end, killing scores of mature trees. The dead oaks and pines eventually topple onto the sand, where their leafless skeletons silver in the sun and salty air. Although the boneyard beach is beloved by photographers and artists, it is a grim reminder that north Jekyll is steadily washing away.

major storms in the twentieth century, and the coast has dodged the big one in the twenty-first century, at least through 2015.

Although surfing-worthy waves are uncommon on Jekyll's beaches except during storms, the Georgia Bight gives the island and its neighbors the most radical tides on the Atlantic Seaboard south of Maine. As a bulge of seawater presses toward the continent on incoming tides, it first meets land at either end of the bight. The water takes the path of least resistance, funneling into the bight and piling up at the westernmost part of the curve, pushing tides as high as nine or ten feet on Jekyll, depending on the phase of the moon. Tides during full and new moons, called spring tides, are the most extreme, rising higher and falling lower than at any other time of the month. Spring tides, which have nothing to do with the season, occur year-round. They are so named

LEFT: The entrance to Clam Creek, which marks the remnants of a much larger coastal sound that once separated Jekyll from St. Simons to the north, predating St. Simons Sound.

RIGHT: High tide at Clam Creek.

because the tide is springing up and down. Neap tides, called nip tides in the colorful Gullah Geechee creole of the coast, are the least radical of the month. When fishermen describe the stage of the tide in coastal Georgia, they say it is ebbing or flooding.

The radical tides of coastal Georgia have graced the state with a broad and luxurious carpet of salt marsh that forms an expansive landscape between the mainland and the sea islands. Although the state's coast is a little more than one hundred miles long, an ornate embroidery of twisting rivers and curving creeks gives Georgia more than nine hundred miles of tidal waterways. Humps of land called hammocks are islands in a sea of marsh that shades from green to gold to lavender with the changing seasons. The hammocks, which range in size from a lone cedar tree and a few shrubs to a thousand acres of forested land, provide refuge for myriad marsh creatures. Diamondback terrapins lay their eggs on hammocks above the high-tide line; egrets and herons roost in hammock trees; raccoons prowl, catching fiddler crabs at the edge of the marsh.

Aside from its stunning beauty, a salt marsh is among the most important and productive acreage in the world, and not only in food production. Marshes buffer the mainland against coastal storms, help control flooding, and filter pollutants. Not many plants can tolerate the harsh conditions between land and sea, but Georgia's dominant

Spectacular view of the Sidney Lanier Bridge, which crosses the Brunswick River between Brunswick and Jekyll.

Fiddler crabs, several species of which colonize Jekyll's marshes.

marsh species, *Spartina alterniflora*, or smooth cordgrass, has adapted perfectly to the twice-daily floods of salt water and corresponding periods of exposure to drying sun and wind. On the ebb tide, water pours out of the marsh through millions of guts and rivulets, creeks and rivers, bearing a rich broth of plant and animal matter that nourishes countless creatures of land, air, and sea. The detritus affects the clarity of inshore waters, making them look dirty, but people now recognize the cloudy olive green as the color of the coastal life-support system. Protected by state law since 1970, Georgia's 700,000 acres of salt marsh represent one-third of the tidal marsh remaining on the Atlantic coast. In spite of laws protecting them, the marshes are still threatened by oily runoff from highways and parking lots, fertilizers and pesticides that flow downriver from inland farms, spills of gas and oil from boat marinas, and the development of marsh-front lots and larger hammocks.

The Glynn County marshes were immortalized in 1879 by the Macon-born writer Sidney Lanier, who praised their beauty in his well-known poem "The Marshes of Glynn." When he worked on his poems, Lanier liked to sit under a live oak tree in Brunswick and look across the wide marshes toward the distant trees of St. Simons and Jekyll. Today, the view includes the soaring Sidney Lanier Bridge, the highest bridge in Georgia. It arches across the Brunswick ship channel on U.S. Highway 17 near the entrance to Jekyll's causeway. The bridge offers stunning views of St. Simons and Jekyll, and St. Simons Sound between the two islands, as well as the marshes of Glynn.

Lanier came to Brunswick to stay with relatives in the hope that his tuberculosis would be cured or at least relieved by the clean, salty air. The poet's disease proved fatal, but the marsh does smell healthy, with its fresh, briny odors of fish and crabs, wet green vegetation, and sulfur-scented mud, the signature perfume of the sea islands.

Jekyll remains the least developed of the four Georgia Golden Isles that are linked to the mainland by causeways. Wildlife watching is a popular pastime for Jekyll residents and visitors. Rare and endangered species find refuge in island marshes and woodlands, freshwater ponds, beaches, tidal waterways, and the ocean. More common creatures, including white-tailed deer and flocks of wild turkey, feed along Jekyll roadsides, in the woods, and in the carefully landscaped yards of private houses, motels, and historic sites. Deer wander everywhere, even on the bare sand beach, probably trying to escape pests such as deerflies and horseflies. The high season for deerflies is May; horseflies hang around through the summer and into fall. Both types breed over damp ground in vegetated areas, which describes a large swath of the coastal landscape.

In early morning and late afternoon, the flies lurk in shady areas under bushes and trees, waiting for an unlucky host to happen by. Mosquito and gnat bites are irritating and itchy; bites from horseflies and deerflies are downright painful. They also bleed, because the flies take chunks of flesh with their scissor-like mandibles. On neighboring Cumberland Island, feral horses called marsh tackies favor the beach, where sea breezes help keep the biting flies away. When the breeze dies, the marsh tackies sometimes wade neck-deep into the ocean to escape the pests.

Some of the island's wildlife is hard to admire because it rarely makes an appearance. David Dallmeyer, a geologist and professor emeritus at the University of Georgia, leads students and others on tours of Jekyll's natural areas. Dallmeyer usually points out the burrows of ghost shrimp on the island's low-tide beach. The burrows are marked by tiny sand volcanoes centered on dime-sized craters. The volcanoes, surrounded by dark, cylindrical fecal pellets that resemble shiny chocolate sprinkles, erupt periodically as the shrimp eject wastes and water from their homes. Ghost shrimp, only a few inches long, dig burrows ten or fifteen feet deep in the damp sand, and then create and maintain a complex network of tunnels at the bottom. It is an astonishing feat of engineering, comparable to a human digging a hole more than 300 feet deep without using tools, then adding extensive corridors far underground.

Ghost shrimp refine their burrows by reinforcing the walls with balls of muddy sand stuck together with shrimp spit. They then smooth the balls, much like a human finishing a rough wall with plaster. Even the most ardent beachcombers rarely see ghost shrimp, because the small creatures spend their lives so far below the surface of the sand. In his book *Life Traces of the Georgia Coast*, Tony Martin describes how fossilized ghost shrimp burrows in the sand hills of Georgia's coastal plain helped Sapelo researchers identify the locations of the state's ancient shorelines.

Higher up on the dry sand beach, larger holes mark the homes of pale ghost crabs, which scurry around, primarily at night, to feed on microscopic plants and animals. Their burrow entrances are ringed by round sand balls containing their wastes. Ghost crabs are speedy little crustaceans whose scientific name means "fast foot" in Greek. A couple who camped one night on a remote Golden Isle beach woke the next morning to find their sleeping bags surrounded by a complicated calligraphy of ghost crab tracks. It was clear that a number of crabs had checked them out during the night, probably to see whether they were edible.

Controversial fauna: the almost-tame, native white-tailed deer on Jekyll Island.

Other invisible beach creatures live in the undulating lines of marsh wrack, dead brown *Spartina* stalks deposited on the upper beach by twice-daily high tides. The wrack line is always filled with a variety of things, natural and unnatural, that wash up routinely on sea island beaches: dead fish and crabs; Styrofoam cups and takeout boxes; fishing floats and tangled balls of monofilament line; the gracefully spiraling egg cases of whelks; brightly colored sea whips, which resemble plants but are related to corals; dead jellyfish; seashells; bits of driftwood crusted with barnacles; and whatever else the tide brings in. On some developed sea islands, beaches were once cleared of marsh wrack to beautify them for tourists, until researchers discovered that the line of dead grass catches blowing sand and helps build dunes. Sand dunes protect the interior of the sea islands from storm winds and tides and are important components in the ecology of the coast.

Georgia's wide coastal plain, representing more than half the area of the state, is composed of deep layers of sand, silt, seashells, and fossilized animal teeth and

Dead marsh grass called marsh wrack piled up at the top of the tide line. A former member of the Jekyll Island State Park Authority thought the wrack was unsightly and had it raked up and removed every day. But in fact, dead grasses trap the blowing sand that builds dunes and helps stabilize Jekyll's ever-moving beaches.

skeletons laid down over millions of years by ancient rivers and seas. The coastal plain is famous worldwide for the variety of whale fossils excavated from its sediments. The fossils are often found during mining operations or large construction projects. When Plant Vogtle, the nuclear power plant near Waynesboro, was being built, scientists unearthed the oldest whale fossil ever found in North America. A model of the forty-million-year-old skeleton, given the scientific name *Georgiacetus vogtlensis* to honor the state and site where it was found, is now on display at Georgia Southern University's museum in Statesboro. The fossil, which resembles the skeleton of a giant alligator more than that of a modern whale, illustrates a link between whales and land mammals. Whales first appeared during the Eocene epoch, which spanned more than twenty million years, ending about thirty-five million years ago.

Large whales still cruise the ocean off Jekyll. Highly endangered North Atlantic right whales migrate south during winter months to bear their calves in the warm shallows east of the island, usually within fifteen miles of shore. They are so named because whalers considered them the "right" whales to hunt: they favored near-shore waters, were buoyant with blubber, moved slowly, and floated after they were killed, making them easy to harvest. The worldwide North Atlantic right whale population is now fewer than four hundred individuals; the whales, which were hunted to the brink of extinction, are still at risk of being killed by ship strikes or entanglement in commercial fishing gear.

In winter, people sometimes spot the fifty-foot-long mother whales and their calves from Jekyll's beach. Researchers with the Georgia Department of Natural Resources photographed a right whale named Foster just a mile south of the island on Valentine's Day 2013. Scientists at the New England Aquarium in Boston who study the whales track them from the air, identifying individuals by the pattern of callosities, or rough patches, on the tops of their heads.

Right whales have calved in Georgia waters for centuries. Early Spanish explorers named one of the sounds flanking Jekyll the Bay of Whales because of the large number of right whales that gathered there every winter. Old maps indicate the name was given to St. Andrews Sound south of Jekyll, but experts today say that St. Simons Sound north of Jekyll was most likely the bay where the whales congregated. Island lore says the whales were so numerous at times in the Bahia de Ballenas, wherever it was, that people could walk from island to island on their broad backs. Other whale species have been recorded in the waters east of Jekyll, including the fin whale, which

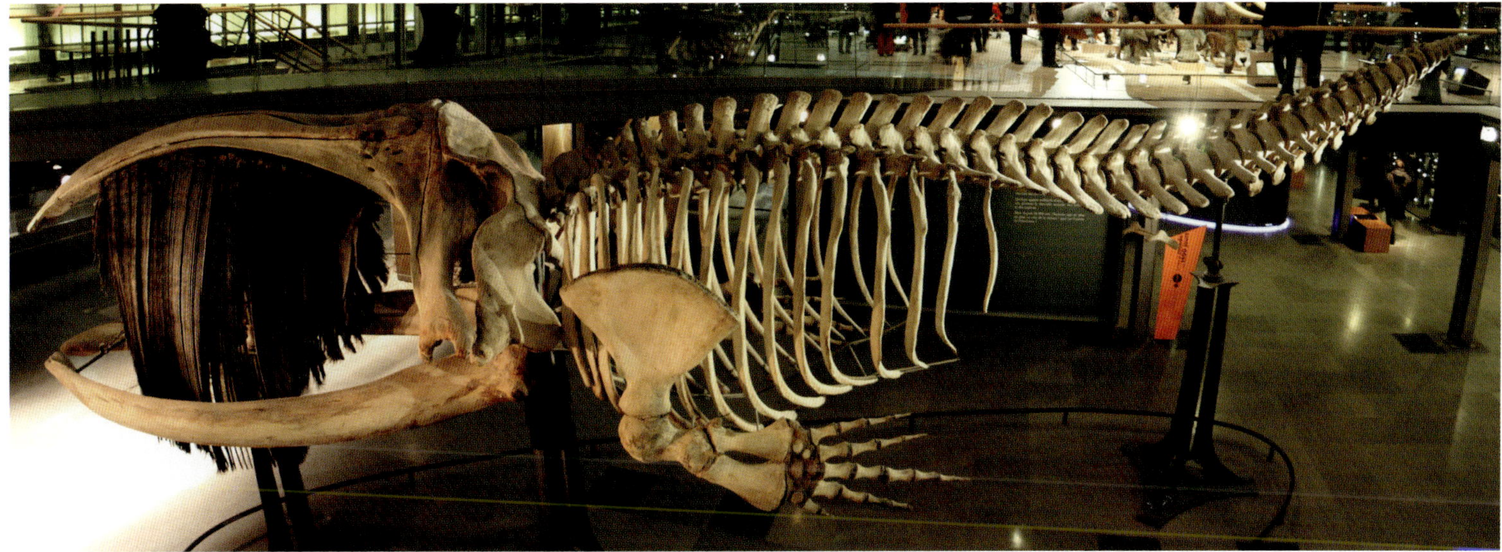

The oldest whale fossil found in Georgia, housed at the science museum at Georgia Southern University in Statesboro. It was given the scientific name *Georgiacetus vogtlensis* to honor the state as well as the site where it was unearthed in 1983 during the building of Plant Vogtle, a nuclear power facility near Waynesboro. *G. vogeltensis* provides a missing link between land mammals and whales. (Thesupermat, Wikimedia Commons)

ranges up to ninety feet long and is the second-longest creature in the world. Only giant blue whales are longer.

Pods of bottlenose dolphins feed near Jekyll's beach and in sounds, tidal creeks, and rivers around the island. Sometimes a pod of dolphins will herd a school of mullet or menhaden onto a muddy riverbank and then propel themselves up the slick mud to feed on the stranded fish before wiggling back into the water. It is against federal law to feed or disturb any marine mammal—penalties range up to twenty thousand dollars per violation, plus jail time—but visitors to Jekyll's south beach have been known to coax dolphins into shallow water by offering them fish. Videos posted on the Internet show people in waist-deep water feeding a dolphin while fascinated spectators taking a tidewater tour of Jekyll watch from a nearby excursion boat.

Human contact with wild creatures can be bad for both. Dolphins that associate with people are more likely to be injured or killed by becoming entangled in fishing gear or swallowing baited fish hooks. Dolphins are large animals with powerful bodies and big teeth. They can behave aggressively toward swimmers who do not supply them with food in areas where they have come to expect it.

Endangered manatees, near relatives of elephants, are gentle tropical giants that feed from April to October in Georgia's coastal waters, most commonly in Camden, Glynn,

A great blue heron flexing his wings as he fishes from the muddy banks of Jekyll Creek.

and McIntosh, the three southernmost coastal counties. In the waters around Jekyll, they feed around boat marinas on aquatic plants and drink freshwater from dock hoses when somebody offers it to them. An Internet video shows people at a Jekyll marina rubbing a large manatee's back and belly. Mature manatees average ten feet in length and weigh up to a ton. The people clearly mean the animal no harm, and the manatee is obviously enjoying the attention, but such activities are illegal, again because they alter natural behavior. Since the slow-moving mammals often loll just under the water's surface, they are frequently injured or killed by whirling boat propellers. They also die from ingesting man-made items. People who boat around Jekyll are advised to keep a careful watch for manatees whenever the animals are likely to be in the area.

Jekyll is listed as one of Georgia's premier birding locales because it is accessible by causeway and because so much of the island remains undeveloped. Hundreds of species of land birds, shorebirds, and seabirds feed, roost, and nest on Jekyll, some seasonally, some year-round. The island, which lies on the Atlantic Flyway, is an important feeding and rest stop for thousands of migratory birds every fall and spring. Resident birds include painted buntings and cardinals, which flaunt their bright colors at island feeders; red-winged blackbirds, which patrol the edges of the marsh; and dun-colored clapper rails, known locally as marsh hens, which weave through the tall cordgrass,

Screech owl. (U.S. Navy photo by Aviation Structural Mechanic [Equipment] Second Class Shanon Kollmar)

occasionally emerging on a muddy creek bank to spear a fiddler crab with their long orange bills. The call of the clapper rail sounds like the creaking of a rusty gate hinge or a small hammer pounding a piece of tin. A pair of ospreys nest regularly on a platform near an island boat launch, the adults peering down haughtily at interloping visitors. If birders arrive at fledging time, they can watch the young ospreys perched on the edge of the nest, teetering back and forth as they work up the courage to test their wings.

At night, Jekyll's woodlands are filled with the voices of owls. Since the nocturnal birds are more often heard than seen, it helps to know what the different species sound like in order to identify them. Barred owls caterwaul, trill, or cry *woo woo woo woooooo*, which the Ornithology Lab at Cornell University translates as *"Who cooks for youuuuuu?"* When they stake out territory, female great horned owls sound like cats meowing. The usual call of both sexes is a muted, harmonic *koooooo*. Barn owls hiss like steam valves and make high-pitched, earsplitting shrieks that sound like saws cutting through metal. They soften the shriek to a purr when they want something, as when a female asks a male for food or when a male tries to coax a female to check out his nesting sites.

The volume of calls produced by small Eastern screech owls suggests they are much larger birds. The owls are misnamed; they do not screech, but whinny like horses or ululate like Middle Eastern women at a wedding. The males and females talk back and forth throughout the night. Humans who mimic their calls can sometimes carry on a conversation with the birds, at least until the owls catch on. The writer William S. Service and his family spent a year caring for an orphaned screech owlet, an experience that Service recounted in his delightfully quirky book *Owl*. He described the bird as about the size of a beer can with the staid personality of a bank president.

Shore- and seabirds often nest in dunes and bare scrapes in sand. In 2007, a grassroots effort led to increased protection for Jekyll's south beach area, where much of the nesting takes place. Volunteers have operated a banding station on the island every autumn for almost four decades, gathering and recording valuable information on small migratory birds that they trap in fine-meshed mist nets spread in brushy swales behind the dunes. After the volunteers fit a bird's leg with a tiny metal bracelet containing identification data, it is released to continue its journey, having contributed another bit of scientific information that might help conserve its species.

Bald eagles, once almost gone from coastal Georgia because the pesticide DDT inhibited their eggshells from developing, again nest around the island. Pelicans dive-bomb fish from above, scooping them up in the wrinkled pouches below their long

bills. Laughing gulls, herring gulls, terns, oystercatchers, and black skimmers work the waves, and sanderlings and sandpipers race up and down the low-tide beach like windup toys, pecking at invisible creatures in the wet sand. Cormorants dive for fish, and anhingas, commonly called water turkeys, pose on Intracoastal Waterway day marks (channel markers on poles), spreading their dark wings to dry.

Common loons, which nest near northern lakes, spend winter months at sea off the Georgia coast, where boaters sometimes spot them. Before laws were enforced to prevent passing ships from dumping oily bilge, loons with gummy, oil-soaked feathers often took refuge on Golden Isles beaches. Jekyll residents tried to rescue many of the oiled birds, cleaning their feathers and keeping them supplied for months with live fish. Loons are large birds with gleaming red eyes and long, intimidating beaks powerful enough to kill a fox, so caring for them takes a bit of courage. One oiled loon that washed up on the beach was named Clair de Loon by its rescuer. It lived for a time in the sandy dog run adjacent to a beach house, gobbling down thirty or more large, live minnows and a squirming eel or two every day. The loon grew so tame that she would take food gently from her hosts' palms. In an interesting predator-prey role reversal, neighborhood cats attracted to the fenced run by the fishy smells soon found themselves scrambling to escape from a large territorial bird. Clair's haunting calls had a lonely, foreign sound, especially when it came time for loons to migrate back to their northern homes. Loons, which are awkward on land, need to take off from water when they fly, so Clair was taken often to a tide pool behind the seawall of loose granite boulders for practice takeoffs. Clair de Loon lived for almost three months before becoming a casualty of the oil. She had ingested large amounts while trying to preen her feathers when swimming to the beach. A necropsy indicated the oil had destroyed her liver, a fate that befell many of the beautiful birds.

The freshwater pond near the old Jekyll Island Amphitheater is a birders' paradise. Endangered wood storks, herons (green, tricolored, little blue), and night herons (yellow-crowned and black-crowned) share roosting or nesting space with egrets (snowy egrets have yellow feet; American egrets' feet are black); white pelicans, which are visitors from Florida; and roseate spoonbills, spectacular tropical wading birds that have recently made an appearance in coastal Georgia.

Roseate spoonbills, immigrants from Florida, summering in the marshes and freshwater ponds of Jekyll. (Courtesy of Melvin Geer)

Rare and Rosy Newcomers

IN THE LATE 1990s, Jekyll and its environs became the summer home for flocks of roseate spoonbills, which feed in pink splendor in the marshes along the Jekyll causeway and on the chocolate-colored mud banks of Jekyll Creek. The birds, refugees from environmental changes in Florida, are still uncommon in Georgia, although their numbers are increasing. Bird-watchers report seeing flocks of more than one hundred spoonbills along the state's coast in recent years.

Tim Keyes, a wildlife biologist with the nongame conservation section of the state Department of Natural Resources in Brunswick, first spotted spoonbills nesting in Georgia in 2011 in St. Marys, a small town on the Georgia-Florida line. As the spoonbill flies, St. Marys and Jekyll are only about twenty miles apart. In 2012, several spoonbill pairs on Jekyll exhibited nesting behavior, the male birds presenting sticks to their partners as part of their courtship ritual, but by 2014, spoonbills had still not nested on the island. Keyes said the Jekyll Island State Park Authority is considering improving nesting habitat on Jekyll to encourage wading birds, including spoonbills and woodstorks, to nest on the island. Wading birds prefer to nest above water in order to reduce the chances that raccoons will raid the nests.

Because of their rosy feathers and size, spoonbills are easy to spot, even for amateur birders. They reach heights of more than thirty inches, with wingspans almost five feet wide. Keyes said the tropical birds are seeking new feeding and nesting habitat in Georgia because so much of Florida's natural hydrology has been altered by human activities, including the draining of wetlands and the dredging of canals to create expensive waterfront property. In addition, many spoonbill nesting sites in Florida have been damaged or destroyed by the hurricanes and tropical storms that regularly rake the peninsula. Spoonbills now spend summers along the length of the Georgia coast, feeding and roosting as far north as the Savannah National Wildlife Refuge on the Georgia–South Carolina line.

Roseate spoonbills were almost wiped out in the United States in the nineteenth and early twentieth centuries by plume hunters who sold the pink feathers for ladies' fans and hats. The birds' numbers have been on the increase since plume hunting was outlawed about a century ago. Now the major threat to spoonbills is destruction of their habitat, along with mosquito control programs, which eliminate some of their food supply.

The rosy birds feed in muddy shallow-water areas such as the banks of Jekyll Creek, using their spoon-shaped bills to filter-feed, sweeping their heads back and forth with great enthusiasm. Their diet consists of algae, small fish, shrimp, crabs, mollusks, aquatic insects, slugs, and aquatic plants. Spoonbill feathers get their rosy glow from the food they eat. Algae contain carotenoids, organic pigments that give carrots, tomatoes, and autumn leaves their color. The more carotenoids a spoonbill consumes, the pinker its plumage.

A great white shark. OCEARCH, a scientific research organization, tracks them around the world; several have cruised near Jekyll during winter months. (Courtesy of Terry Goss, Wikimedia Commons)

On summer nights, Jekyll's beaches provide nesting territory for three-hundred-pound loggerhead sea turtles that lumber ashore to lay their eggs at the edge of the dunes above the high-tide line. Loggerheads are an ancient species; their ancestors probably laid their eggs on Georgia's earliest sea islands. Jekyll is now home to the Georgia Sea Turtle Center, the only facility of its kind in the state and one of the few such centers in the world.

In recent years, scientists have begun tagging and tracking great white sharks in the Atlantic Ocean and beyond, including several that cruise off the Georgia coast. One is named Mary Lee after the mother of a researcher. The shark has her own Twitter account, which alerts her thousands of followers to her whereabouts. Mary Lee is a mature female, sixteen feet long and weighing 3,456 pounds—almost two tons. She was tracked to within a few miles of Jekyll's beach in January 2013. She swam even closer to Jacksonville Beach in northern Florida, entering the surf line a few hundred yards offshore. Officials ordered swimmers out of the water until the giant shark moved on. Another large female, named Katherine, cruised around Cumberland Island in February 2014. Researchers once thought the great whites, which prefer colder waters, might be drawn to the southeastern coast by calving right whales. Now they are not sure; the tracking program is designed to provide researchers with more

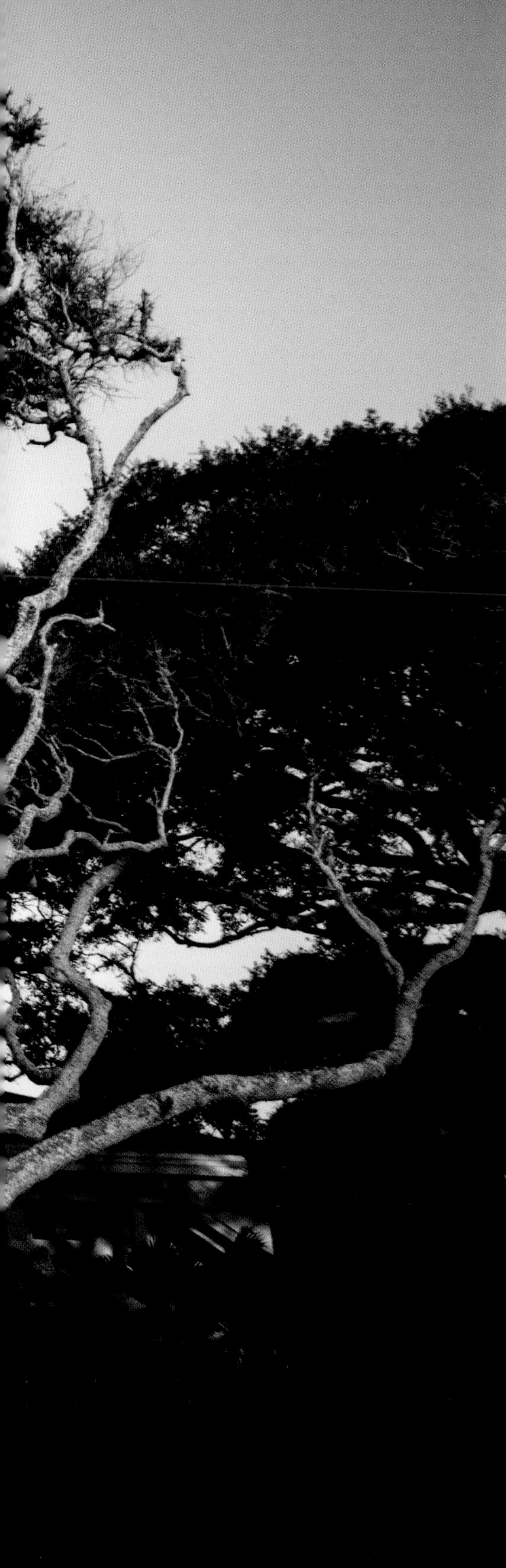

information. Like right whales, great white sharks are listed as an endangered species because their numbers have dropped to critical levels. Scientists say Mary Lee and others of her kind need protection because they are vital parts of the ocean's ecosystem. The OCEARCH website reports the movements and displays pictures of all the sharks they tag. It may reassure locals and visitors to know that the great whites have probably always been off coastal Georgia in winter months, and there has not been a fatal shark attack in Georgia waters since record keeping began more than a century ago.

Great white sharks are the top ocean predators today, but an even bigger shark, *C. megalodon*, occupied an ancient sea that covered Georgia's coastal plain millions of years ago. Its fossilized teeth indicate the gigantic size of the animal: scientists figure ten feet of shark for each inch of tooth, so a shark that grew a seven-inch tooth was longer than a standard freight train boxcar. People find *C. megalodon* teeth and smaller fossilized shark teeth on a narrow crescent of riverine beach near Jekyll's Summer Waves Water Park and in places where erosion or dredging has exposed old sediments. Researchers who study and tag other feared creatures on the island, including diamondback rattlesnakes and alligators, hope to teach people not to kill or molest them, because they also play important roles in island ecology.

The Georgia coast was surveyed in recent years to determine whether sustained wind velocities could support wind farms—installations of giant windmills—to generate clean electricity. Only two areas qualified: the ocean off Tybee Island near Savannah, where sailing events were staged during the 1996 Atlanta Summer Olympics, and the Atlantic off Jekyll Island. Islanders and visitors can observe one effect of Jekyll's brisk ocean breezes. Wind and salt spray have clipped the canopy of the island's ocean-side forest to topiary-like smoothness.

St. Andrews Sound

One of Jekyll's most spectacular natural features flanks the south end of the island. Two and a half miles wide, St. Andrews Sound is a stretch of sparking salt water separating Jekyll and Little Cumberland Islands. The sound, one of Georgia's largest, is wild and beautiful, but many boat captains who travel the Intracoastal Waterway consider it one of the most dangerous stretches to navigate on the entire Eastern Seaboard. A huge underwater sandbar called Horseshoe Shoal blocks direct passage across the sound, requiring captains either to run out into the open ocean through a gantlet of big breakers or else take an alternate route that adds miles to their trips and requires navigation of a marsh creek that is shallow in places, especially at low tide.

The easterly winds that prevail on the Georgia coast always kick up rough water in St. Andrews, especially on the ebb tide, when the wind and tide are in opposition. The most dangerous stretch is near Buoy R 32, a red, lighted beacon that marks the eastern end of Horseshoe Shoal. The buoy sits uncomfortably close to another large sandbar, one of several guarding the mouth of the sound. In recent years, the sandbar has been edging closer to the buoy, forcing boaters to pass west of the marker and closer to Horseshoe Shoal. Trains of big breakers roll through the area, making the narrow passage between the shoal and the sandbars the southern Georgia version of Scylla and Charybdis, the sea monster and giant whirlpool that in Greek mythology guarded the narrow strait between Sicily and the Italian mainland and sent many ships to their doom.

One southbound Intracoastal traveler who planned to cross St. Andrews rounded Jekyll's south end, took one look at the sound's rough water and the breakers near Buoy R 32, and opted for the alternate route. The captain later recorded his impression of St. Andrews on Cruisers' Net, a website for boaters, describing the breakers as "giant elephants." Another mariner who made the crossing on a strong southeast wind likened it to being inside a washing machine. One area towboat captain refuses to answer distress calls from St. Andrews for fear of losing his boat and his life. Local experts advise boaters to wait for favorable conditions to make the crossing or else take the longer, alternate route through Umbrella Cut.

On its best days, St. Andrews Sound is beautiful, its olive-blue waters sequined with sunlight and whitecapped by brisk sea breezes. Views of the sound are spectacular from Jekyll's south beach, especially when dawn tints the water pale pink or winter sunsets drench the swells with gold. Because St. Andrews lies between two mostly undeveloped Georgia sea islands, wildlife rules. Bald eagles soar, trying to steal fish caught by the more enterprising ospreys. An occasional shark fin carves the waves, a reminder that the Deep Hole just south of Buoy R 32 was once a favored fishing spot for large sharks: tigers, hammerheads, and bulls. Today, conservation groups around the world lobby

to protect big sharks because commercial fishing has reduced their numbers to critical levels. St. Andrews Sound has long been rumored to be the premier shark-breeding ground on the Eastern Seaboard, but Susan Shipman, the former chief of the Georgia Department of Natural Resources' Coastal Division in Brunswick, said samplings indicate the shark population in St. Andrews is no greater than in other Georgia sounds, although she agreed that high numbers of juvenile sharks turned up in the samples.

St. Andrews is flanked to the south by Little Cumberland Island, where sand dunes soar fifty or sixty feet above the beach, higher than any other dunes on the Georgia coast. A historic lighthouse, built in 1838 and called St. Andrews Light before the Civil

War, is almost hidden by Little Cumberland's mountains of sand. Only the top few feet of the tower are visible from the south beach of Jekyll, one of two places where the lighthouse can be viewed from land other than on Little Cumberland itself. The lighthouse was deactivated in 1915 and fell into disrepair, but was restored in recent years by the Little Cumberland Island Association and is now listed on the National Register of Historic Places. The association owns the island, limiting membership to one hundred conservation-minded people of means, whose houses are built to blend with the natural surroundings. Little Cumberland is the Holocene younger sister of the near-pristine Cumberland Island National Seashore, and its owners aim to keep 90 percent of the smaller island undeveloped. Little Cumberland and the lighthouse are private, open only to association members and their invited guests. Although all Georgia beaches below the high-tide mark are public, regulations prevent powerboats from coming within one thousand feet of many sea island beaches.

Raccoon Key offers the only other land view of the Little Cumberland lighthouse and St. Andrews Sound. The key, which is surrounded by marsh in the sheltered western reaches of the sound, is accessible only by boat. During the 1940s, the 1,750-acre, low-lying marsh island was owned by a commercial seafood producer who built half a dozen impoundments in the marsh to raise fish, shrimp, lobsters, and crayfish. The long-abandoned seafood farm is now open for day trips or conferences at the lodge, which sits beside the largest of the freshwater lakes. The lakes are stocked with bream and bass. Raccoon Key also boasts a narrow shell-strewn beach and great bird- and wildlife watching, including the occasional alligator, manatee, and large populations of raccoons and pelicans. Boat trips to the key are offered at the Jekyll Marina.

The Satilla River is St. Andrews's major distributary. The blackwater stream rises in Ben Hill County near Fitzgerald and meanders for 235 scenic miles across Georgia's coastal plain. Stained by tannic acid leached from decaying vegetation, the Satilla's water is the dark red color of Burgundy as it flows over sugar-white sandbars, shading to black in the deeps. During the early days of European exploration, mariners braved St. Andrews Sound in order to fill their ships' casks from the Satilla, because the acidulated water was slow to spoil on long sea voyages.

CHAPTER II Jekyll Natives and Newcomers

[c. 12,000 years ago to 1735]

NOMADIC PALEOINDIANS roamed the Southeast at least twelve thousand years ago, when Jekyll, like the other Silver Bluff islands, was a sand hill on the mainland. In those days, the climate was much drier and colder than now, and early people moved often to find fresh water and food. Paleoindians were hunter-gatherers who traveled in small family groups, searching for big game such as mastodons, woolly mammoths, giant land tortoises, elephants, camels, and buffalo, and gathering plants, berries, and roots as food. To date, no artifacts from the period have been found on any sea island, possibly because the material has been deeply buried over time.

During the Late Archaic period, from about five thousand to three thousand years ago, people began settling on the coast, which may have borne only a slight resemblance to the Georgia coast today. The coastal geologist Tim Chowns of the University of West Georgia believes that all the Georgia sea islands, including Jekyll, were joined in two long, unbroken strands, one that stretched about seventy miles from modern Tybee Island near Savannah to what was then the south end of Jekyll. The other strand encompassed Cumberland Island and several sea islands in northeastern Florida, including Amelia and St. George.

Sherds of prehistoric Native American pottery unearthed on Jekyll. (Courtesy of the Jekyll Island Museum Archives)

At the time, Chowns says, the ancestral Altamaha River, fed by its major tributaries—the Ogeechee, the Satilla, and the St. Marys, which today marks the easternmost stretch of the Georgia-Florida border—ran west of the two island strands for miles. It carved a broad river valley and emptied into the Atlantic Ocean between Jekyll and Big Cumberland Islands, in the same general location as St. Andrews Sound today. The tons of silt and sand carried downstream by the giant river settled in a huge delta at the mouth of the sound and formed the footing for Little Cumberland Island.

The ancestral Altamaha cleared the path occupied today by a wide band of what Chowns calls "unusually featureless" salt marsh, which separates the Georgia sea islands from the mainland, supporting his theory that the area was once occupied by the giant river's paleovalley. In addition, the Brunswick archaeologist Fred Cook has found cypress tree stumps and Native American artifacts in abundance on the northwestern side of Jekyll, indicating the former presence of a freshwater swamp where salt marsh and tidewaters exist today.

The old floor of the swamp, complete with preserved tree roots, now lies hidden below marsh mud. Cook found projectile points and knives scattered along about a mile of eroding shell bank, indicating that Late Archaic people hunted in the swamp extensively. The oldest of the artifacts dates to about 5,500 years ago; the youngest is about 2,500 years old.

As sea levels rose and storms struck the coast, the ancestral Altamaha and tidewaters eroded the long island strands, carving them into separate islands. Chowns found evidence that Jekyll and St. Simons remained joined as a single island up to several thousand years longer than the rest of the islands. As new inlets opened, salt water invaded the Altamaha's paleovalley, mingling with fresh river water and creating brackish estuaries that provided ideal habitat for fish, shellfish, and a wealth of other marine life. Since the first major breaching of the island strands occurred about the time when people settled on the coast, the newly formed estuarine environment is probably what attracted them. At any rate, Late Archaic people found such a good life on the coast that they formed some of North America's first permanent communities on the sea islands of Georgia.

On Jekyll, the diet of early islanders included deer, wild turkey, bear, and smaller game as well as a variety of wild plants, including nuts, acorns, berries, persimmons, and muscadine grapes. Seafood, especially oysters, was their dietary staple. Oysters were high in protein, plentiful on almost every intertidal creek bank, and easy to

harvest at low tide. The shellfish were also versatile: they could be eaten raw; roasted or steamed in their shells over hot coals; used to make soups and stews; or dried, smoked, and stored for future use. Sharp oyster shells made good hide scrapers and cutting tools.

Late Archaic people left scores of oyster shell mounds on Jekyll, close to the banks of creeks and marshes where they harvested and ate the shellfish. Many of the mounds have long since been covered by topsoil, but cedar trees, which thrive in the alkaline environment created by the shells, often mark the location of old shell mounds. Some of the smaller hammocks, islands in the marshes west of the sea islands, were built up on a foundation of shells colonized over time by shrubs, trees, and wildlife.

Most of the shell mounds were simple kitchen middens, or trash dumps, but Late Archaic people on the southeastern coast also constructed huge circular C-shaped and U-shaped structures, primarily along the coast of South Carolina and Georgia, but also in Florida and Mississippi. Collectively called shell rings, many are massive, several hundred yards in diameter and up to twenty feet high. Since they have been subject to settling, erosion, and other disturbances over the ensuing thousands of years, they were almost certainly even higher when originally built. In addition, many shell rings were raided by colonial settlers, coastal planters, and modern people, who used the shells to make a concrete-like building material called tabby and to pave sandy island roads. Marsh has now encroached on a number of the rings, including two on north St. Simons that may have been built when Jekyll and St. Simons were still a single island or even part of the long island strand. In 2008, an archaeologist conducting a dig on St. Simons found what may be a third shell ring in the marsh east of the island. The Glynn County shell rings will probably become submerged in the next fifty years as sea levels continue to climb. Since the Cannon's Point ring on north St. Simons is the only one that has been explored to date, any archaeological treasures the others might contain will be lost for good.

Some researchers believe that shell rings formed naturally around circular aboriginal villages as the occupants disposed of empty oyster shells behind their homes. But some of the rings either evolved into more than garbage dumps or were built deliberately for ceremonial or practical reasons. Because the rings provided some of the highest land on the low-lying coast, houses and entire villages were built on top of them, above the range of storm tides. The rings no doubt served as lookout points and retreats where sea breezes kept the coastal mosquitoes and sand gnats at bay.

Some experts say the giant rings were built as ceremonial sites of significance and should be listed National Historic Landmarks because the early Native Americans, whose religious beliefs were closely linked to the natural world, conducted important rituals in the center of the rings. They met there with people from other villages and chiefdoms to trade valuables, hear leaders speak, hold religious feasts and dances, and find mates. The size of some rings argues against incidental construction. When rings reached a certain height, it would have been necessary to carry additional shells to the top of them. If the rings were used only for disposal, it would have been much easier to spread the shells on the ground than to carry heavy baskets of them up a slope made of sharp, shifting oyster shells. Whatever their function, shell rings on the southeastern coast predate the pyramids of Egypt and the giant earthen mounds built by southeastern Native Americans inland.

Probably the most impressive invention of the Late Archaic people on the Georgia coast was pottery, the first ever crafted in the Americas. Ken Sassaman, a pottery expert at the University of Florida, is convinced that pottery was initially made on or near St. Simons Island, in part because some of the oldest potsherds found in a shell ring came from the Cannon's Point ring on north St. Simons. Sassaman's theory is that sea island women invented pottery in response to a shortage of the stones they used for cooking. Indian women traditionally cooked food in hollowed soapstone slabs first heated in open fires, or else dropped heated fist-sized stones into cooking vessels—tightly woven baskets or containers made of wood or hide—of food and water. The stones kept soups and stews hot and simmering until the food was cooked. Both methods were forms of cooking with indirect heat; pottery gave Indian women a more efficient way to cook.

Soapstone slabs and boiling stones were hard to come by on the sea islands, which have no natural surface stone. Indian men either had to paddle long distances upriver against strong currents to collect stones, which they used to make weapons and tools, or had to trade valuable items for them. Indian men may not have considered weighty cooking stones a priority.

The raw material for making pottery was available on the coast. Marine clays, different in mineral composition from clays washed downstream from the Piedmont, are abundant in the marshes of Glynn. At first the female potters probably attempted to replicate real stones with artificial stones crafted of clay. There is still debate about how the fake stones were used. Some say fist-sized clay balls were used as boiling stones; others claim the hot clay would have shattered when plunged into colder water. Clay stones might have been used to heat earthen ovens, as real stones were. Over time, Indian women learned to craft shallow bowls of clay that could be filled with food and placed directly over a fire. Direct cooking was a major breakthrough.

As the potters' skill increased, their wares became more elaborate and multifunctional. Indian women learned to temper the clay with Spanish moss in order to keep it from cracking when fired. Later they began using sand or crushed pottery, called grog, as tempering agents. The women used a variety of tools, including corncobs, carved wooden paddles, and sharp-pointed objects, to press, punch, or incise complex and beautiful designs in the damp clay. By the time the first Europeans arrived in coastal Georgia in the early 1500s, the art of making pottery had spread to every part of the

Americas. Archaeological digs on Jekyll have turned up sherds of pottery, including the earliest fiber-tempered type, which was either made on the island or brought there by indigenous people who visited or settled on Jekyll thousands of years ago.

Late Archaic people were well known for their creativity. They used the mortar and pestle, a tool still in use today, for a variety of purposes, including pounding shelled acorns into flour. In autumn, coastal Native Americans gathered carbohydrate-rich acorns in great quantities. Early people favored live oak acorns over other varieties because of their lower content of bitter tannins. After harvesting the acorns available on sea islands—squirrels, deer, birds, and rodents would have taken a large share of the crop—islanders probably paddled to the mainland in dugout canoes in search of more.

The Brunswick archaeologist Fred Cook discovered a major acorn-harvesting site in the Old Town historic district on the southern end of the Brunswick peninsula, only a few miles from Jekyll. After gathering the acorns, Native Americans dried them as quickly as possible in order to prevent mold, turning them so they would dry evenly. They made ingenious use of a natural feature of coastal soil during the drying process, which took several days. They spread the acorns on hides or blankets over patches of Cainhoy soil, which heats up faster than other coastal soils. Sandy Cainhoy is so permeable that water does not collect and evaporate on its surface, which would have a cooling effect. Instead, water drains off quickly, allowing the sun to heat the soil surface. Cook found quantities of Cainhoy at the acorn-harvesting site in Brunswick, suggesting that Native Americans may have used the area as a drying site as well as a harvesting site.

When the acorns were dry, indigenous people shelled them and then pounded them to powder with a mortar and pestle. They leached the acorn flour with cold water to remove tannins and then dried it again for storage. The flour was often used to make small fritter-like cakes.

Smilax was another important food for early people on the Georgia sea islands, where it grows in abundance and today is considered a noxious weed because it is so hard to eradicate from gardens. The plant produces long vines with sharp briars that ramble everywhere, entangling other plants in strands of natural barbed wire. On Jekyll, Native Americans cooked tender smilax shoots and ate them; they are said to taste like fresh asparagus. They also ate the starchy smilax tubers, which grow like potatoes underground. The famed naturalist William Bartram, who visited Georgia sea islands during his travels through the south in the 1700s, said Natives chopped the reddish tubers into pieces, pounded them to powder, mixed the powder with water, and left it to settle. The sediment was drained and dried to a flour, which, when mixed with water and honey and cooled, produced "a beautiful, delicious jelly." Bartram called the plant "conte," but it was usually referred to as "coontie" or "koonti" by southeastern Natives, who may have used the same name for several similar plants, including arrowroot, depending on which was most common in their part of the country. Coontie flour could be mixed with corn flour, patted into small cakes, and fried in fresh bear grease to make "very good hot cakes or fritters," Bartram reported. Native Americans also made sofkee, a pudding-like gruel or thick stew, from smilax flour.

After they began cultivating maize, indigenous people often substituted corn flour for acorn or smilax flour, in part because corn was easier to process. Later, Europeans urged Native Americans to cultivate corn, which the Europeans preferred to wild plant foods. On Jekyll and the other Georgia sea islands, early people grew the so-called three sisters—corn, beans, and pumpkins or squash—but only to a limited extent, because sandy island soil lacks fertility. Coastal Natives may have continued to use acorns and smilax roots to make flour well after people living on fertile farmland in the interior switched to corn flour for most of their needs.

Courtesy of Carsten Niehaus, Wikimedia Commons

For more than five thousand years, Georgia's sea islands have had human occupants. But scholars speculate that indigenous people abandoned the islands for several centuries during a relatively short planetary cold cycle that began about 2,800 years ago, a mere blink of the eye in geological time. Sea levels dropped as much as a dozen vertical feet or more as polar ice sheets expanded. The shoreline crawled eastward across the gently sloping continental shelf, depriving the marshes behind the islands of their lifeblood: the twice-daily influx of tidewater. The estuaries were replaced by freshwater swamps and woodlands, and the rich seafood resources of the coast vanished.

Nobody knows where early people went when they abandoned the sea islands. They could have dispersed inland. Maybe they congregated at the mouths of the Savannah and Altamaha Rivers, where estuaries followed the retreating sea. The shoreline would have looked very different from the coast that native people had known before. Sea islands form only when sea levels are rising, so the newly exposed shore would have been a flat plain of muddy sand with a line of vegetation creeping eastward and expanding the mainland as rains and rivers washed salt from areas formerly covered by the Atlantic.

Over the next few centuries, as the planet warmed, sea levels began climbing again. Salt water invaded the freshwater swamps and woodlands, turning them back into estuaries. When the seafood-rich estuaries returned, so did Native Americans. They may have been the descendants of early sea islanders or people whose ancestors had always lived inland. Jekyll was reoccupied sometime between 2,500 and 1,300 years ago, according to Ray Crook. The newcomers lived in much the same way that people on the sea islands had done since the Late Archaic, hunting, gathering, and harvesting the bountiful resources of the coast.

By the early 1500s, when the first Europeans arrived on the Georgia coast, Jekyll was occupied by the Mocama people. The Mocama were one of many Timucua-speaking groups that occupied about nineteen thousand square miles of southeastern Georgia and northeastern and northern Florida. The archaeologist Jerry Milanich, a Timucua expert, estimates that as many as two hundred thousand people belonged to the confederation before contact.

Like most Native Americans, the Timucua probably had no name for themselves, nothing comparable to terms such as "Americans" or "Georgians." When early European explorers asked what the people called their confederation, they answered, "We are us" or "We live on this land." The French apparently named them "Timucua"

because of a misunderstanding. The name probably derives from "Thimogona," which translates as "terrible enemy." When one of the Frenchmen asked a Mocama chief where he had acquired a silver ingot, the chief answered that it came from Thimogona, meaning from his enemy. The chief had probably acquired the ingot in a raid on an enemy village. Since neither Florida nor southern Georgia have silver deposits, the ingot most likely came from the wreckage of a Spanish treasure ship. The French, who were eager to find the source of the silver, concluded that it had been mined in the land they thought was called "Thimogona."

Language is a defining feature of the Timucua people. It is considered an isolate because it cannot be linked to any other indigenous language in North America. In the Southeast, most Native people spoke Muskogean languages, which are as different from Timucua as Japanese is from English, according to Jerry Milanich. Mocama was a Timucua dialect spoken by people who lived on the sea islands, including Jekyll, and a fringe of coastal mainland, south of the Altamaha River and into today's northeastern Florida. "Mocama" translates as "saltwater people" or "people of the sea."

Although the Timucua language and its dialects are now extinct, they are known today because of work done by Father Francisco Pareja (c. 1570–1628), a talented Franciscan linguist. Based at a Mocama mission in northeastern Florida for more than thirty years, Pareja translated Mocama and eight other Timucua dialects into Spanish so that friars assigned to the scattered missions could teach Catholic catechisms and other church doctrines to people they considered heathens. In 1612, Pareja published a book of translations from a Timucua dialect into Spanish. It was the first book devoted to an indigenous language published in North America. Decades earlier, a Jesuit friar assigned to a Guale mission on St. Catherines Island wrote a dictionary translating Guale into Spanish, but the book was never published and has never been found. The Timucua mission

friars, using Pareja's book and subsequent publications, taught adult Mocama men and women to read and write, often in as little as six months. The Spanish friars were impressed by how quickly the Native people learned a skill that had no precedent in their culture.

There is an ongoing debate whether Jekyll ever had a permanent Mocama settlement or mission. Ray Crook said the largest and most important aboriginal sites on the island have never been fully explored. They are located in the same areas as—and in some cases, under—more recent historic sites, including the Jekyll Island Club Hotel and other buildings in the island's National Historic Landmark District. Exploring Native American sites under and around newer historic sites while preserving both would be difficult. Crook found evidence that Jekyll had a council house, a central feature of all aboriginal villages in the Southeast, which suggests a period of lengthy occupation of the island. Even if Jekyll had no mission, Franciscan friars would have visited any Natives living year-round or part-time on the island, and people on Jekyll would have paddled across the mile-wide St. Simons Sound to attend mass at San Buenaventura de Guadalquini, the large Mocama mission established on south St. Simons in the early 1600s.

Where the island meets the marsh.

Like their counterparts on the other sea islands, indigenous people on Jekyll ate great quantities of seafood and game. They employed a unique way of hunting

white-tailed deer. To creep within range of the skittish animals, they covered themselves with deer hides and heads, peering out through the empty eye sockets as they stalked their prey. Native Americans used the inedible parts of land animals and sea creatures to craft tools and decorative items. Long bones became scrapers; triangular shark's teeth served as arrow and spear points. Shiny fish bladders were dried, inflated, painted red, and used as earplugs. Europeans referred to them as carbuncles, or rubies. Whelk shells served as ceremonial drinking cups, or were crafted into hoe blades or signaling horns whose deep bellow carried over long distances. Beads were carved from columellas, the hard central spirals of whelk shells, and gorgets—large pendants worn by Indian men—were crafted from seashells or copper obtained through trade. Shells and items made of shell were popular with indigenous people who lived inland. Islanders traded the prized leaves of yaupon holly, also called cassina (*Ilex vomitoria*), which grows wild on the southern coast, with people inland. The cassina leaves were toasted and then steeped in hot water to make the black drink Native people in the Southeast consumed in great quantities. They then vomited up the liquid in order to purify their bodies. Maintaining a state of purity was essential to southeastern Natives. In trade for toasted cassina leaves, the Mocama received stone, copper, and other desirable items unavailable on the sea islands.

Coastal Natives knitted long seines from plant fibers, weighted them along the bottom with stones, bones, or shells, and pulled them through the shallows. At times they netted more fish than a whole village could consume immediately. They dried the surplus over smoky fires on a high wooden framework the Spanish called a "barbacoa," a name they adopted from indigenous Arawak people in the Caribbean. On Jekyll, people still seine for fish and shrimp on the island's south end, although they use monofilament nets and fill plastic or Styrofoam coolers instead of hand-woven baskets with their catch, and cook it over charcoal or gas-fired grills rather than barbacoas. Visitors today can join summer seining expeditions and other year-round activities at Jekyll's 4-H Tidelands Nature Center.

In the first half of the sixteenth century, French and Spanish explorers became the first Europeans to make contact with the Mocama on Jekyll. They gave the island its first documented names.

By the early 1520s, European explorers—Spanish, French, Italian, Portuguese, and others—were regularly sailing up and down the Eastern Seaboard, stopping on sea islands such as Jekyll to replenish supplies of fresh water and food, to capture Native

Naming an Island

NAMING LAND is a way to claim it. The Spanish called Jekyll the Isla de Ballenas, or Whale Island, because of the abundance of North American right whales that calved around the island during winter months. The Satilla River, which flows into St. Andrews Sound south of Jekyll, was called the Great St. Illa a century or two ago. The name "Satilla" is said to be derived from a Spanish surname, but at least one scholar says Native Americans gave the river a name later anglicized to "Satilla." When the Spanish temporarily suspended their settlement efforts in the Southeast, the French moved in and tried to claim the area. The explorer Jean Ribault marked the Satilla River on his charts as the river Somme, and named Jekyll the Ile de la Somme. Since *somme* can be translated as "slumber" or "doze," perhaps Ribault was struck by the sight of the slow-moving, blackwater river and nearby Jekyll dozing under the hot Georgia sun.

Villa Ospo, one of the restored cottages in Jekyll Island's National Historic Landmark District. "Ospo" was once thought to be the name given the island by prehistoric inhabitants. Researchers now believe Ospo was an aboriginal town unrelated to Jekyll.

General James Oglethorpe, Georgia's British founder, gave Jekyll its present-day name. In 1734, he named the island for Sir Joseph Jekyll, an English nobleman and a major financial backer of the Georgia colony. Sir Joseph, however, died before word reached England that a sea island across the Atlantic had been named in his honor. The island's name was routinely misspelled for years, even by the Provincial Council in Savannah in 1765, which dropped the final *l* in a document referencing "Jekyl." The name of the island continued to be spelled with one *l* until an act of the Georgia Legislature in 1929 officially reestablished the official, two-*l* spelling.

There is some evidence that the Mocama people called Jekyll "Peraban." In recent years, the anthropologist John Worth, who specializes in archaeology and ethnohistory at the University of West Florida, discovered a number of documents in the Archives of the Indies in Seville, Spain. The voluminous archives consist of millions of detailed records kept by the early Spanish, describing their sojourns in the New World. In a document collection probably not examined since it was filed centuries ago, Worth found a report listing the coastal Guale and Mocama sea islands or missions from north to south. On the list, Peraban is listed between the missions of Guadalquini on south St. Simons and San Phelipe on north Cumberland, in the same location as Jekyll.

Earlier researchers incorrectly reported Jekyll's Indian name as "Ospo." A number of publications and websites today perpetuate the error. John Worth says Ospo was a Guale Indian village located on Sapelo Island and named for the village chief there. Ospo may later have been relocated farther north up the coast. When chiefs moved to other locales, the names of their villages often moved with them. Based on the erroneous reports, however, a millionaire member of the exclusive Jekyll Island Club named his luxurious, ten-bedroom cottage Villa Ospo when it was built in 1928. Today, one of the charter boats at the Jekyll Marina is called the *Ospo*. The name is now firmly entrenched in the island's history, even though it is unlikely that Ospo was ever Jekyll's name, except in twentieth-century history books.

people and take them away as slaves, and to explore and claim territory on the newfound continent. The first known European settlement in what is now the United States was probably located in coastal Georgia about thirty miles north of Jekyll. There has long been scholarly debate over the location of San Miguel de Gualdape (wall-DOP-ay), but many experts now think it was somewhere near Sapelo Sound between Sapelo and St. Catherines Islands.

A wealthy Spanish sugar planter and judge from Hispaniola, Lucas Vázquez de Ayllón (EYE-on), brought about six hundred people with him on three ships to establish San Miguel de Gualdape in 1526. St. Augustine, Florida, the oldest continuously occupied town in the country today, was founded almost forty years later, and James Oglethorpe, the British general, established the colony of Georgia more than two centuries after the Spanish founding of San Miguel de Gualdape.

The immigrants who accompanied Ayllón included women and children as well as Dominican priests and about three hundred Africans—the first ones brought to the future United States as slaves. The Africans were skilled in a variety of trades. At San Miguel de Gualdape, they staged North America's first known slave uprising in 1526, burning some of the settlement's buildings, including the church, a storeroom, and rough-hewn housing, before fleeing into the woods.

Just a few months after founding the colony, Ayllón and many other settlers had died from illness, unusually harsh winter weather, a shortage of supplies, hostile conflicts with Natives, and starvation. The Europeans refused to eat unfamiliar foods, instead demanding corn from the Natives. At first they supplied it willingly. But when some of the settlers tried to take the corn by force, the Native people killed them. About 150 desperate Spanish survivors set sail for Hispaniola, most likely abandoning the Africans to their fate. Most of them probably perished, but a few may have been captured by Native Americans and enslaved again—at least temporarily. It was common for slaves to gain freedom by marrying into the Native American group that had enslaved them. A skeleton unearthed in coastal Georgia and dated to the time of the Gualdape settlement is of mixed African and Native American ancestry.

The Ayllón colonists imported about one hundred horses and other kinds of livestock to Georgia, some of the first European animals brought to North America. Few if any would have survived. The starving colonists ate most of them, and the Native people no doubt killed any horses that escaped the stew pot. When indigenous people first saw mounted Spaniards, they were terrified, believing them to be part man, part large, four-legged beast.

Hernando de Soto led his expedition through Florida, Georgia, and the Southeast a few decades after the failure of San Miguel de Gualdape, traveling with a large contingent of conquistadores, priests (to minister to the explorers and convert the Native Americans), giant war dogs and horses, and hundreds of pigs, which "multiplied greatly" on the journey, according to a Soto chronicler. Many of the pigs escaped into the woods, where they found an abundance of acorns, roots, and other wild food. Soto also gave breeding pairs to Native chiefs. The Spanish leader's death ended the expedition, but the pigs flourished. Some of the fierce and feral razorback hogs of the southeastern United States are thought to be descendants of Soto's pigs.

Following several ill-fated attempts to colonize the Southeast, the Spanish temporarily abandoned the effort on order of their king. French Huguenots—Protestants fleeing persecution by Catholic monarchs—quickly sailed in to fill the void. The French explorer Jean Ribault led an expedition of three ships to the southeastern coast in 1562. He promised the friendly Natives he met that he would return, and then sailed north along the Georgia coast, renaming the rivers and sea islands he passed.

Ribault's party founded a colony they called Charlesfort, which archaeologists have located on present-day Parris Island, South Carolina, identifying it in part from sherds of French pottery found at the site. While Ribault traveled back to France for additional supplies and colonists, his lieutenant, René de Laudonnière, returned to the expedition's original landing place to build Fort Caroline. France's toehold on the southeastern coast was brief. Neither Charlesfort nor Fort Caroline survived. Ribault was gone much longer than he expected. Starving and desperate, the colonists at Charlesfort sailed for France, becoming hungry enough to eat one of their comrades on the journey.

Fort Caroline lasted less than two years. Pedro Menéndez de Avilés, the Spanish captain who had founded St. Augustine in 1565, stormed the French fortress with his soldiers and killed the occupants. The majority of Ribault's troops escaped the attack because they had sailed south shortly before, intending to invade newly established St. Augustine. Instead, a hurricane wrecked their ships, marooning Ribault and scores of other survivors on a beach south of an inlet. Menéndez spent several days marching his troops from Fort Caroline to the north side of the inlet. Menéndez tricked the French into crossing the inlet in small numbers, and then had his men take them behind sand dunes and slaughter them, out of sight of the remaining French. Ribault himself was among the victims. Catholics at the time believed that Huguenots were heretics aligned with Satan. The massacre site has long been identified as Matanzas Inlet, about fourteen miles south of St. Augustine. "Matanzas" means "killings" or "slaughters" in Spanish.

As Europeans were fighting over territory in the New World, indigenous people were dying in devastating numbers in the Caribbean, Central America, South America, and the Southeast. In the two centuries after Columbus landed in the Bahamas, southeastern Natives were virtually wiped out by diseases imported to the New World by early explorers, settlers, and priests. Indigenous people whose ancestors had crossed the Siberian land bridge thousands of years before the rise of cities in Europe and Asia had no inherited or acquired immunity to such diseases as bubonic plague, smallpox, measles, influenza, or even the common cold. According to recent studies, at least 90 percent of the people native to what is now the southeastern United States died from imported diseases. Powerful indigenous chiefdoms that had lasted for centuries collapsed almost overnight, their people done in by germs and viruses that even their finest warriors had no weapons to combat. Other Native people died from overwork after being conscripted by the Spanish in St. Augustine to grow crops, build roads, operate ferries, and help construct the Castillo de San Marcos, the magnificent coquina and tabby fortress that still stands today. Between the late 1500s and the mid-1600s, Franciscan friars established about 150 Catholic missions in Native villages inland and on the coast, primarily in today's Florida and Georgia. Many bore now-familiar names that were used centuries later for missions in the western United States: San Francisco, San Antonio, San Pedro.

The Native people came under siege from another quarter, one that helped destroy the Spanish mission system for good. Starting in the 1650s, Chichimeco-Westo people, probably driven from their homeland in the north by European expansion, joined forces with British planters in Virginia, and later in the Carolinas, to kidnap slaves from Georgia's most vulnerable interior chiefdoms: those unaligned with the Spanish.

The British supplied the slave raiders with muskets as well as branding irons to mark their captives. In 1661, British-allied Natives launched their first attack on a Spanish mission on the Georgia coast. About one thousand Chichimeco-Westo warriors paddled down the Altamaha River to invade Santo Domingo de Talaje (ta-LA-hay), near today's Darien. The mission, founded in 1598, was an amalgam of two Guale towns, Santo Domingo de Talaje and Asajo (ah-SAH-ho), whose chiefs at the time were brothers. When the Chichimeco-Westo attacked the mission more than half a century later, the missionized Native Americans and the priest at Santo Domingo de Talaje fled to Sapelo Island, pursued by about seventy raiders in a boat they built with wood salvaged from the mission church and convent. The hastily built boat was caught in strong currents in Doboy Sound and swept into the open sea. The boat broke apart, and all on board drowned in sight of the Santo Domingo de Talaje refugees. According to a period account, the refugees shed no tears for their attackers but did admire their valor. The rest of the Chichimeco-Westo retreated inland; many "died of hunger on the roads," according to a Spanish account of the time.

The failure of the raid on the Santo Domingo de Talaje mission must have discouraged the slave raiders, since there were no more attacks on coastal mission villages for some years. Non-missionized interior villages continued to be prime targets, however. Some of the Native Americans known as Yamasees took refuge in the coastal Guale and Mocama provinces, where Spanish soldiers could better protect them. Because the Yamasees refused to convert to Catholicism, the Spanish referred to them as pagans. Two refugee groups, one from the interior town of Colón, were resettled on the west side of St. Simons in about 1660. One village was called Ocotonico, perhaps the name of a Yamasee village or chief; the Spanish named the other village San Simón, a name later anglicized to St. Simons by the British. It is ironic that the island's name today derives from a village occupied by Yamasee people, who were not native to the Georgia coast and whose presence lasted on the island for only a few decades.

Guale people who took refuge on Sapelo Island from the Santo Domingo de Talaje mission were also resettled on St. Simons. That mission, relocated to the island's north end, was renamed Santo Domingo de Asajo, a name change that confused scholars for centuries. Because Asajo and Talaje, the villages incorporated into the original mission near today's Darien, were Guale, researchers concluded incorrectly that precontact St. Simons and Jekyll were both part of the Guale province. Early historians also reported that the Native American name for St. Simons was Asajo, when in fact the island's

Pirates

PIRATES WERE frequent visitors to the Golden Isles. Jekyll legend holds that a buccaneer buried treasure somewhere on the island. According to the legend, the treasure's location was marked with a copper hook set into a tree. Neither the hook nor the treasure has ever been found, but island managers now stage annual hunts for another sort of treasure. They hide colorful handblown glass balls around Jekyll each January and February for residents and visitors to find. Every ball is a unique work of art. They refer to the time on the island when glass fishing floats were used by coastal fishermen in the days before Styrofoam.

Handblown glass balls hidden around the island by Jekyll workers every January and February for residents and visitors to find. The balls, reminiscent of the glass fishing floats once used for fishing nets, also hint at pirate treasure allegedly buried somewhere on Jekyll by seventeenth-century buccaneers who regularly visited Georgia's Golden Isles.

A British privateer known to the Spanish as Thomas Jingle was the leader of a group of pirate captains who planned to attack St. Augustine in 1684. Five of Jingle's eleven ships were scattered by a storm that hit just as the fleet was massing offshore for the attack. A crewman, Andrew Ranson, and ten other pirates rowed ashore in a small boat to steal corn from a Mocama mission south of Jekyll, but were captured by Spanish troops. Jingle led his remaining six ships up the coast to plunder the Golden Isles, stopping on sea islands such as Jekyll to repair his storm-damaged vessels and replenish supplies of fresh water and other provisions.

Ranson was taken to St. Augustine and sentenced to death by garroting. As Ranson was gasping his last, the garrote broke, sparing the pirate's life. Catholic priests claimed Ranson's survival was a miracle and gave him sanctuary. For years, Spanish authorities tried to get the priests to surrender Ranson so that his death sentence could be carried out, but the priests stood firm. When the Spanish later learned the pirate was an accomplished draftsman, they offered him a pardon in return for his help in designing and building the Castillo de San Marco.

Jingle's ships left the Jekyll area and headed for Guale territory north of the Altamaha River, where they spent several weeks planning to besiege the missions of Sapelo Island. Many mission natives from both Guale and Mocama provinces had already relocated from the sea islands to the mainland to escape the buccaneers. Jingle and his crewmen sacked Sapelo's mission village before sailing north to Charleston, leaving the pirate captain Jacob Everson and his frigate behind. Everson and his crew raided the abandoned Mocama mission of San Buenaventura de Guadalquini on south St. Simons, stealing anything of value. The pirates then burned the mission buildings to the ground.

first known name was Guadalquini. Once the Chichimeco-Westo slave raiders began attacking missions as well as non-Christian villages in the interior of Georgia, the Franciscans relocated all the missionized people and other Native refugees to the sea islands, where they were less vulnerable to the slave raiders. But the moves left the refugees vulnerable to another threat.

After the destruction of San Buenaventura de Guadalquini, the Natives of coastal Georgia as well as inland refugees who wanted to tag along were relocated farther south toward St. Augustine, where they would be closer to Spanish troops. After 1684, the Georgia coast was never again occupied by its native Guale and Mocama people.

The Island Refuge

WHEN GEORGIA'S FOUNDER, the British General James Edward Oglethorpe, arrived on St. Simons in 1736 to establish Fort Frederica, he saw fires burning on Jekyll Island. Knowing the island was supposed to be deserted, he explored and found a smoldering campfire in an abandoned Native American village. Oglethorpe followed footprints leading away from the fire until they disappeared into the underbrush.

The identity of the person or people who built the campfire on Jekyll remains a mystery. They might have been Native Americans who had come to the island to hunt or gather seafood but fled when Oglethorpe's ships arrived. Perhaps they were escaped African slaves making their way south from the Carolinas to freedom in Spanish Florida.

After the Georgia coast was abandoned by its original Mocama and Guale inhabitants, sea islands such as Jekyll provided a refuge for displaced and desperate people in a greatly changed and still-changing Southeast. By Oglethorpe's time, the coast had been repopulated by Indians of the Creek and Yamasee nations, neither of which existed before 1492. The Creeks and Yamasees rose from the ruins of small interior chiefdoms—Alachua, Altamaha, Arapaja, Cachipile, Colón, Ichisi, Ocute, Shawnee, and others—in the general area of today's Georgia and Alabama. Unable to maintain their culture or even to produce enough food to keep from starving, the ragtag survivors banded together and agreed to live in peace, even though their chiefdoms might have been bitter enemies in earlier years.

Once the slave raids on Native Americans began in earnest in the Georgia interior during the mid-1600s, some indigenous groups sought protection in coastal Spanish missions. They refused to convert to Catholicism, so the missionaries considered them pagans. By 1663, they had become known as Yamasees, although the origin of the name is still under debate. After the final collapse of Georgia's coastal mission system in 1684, some of the Yamasees migrated to South Carolina, where they joined other Muskogee-speaking people and allied with the British. Others fled south and banded together with Native American fugitives in the Florida outback, who herded cattle, farmed, and fought Europeans. The Spanish called them *cimarrónes*, meaning "runaways" or "wild ones," a name later changed to "Seminoles."

The history of the Creek confederation is similar. Indigenous people from a number of precontact interior chiefdoms joined forces for survival. One group settled in the old Tallahassee mission province centered on the northern Florida–southern Georgia border, miles from the coast, where they could be protected by Spanish troops. When the Natives began dealing with British traders, the Spanish sent soldiers to punish them. To continue their lucrative trade with the British, many of the Natives abandoned their erstwhile Spanish allies and relocated farther north. By 1690, a large group had settled in Middle Georgia near today's Macon at a Scottish trading post on the Ocmulgee River, then known as Ochese Creek. The creek's name was a corruption of "Ichisi," the prehistoric Indian town visited in 1540 by the Spanish conquistador Hernando de Soto. Fur traders began referring to their Native trading partners as Ochese Creek, a name soon shortened to Creek. The Creek confederation was later expanded to include a number of southeastern peoples who spoke one of the Muskogean languages. By the late eighteenth century, the Creek nation was the largest Native American confederation in today's Georgia and Alabama, numbering as many as ten thousand people.

By the time Oglethorpe arrived in Savannah in 1733, most of the indigenous people he encountered were Creeks, Yamasees, or Yamacraws. Georgia's coastal Natives, Mocama and Guale, were long gone. Tomochichi, the Indian leader who helped Oglethorpe acquire land for the colony of Georgia, was Creek-born, but later founded his own small Yamacraw band with Creeks and Yamasees whose ancestry was rooted in a variety of collapsed chiefdoms.

After the British founded Charles Town, now the coastal city of Charleston, South Carolina, the character of the Southeast changed in another major way. Settlers began establishing large and lucrative rice plantations on the Carolina coast. At first they used Native American slaves, most of them kidnapped from interior Georgia, to labor in the rice fields, but they soon began importing slaves from the west coast of Africa who were experts at growing rice in tidewater areas. As an added advantage to the planters, many of the Africans had inherited the sickle-cell trait, which provides partial immunity to malaria, a disease brought to North America by Europeans and spread by the mosquitoes that infested the wetlands of the coast.

By the late 1600s, Spanish Florida had become a haven for African slaves who escaped from Carolina plantations. The first recorded group of eight slaves, including a nursing baby, arrived in St. Augustine in 1687, just three years after the Georgia coast was abandoned by its Native people. Historians have documented more than one hundred Africans who escaped by way of the southbound underground railroad, which predated its more famous and much larger counterpart by almost a century. The railroad to Spanish Florida continued to run through Georgia until after the American Revolution. Instead of hiding in safe houses, Africans who traveled the railroad's coastal route hid from pursuers in the maze of tidal waterways that wind through marshes behind the islands, and on abandoned sea islands such as Jekyll, where they could rest and find fresh water and food. Writing about coastal scout boats used during Georgia's British colonial era, the Reverend Thaddeus Mason Harris noted that the strongly built, ten-oared boats, each armed with three swivel guns—small cannons—were sometimes used to repel "the predatory attempts of runaway slaves who sometimes lurked round and infested the coast."

A few years after Oglethorpe built British forts on St. Simons, Cumberland, and Amelia Islands, the governor of Spanish Florida established a small military outpost a few miles north of the Castillo de San Marcos in St. Augustine. Designed to guard against sneak attacks by the British, the fort was staffed by escaped African slaves who had trained as soldiers at the Castillo. Called Gracia Real de Santa Teresa de Mosé (moh-say), it was the first sanctioned settlement of free black people in what later became the United States. The first Fort Mosé was destroyed in 1740 when Oglethorpe attacked St. Augustine. It was rebuilt a decade later in a slightly different location. Although no trace of either outpost remains aboveground today, Fort Mosé artifacts were recovered by a team led by Kathleen Deagan, an archaeologist at the Florida Museum of Natural History at the University of Florida in Gainesville. The small marsh hammock where the second Fort Mosé was located is now a National Historic Landmark and an important stop on Florida's Black Heritage Trail.

Courtesy of Ebyabe, Wikimedia Commons

Fort Mosé became a beacon of freedom to Carolina slaves, but many never made it to Spanish Florida. A year after the outpost was founded, the notorious Stono Rebellion erupted near Charleston, led by slaves hoping to travel south through Georgia to reach Fort Mosé. The rebellion, named for the river where it began, was the largest colonial uprising in mainland America before the Revolutionary War. The eighty or so slaves involved were ultimately defeated by the Carolina militia. Rebels who were not killed in battle were captured and executed; a few were sold to buyers in the West Indies. The Stono Rebellion led to the passage of the draconian Negro Act of 1740, which imposed severe restrictions on slave movements, assemblies, and education.

CHAPTER III The Struggle for Jekyll

[1736–1800]

WILLIAM HORTON, the soldier-entrepreneur who established the first English settlement on Jekyll and left his indelible mark on the island, was a redhead with a taste for adventure and a desire to succeed. In just a dozen years, he became the right-hand man for the Georgia colony's founder, the British general James Edward Oglethorpe. In 1735, Horton left his wife and two small sons in England to travel with the general and other colonists to Georgia. Unlike Great Britain's other royal colonies in America, Georgia was a bold experiment in eighteenth-century social engineering designed by Oglethorpe after he watched a close friend die in debtors' prison in London. In Georgia, he wanted debtors, the "worthy poor," and other ambitious people to work hard and do well. If the Georgia experiment succeeded, Oglethorpe thought it might offer a way to clean up the dreadful slums of London. He envisioned slum dwellers being shipped to the newest American colony and then given land, tools, and a chance to make something of themselves.

Oglethorpe and other members of the Board of Trustees did not select people from the slums as the initial Georgia colonists, however. They chose them with care, looking for people of good character with a variety of useful skills. In the end, none of those

Tabby ruins of Frederica, the colonial-era fortified town built on St. Simons by Georgia's founder, General James Edward Oglethorpe, in 1736. Oglethorpe's top aide was Major William Horton, who built his plantation on a land grant on Jekyll. When Oglethorpe left for England, he put Horton in charge of the soldiers and civilians at Frederica.

chosen had ever been in debtors' prison, although many were poor and some were from rough neighborhoods. The trustees paid passage for at least half of them; the rest funded their own trips and even brought servants along.

There is no record of why Horton applied to immigrate. He hailed from the rural area of Herefordshire, northwest of London, where he held a responsible, middle-class position as undersheriff. Perhaps he liked the idea of joining the landed gentry. In Georgia, he would have the opportunity to farm virgin territory and create his own estate. All the colonists would receive fifty acres of farmland, plus lots where they could build houses and have small gardens. Because Horton paid his own passage to Georgia, he was eligible for a larger grant, and so petitioned the trustees for land. Noting that Horton was a gentleman worth three thousand pounds, the Trustees awarded him five hundred acres on Jekyll, just south of St. Simons where Oglethorpe planned to establish the fortified town of Frederica. Since Horton received the maximum amount of land awarded initially to any of the Georgia colonists, he was required to bring ten indentured servants to work for him until they served out their terms of indenture, usually about five years. Afterward, they would be free to acquire farmland of their own or to pursue trades. Horton could then contract to import other indentured servants who wanted to come to Georgia.

He lost one of his servants even before his ship left England because of complaints about the woman from the evangelical British brothers John and Charles Wesley. The Wesleys signed up to travel to Georgia on the 220-ton *Symond* with Horton, Oglethorpe, and about two hundred other colonists. The brothers took it upon themselves to monitor and critique the behavior of their fellow passengers. They earned Horton's lasting enmity when they accused his indentured servant, Elizabeth Wheeler, of being a "known drunkard" whom they suspected, for unspecified reasons, of "theft and unchastity." The brothers demanded that Oglethorpe put her ashore, which he did. Although he offered to provide Horton with a replacement servant, Horton was furious at the Wesleys for interfering. He got his revenge by dancing hard on the *Symond*'s deck over the brothers' sleeping quarters in the middle of the night, jolting them awake. Even though he apologized the next day, perhaps at Oglethorpe's instigation, Horton and the Wesleys never got along after that. Since the three men were among the dozen gentlemen who dined daily at Oglethorpe's table on the ship, mealtime conversations must have been a bit strained.

Blocks of eroded tabby, a unique coastal building material made of oyster shells, sand, water, and lime made from burned shells. These mark the location of some of the buildings on the Horton plantation, the site of Georgia's first brewery. Horton produced beer and ale for the soldiers and civilians at Frederica.

The Wesleys, later renowned as the founders of Methodism, the forerunner of the United Methodist Church, were young ministers full of energy and religious fervor. Charles, twenty-eight and newly ordained, had been hired as Oglethorpe's secretary and as the colony's secretary for Indian affairs. He would also preach to the soldiers and settlers at Frederica. John Wesley, the elder brother, agreed to stay for a time in the new town of Savannah as the religious leader of the colony as a whole, although he was unhappy with his assignment. The chief goal of the Wesleys was to convert Native Americans to Christianity. It must have seemed more exciting and rewarding to contemplate saving the souls of people whom they considered savages "of almost a different species," as John Wesley described them, than to preach to their fellow Europeans. Although old paintings depict the Wesleys preaching to indigenous people, neither ever did. Wiser heads may have realized that the brothers, rigid in their beliefs and unrealistic in their expectations, were more likely to stir up trouble with the Natives than convert them.

When the *Symond* was loaded with colonists and supplies, it proceeded to the port town of Cowes to rendezvous with its sister ship, the *London Merchant*, and the

man-of-war *HMS Hawk*, the armed sloop that would escort both ships to America. The *Hawk*, captained by James Gascoigne, was a fast shallow-draft vessel, ideal for navigating the shoal waters of Georgia. The man-of-war design was popular with the military and with coastal outlaws, including pirates who frequented Jekyll and the other Georgia sea islands. Today, a stretch of marsh tucked into the lee of Jekyll's southwestern side is called Man-of-War Marsh, possibly in memory of the small ships that played a significant role in Georgia's colonial history.

The *Symond* and her companions lay at anchor for weeks on the English coast, waiting for favorable weather. During the delay, Oglethorpe tried to keep everyone on board comfortable. He had fresh water brought to the ships so that the passengers could wash their clothes. He ordered flour and "plumbs" so they could have "puddens" as a treat. Even so, the colonists—crowded, bored, ill with a variety of fevers, and eager to start their new lives in Georgia—became contentious and rowdy.

Because Oglethorpe believed his earlier Georgia colonists had gotten sick from drinking rum, he and the other trustees had banned it from the colony, along with both slavery and the ownership of large tracts of land. They also banned lawyers, believing they caused too many problems. The land restriction was to prevent wealthy people from buying up smaller tracts and consolidating them into huge plantations such as those in the Carolinas and Virginia that were worked by thousands of African slaves. Georgia colonists were supposed to perform labor themselves, operating small farms, blacksmithing, baking, candle making, tavern keeping, and engaging in other trades. Those on the *Symond* were a mixed crew: Moravians from today's Czech Republic, kilted Scots Highlanders armed for battle, pacifistic Lutheran Salzburgers driven from their homeland by the Catholic bishop of Salzburg, other German-speaking refugees seeking religious freedom in America, middle-class people such as Horton, a handful of people from the slums of London, and a number of indentured servants. Several men on board were considered gentlemen, including Horton, because they had nice manners and were able to pay their own passages and that of their servants. Male colonists were expected to augment Oglethorpe's regular troops and help defend Georgia from attacks by the Spanish in Florida, French invaders from Louisiana, pirates, hostile Natives, and anyone else who threatened British interests. Horton and some of the others joined Oglethorpe's Forty-Second Regiment of Foot; others functioned as citizen soldiers, called up only when needed.

As thick fog and contrary winds kept the ships at anchor on the British coast, Oglethorpe fretted about the delay. He worried as the provisions on board, intended to feed the colonists during their first winter in Georgia, disappeared at an alarming rate. He had to pay what he considered an "excessive" price in Cowes to replace the depleted food. Another concern was that the colonists would miss the spring planting. Oglethorpe and his fellow trustees expected the colonists to grow their own food for the following year.

Before Oglethorpe made his first trip to America, in 1733, he described Georgia as a delightful Eden offering farmland so rich that crops almost leapt from the ground and livestock grazed unattended on lush, wild savannas. By the second voyage, his descriptions had become more restrained. He informed Horton's group that coastal Georgia was not the paradise he had described to their predecessors. He said the coast was hot and humid in summer and plagued by mosquitoes, flies, and "little red vermin called potato lice that in the summer crawl up the legs of those that lie in the woods." Oglethorpe was referring to the ubiquitous red bugs, or chiggers, that lurk in brushy areas and in the tattered banners of Spanish moss that hang like limp gray flags from trees and fences on the sea islands and the coastal mainland of the Deep South.

The ships finally left for Georgia on December 10, 1735. The wintertime voyage encountered high winds and rough seas. Almost all the passengers, many already suffering from fevers and other maladies, were seasick. They were terrified when huge icy waves swept over the decks and flooded some of the cabins. John Wesley noted that he welcomed the danger because it made the frightened passengers more receptive to his message of salvation, at least until the weather improved. On February 6, 1736, after about eight weeks at sea, Oglethorpe's ships anchored in the mouth of the Savannah River off Tybee Island, about seventeen miles east of Savannah. Oglethorpe had expected the *Symond* and the *London Merchant* to transport the colonists and supplies to St. Simons Island right away, but the captains refused to budge without a guide to navigate the shoal waters of the sound between Jekyll and St. Simons. Until the ships were unloaded, Oglethorpe had to continue paying for their use, which was fast burning up funds earmarked for other needs of the colony. While the general racked his brain for a solution, he allowed the colonists to go ashore every day on a small uninhabited spit of land now called Cockspur Island near Tybee, where they dug a well, found a freshwater pond for washing clothes, and tried to amuse themselves. They spotted an eagle's nest in a tree and cut the tree down, finding an egg containing a young eagle. There is no record of what they did with it.

They enjoyed a little excitement when Tomochichi, the head of the Yamacraw chiefdom, visited the *Symond* and the *London Merchant*, bringing gifts of milk, honey, and venison. Tomochichi was accompanied by his wife Senauke and his nephew and heir, Toonahowee. They were probably the first Native Americans the colonists had ever seen. Tomochichi, exotic, tattooed, and dignified, was then in his nineties. He had been instrumental in helping Oglethorpe negotiate treaties with the Creek nation, his birth tribe, for land the Creeks claimed in Georgia. Oglethorpe and Tomochichi had learned to trust and respect each other.

Oglethorpe had fresh provisions delivered to the ships every day. He was reluctant to let the colonists loose in the rough frontier town of Savannah for fear they would spend all their money and make themselves ill by "drinking drams and eating trash." Impatient to get work started at Frederica, Oglethorpe purchased the entire cargo of the sloop *Midnight* when it arrived from New York, loaded with goods for sale. The deal was contingent on the *Midnight* delivering Horton and the goods to St. Simons. Oglethorpe, already impressed with Horton, had chosen him to manage a work crew of thirty men to begin building Fort Frederica. Horton headed south aboard the

Midnight on Valentine's Day 1736. Oglethorpe followed a few days later on a scout boat accompanied by a group of Tomochichi's Yamacraw, some of whom helped row after the English oarsmen exhausted themselves. The Native Americans alternated long and short pulls on the oars, an efficient and less demanding method of rowing called the Yamasee stroke, which became popular with many European oarsmen on the Georgia coast.

On St. Simons, Oglethorpe laid out the fort and the town on the west side of the island, on a bluff overlooking the Frederica River and the green expanse of marsh between the island and the mainland. It was probably the same site that had been briefly occupied half a century earlier by the Yamasee refugee town of San Simón. Horton and his crew built a large palmetto-thatched shelter to protect Frederica's food and other supplies, as well as similar smaller structures, called booths, to house the colonists until they could construct their own houses. Although Horton reached Frederica in mid-February, he did not have a chance to visit his land, only a few miles away on Jekyll, until April, because of the many duties Oglethorpe assigned him. He soon became the general's top aide and quickly advanced to the rank of regimental major. Once construction of the fort at Frederica was in progress, Horton traveled south with Oglethorpe to establish smaller fortifications on some of the sea islands between St. Simons and the St. Johns River, which empties into the Atlantic east of modern Jacksonville, Florida. Spanish-occupied territory lay south of the St. Johns.

Great Britain had been reluctant to allow development in Georgia; Spain still claimed it, although the Spanish had abandoned the area in 1684 when their Georgia mission system collapsed. The territory had long been called the Debatable Land because it was claimed by Great Britain and France as well as Spain. In the treaty Oglethorpe signed with the Creeks about fifty years later, they ceded the Debatable Land to Great Britain. The territory stretched from the Savannah River south to the St. Johns River, an area that embraced the entire Georgia coast and part of today's northern Florida. Although the Spanish complained when Oglethorpe settled Savannah, just across the river from British South Carolina, they did not retaliate. But the presence of a fortified town on St. Simons and smaller forts on sea islands even closer to Spanish Florida was a different matter. Oglethorpe knew the Spanish would see the new forts as forerunners of a British attack on the Spanish stronghold of St. Augustine. The Georgia trustees were especially reluctant to allow Oglethorpe to expand south of the Altamaha River. The wild coastal land between the Altamaha and the St. Johns—the

Fort Frederica, built in 1736 by Major Horton on nearby St. Simons Island.

location of St. Simons, Little St. Simons, Sea Island, Jekyll, Big Cumberland, Little Cumberland, and Amelia—had been unofficially off-limits to any European country for decades. Oglethorpe believed, or wanted to believe, that his planned military incursions in the Debatable Land were necessary to protect British interests farther north, including newly founded Savannah.

To get around the trustees' ban on settlements south of the Altamaha, Oglethorpe came up with an ingenious plan. He rerouted part of the river, at least on paper. Oglethorpe argued that the mighty Altamaha's southernmost branch emptied into the Atlantic through the mouth of the St. Johns River, a good fifty miles from the Altamaha's main outlet east of Darien. Oglethorpe even provided the trustees with a redrawn map to strengthen his claim, although he knew that he was stretching the range of the Altamaha to the point of absurdity. Oglethorpe often gave his fellow trustees in London misleading or exaggerated information. He even ignored their direct orders to get what he wanted and needed for the colony. His mission, as he saw it, was to make Georgia successful and to protect it from enemies. His argument regarding

Colonial-era map of the Georgia coast showing the location of Jekyll Island. (From John Cary's *New Universal Atlas, containing distinct maps of all the principal states and kingdoms throughout the World* [London, 1808]; Wikimedia Commons)

the Altamaha's southern branch proved convincing. The trustees not only approved the fort on St. Simons but also granted Horton the acreage on Jekyll even farther south, making him the southernmost British landowner in North America at the time. His land lay in the most precarious location of all.

Oglethorpe expected the Spanish to protest. He began a polite correspondence with the governor in St. Augustine, Don Francisco del Moral y Sánchez, to reassure him that he meant the Spanish no harm. Indeed, Oglethorpe said, his aim was to protect the people of St. Augustine. The British general reminded the Spanish governor that the territory between the Altamaha and the St. Johns had become the province of pirates, renegade Natives, and other bad characters. Oglethorpe claimed that his fortifications and troops were designed to keep the outlaws and hostile Natives from crossing the St. Johns into Spanish Florida. In reality, Oglethorpe's goal was to push the Spanish out of North America for good and to claim their land for the English Crown. But he knew he had to proceed with caution in order to avoid provoking outright war between the two countries, which had been edging toward armed conflict for decades, for reasons including their dispute over ownership of land in the New World.

When Oglethorpe and Horton reached the north bank of the St. Johns, they launched armed patrol boats on the river "within earshot of muskets" from a Spanish outpost on the opposite shore. Oglethorpe again demonstrated his trust of Horton, even though he had known him for only a few months. He sent Horton and a major from his regiment to St. Augustine to deliver letters to Don Francisco. Horton and the major must have known the mission was dangerous. The two had planned to borrow horses at the outpost to ride to St. Augustine, but it was deserted. Horton later explained the absence of Spanish soldiers on the south bank of the river: the Spanish were so afraid of attacks from indigenous people that they rarely ventured north of St. Augustine unless they traveled in groups.

After waiting for four days across the river from the outpost, Horton volunteered to walk the forty miles to St. Augustine. He set out along

the beach one morning, accompanied by two servants. It was spring, but the weather was already hot. One of his servants fell by the wayside, so Horton left him behind. He and the other servant reached St. Augustine that same night and were well received, at least at first. Men were sent to fetch the major, still at the outpost, and the fallen servant. The British emissaries delivered Oglethorpe's letters. Horton reported that the residents of St. Augustine, who had been terrified of an impending British attack, regarded Horton's party as "messengers of their deliverance" after Oglethorpe's reassurances were made public. Civilians might have been persuaded by the general's rhetoric, but Don Francisco and other Spanish military officials were unconvinced.

Horton and the major waited for days in St. Augustine for Don Francisco's reply. They were treated as guests and were even invited to a dance one night at the home of a Spanish official, where they enjoyed themselves until three. Early the next morning, they were awakened in their quarters by the town mayor and a troop of armed musketeers. The mayor charged them with spying and placed them under house arrest "on the false pretense that they had been taking plans of the town and castle," Horton wrote, although it is likely that he and the other soldier were indeed at least observing St. Augustine's military fortifications. The castle referred to was the imposing Castillo de San Marcos, the near-impregnable fortress built in the late 1600s and still standing today. After the men were arrested, Don Francisco sent a scout boat north to reconnoiter. Five days later, the exhausted Spanish scouts returned, having rowed the skin off their hands. They reported that the islands and rivers north of the St. Johns were bristling with British troops, new fortifications, and armed patrol boats. When Don Francisco questioned Horton and the major about Oglethorpe's whereabouts and military strength, the major claimed ignorance, but a defiant Horton declined to answer the governor's questions at all, even when Don Francisco threatened to send him to the notorious mines of South America. Horton's reply was arrogant. He told the governor that his British monarch was powerful enough to guarantee his safety. He might have regretted his remarks years later, after the Spanish attacked St. Simons and targeted Horton's plantation on Jekyll during their retreat to St. Augustine.

After Horton and the major promised not spy on the Spanish or try to escape, their guards were removed. The Spanish counted on the fact that it would have been dishonorable for British officers to break their word. Don Francisco met with St. Augustine's war council and then sent Horton and the others back to St. Simons with a request that Oglethorpe himself meet with Spanish representatives. Don Francisco wanted

Jekyll's popular fishing pier, which faces north across St. Simons Sound.

the conference to take place at Frederica so that his envoys could evaluate the military strength of the St. Simons fortification.

Oglethorpe accepted the invitation but set up the meeting on the north end of Jekyll, overlooking the south end of St. Simons, where the guns of Fort St. Simons guarded the sound between the islands. A group of the "genteelist" Scots Highlanders from Darien wined and dined Don Francisco's two Spanish emissaries, accommodating them on Jekyll for almost a week. Since there were no structures on Jekyll—Horton had not yet even visited his island property, much less built his house—Oglethorpe ordered two elegant canvas-walled tents erected. Each was lined with Chinese silk and a delicate mesh fabric called marquisette, perhaps to keep the mosquitoes away and to give the tents a more elegant appearance. The envoys were supplied with servants to address their needs. Oglethorpe had arranged for the troops on south St. Simons to put on a show of military strength by firing cannons and muskets, posing on horseback in the sand dunes in order to make their mounted troops seem larger in number, and marching around, all in full view of the Spaniards.

Oglethorpe invited the envoys to dine aboard the *Hawk* during their stay. While the lavish meal was in progress, Tomochichi, along with his war chief, Hyllispilli, and about thirty angry Yamacraw warriors, stormed aboard, dressed and painted for war. They demanded revenge for an unprovoked attack by Spanish-affiliated Natives on a group of Natives allied with the British. The attackers had killed the boys by dashing their brains out with clubs, taken the men prisoner, raped the women, and murdered one of them. A wounded man escaped and reported the massacre to Tomochichi. The Spanish seemed horrified by the account. They denied any knowledge of the incident but promised to punish the perpetrators if they could be caught. Hyllispilli's dry response was that he heard what the Spanish said, but would believe it when he saw it.

In the end, nothing was settled during the Jekyll conference. Oglethorpe continued negotiations with Don Francisco, and the two signed a treaty in October, each pledging to control their Native American allies and let their governments settle the Debatable Land boundary dispute. Oglethorpe agreed to remove his troops from Amelia Island north of the St. Johns River, on the condition that the Spanish would not occupy the island and that it would be recognized as British territory. Don Francisco signed the treaty, which so enraged the king of Spain that he recalled the governor in disgrace and had him hanged for making too many concessions to the British.

In April, Horton visited his land on Jekyll Island for the first time. Oglethorpe noted that his aide had been so busy that he had not even had time to change clothes since reaching St. Simons. Dirty clothes and all, Horton took a scout boat to the island, named by Oglethorpe for Sir Joseph Jekyll, a major financial supporter of the Georgia colony. Scout boats were an important form of transportation on the colonial coast. There were few roads in Georgia at the time, other than meandering game trails and narrow paths followed by indigenous people. Travel by water was faster and easier than hacking through dense underbrush and making long detours around freshwater swamps and coastal marshes. The double-ended scout boats, each dug from a single cypress log, were about thirty-five feet long and six feet wide, and were equipped with a pair of gaff-rigged sails, although their main propulsion came from oars rowed by ten scouts. Three small cannons called swivel guns were mounted on each boat. The shallow-draft scout boats were ideal for coastal waters because they were sturdy, lightweight, and fast, perfect for exploration, surveillance, and, if necessary, fighting.

Horton was delighted with his acreage on Jekyll, which he pronounced "exceedingly rich." Others on the scout boat were infected by his enthusiasm. A young gunner fired one of the swivel guns to notify the people on St. Simons that Horton was pleased with the lay of his land. The exuberant gunner kept reloading, each time increasing the amount of powder. The cannon exploded on the third shot, driving shrapnel into the

Remains of the Horton House on Jekyll. The home is one of the few two-story tabby colonial-era homes still standing in Georgia.

poor man's head. Horton rushed him back to Fort Frederica to the regimental surgeon, but he died of his injuries the following day.

Horton, eager to start work on his plantation, soon had his indentured servants clearing land and building shelters. He later learned that he was mistaken about the richness of the island soil. At first glance, sea island soil does seem rich. It supports maritime forests of giant live oaks, magnolias, and pines. Only the top layer of soil is fertile, however; the rest is sandy, barren, and rapidly depleted by crops. Without compost or other amendments, it makes for poor farmland. When cotton was grown extensively on Jekyll and other sea islands after the Revolutionary War, slaves had to dig tons of mud out of the marshes to manure the fields every year, in addition to enriching the fields with animal manure. Horton and his servants soon had crops planted, a sawmill built, and the site selected for his first house on Jekyll.

Horton worked endlessly to make his plantation a success. His most successful crop turned out to be cattle. He may have learned about raising livestock in his native Herefordshire, where cattle were an economic mainstay. Around the time Horton came to Georgia, the now-famous Hereford cattle, with their distinct white faces and stocky red bodies, were being bred for the first time in the shire, although it is unlikely that Horton ever raised prized Herefords on Jekyll.

The Horton House

HORTON'S FIRST HOUSE was built on the site of a large prehistoric Indian shell mound. It was a two-story frame structure, with living areas downstairs and bedrooms above. He probably cut the timber and dressed the boards on Jekyll; a period map shows a sawmill on the island's north end. Horton chose the location for his home and plantation because the land bordered a small but navigable waterway now called Du Bignon Creek. The creek provided easy access to the larger tidal waterways between Jekyll and St. Simons. Horton's plantation was about eight miles south of Frederica, and the creek would have made it easy for him to travel back and forth to attend to his many duties at the fortified town. When working on Jekyll, he could be summoned to St. Simons at any time by a specific number of cannon shots.

After his house was burned, Horton rebuilt. By then, his family had joined him on Jekyll, probably arriving in June 1742. His wife, Rebecca, was no doubt involved in planning the new house, which rose on the ruins of the first. The second home had two stories, too, but was built of tabby, a unique, fireproof coastal masonry made of lime, oyster shells, salt-free water, and sand. Horton would have seen the tabby-making process in St. Augustine, where the Spanish invented it in the late 1500s, adapting local materials and employing techniques used for thousands of years all over the world. Tabby is North America's oldest masonry; Portland cement, the chief component in concrete, came along several centuries after tabby was being made on the southern coast. At Fort Frederica, tabby was used to build the riverfront powder magazine and the entry to the barracks. Some of the colonists used tabby to construct houses in the fortified town. Oglethorpe's only home in America, Orange Hall, was a simple tabby cottage near Frederica.

Because Horton's house was near a Native American shell midden, large quantities of oyster shells were easy to gather. His servants first made lime by piling layers of shells, alternated with layers of wood, in a large log-cabin-like structure called a rick. The rick was then set afire. When the fire died and the pile cooled, lime and ash were dug out, mixed with the other components, and poured wet into wooden forms. After the first layer set, the forms were raised for the next pouring. Tabby was almost as durable as modern concrete. Most tabby buildings, including Horton's, were smoothed over with a coat of lime plaster, not only to make them look more refined but also to protect the rough tabby from weathering. Over time, the lime coat would flake off, revealing the beauty of the tabby, with its picturesque oyster-shell aggregate.

Horton's rebuilt house was about forty feet long and eighteen feet wide. It had a tabby floor and a tabby wall partitioning the parlor from the kitchen. Each downstairs room had its own fireplace. Upstairs there were two bedrooms, one for Rebecca and William, the other for the boys. Downstairs rooms led out to a verandah, and the bedrooms above opened onto a breezy balcony overlooking tidal waterways and marshes. The home's red hipped roof would have made a nice contrast to the soft buff-gray color of the tabby.

The tabby framework of Horton's house still stands, along with the ruins of other outbuildings. One of the two oldest two-story colonial buildings in Georgia, it is listed as a National Historic Landmark, a designation of special significance. The historic marker identifying the tabby ruins on Du Bignon Creek as the remains of Horton's brewery is inaccurate, according to experts, who say the broken tabby blocks were most likely part of a wharf or storage building.

A baby alligator soaking up sun on waterlogged boards.

Because he was so often at Frederica or traveling on Oglethorpe's behalf, Horton probably relied on his indentured servants to do most of the manual labor of growing and harvesting crops, tending cattle and sheep, building his house and outbuildings, and doing whatever else needed to be done. Horton's handful of servants must have felt isolated on the island plantation, and there is little doubt that they were overworked. Four became unhappy enough to steal Horton's boat and run away. Horton may have replaced them with other indentured servants.

In addition to corn and vegetables, Horton grew barley and hops for ale and beer. His brewery, thought to be the first in Georgia and one of the first in the South, was equipped with a large copper kettle and "all Conveniences." There is no indication that Horton ever named his brews, but in recent years, popular television shows have featured Jekyll Island Red Ale, Jekyll Island Lager, and Jekyll Island Root Beer. All three are fictitious brands created by a California company, Independent Studio Services, that provides props for films and television. The Jekyll labels have been featured on the popular television shows *Lost*, *My Name is Earl*, *Dexter*, and *Rules of Attraction*. A skull—a reference to Jekyll's pirate past—marks the labels. A spokeswoman for the company said she could find no record of why Jekyll was selected for the honor. Since the company has a branch near Atlanta, it may be that an employee vacationed on Jekyll and learned about Horton's brewery. Another company, Jekyll Brewing, in

Alpharetta, Georgia, also pays tribute to the Georgia's first brewery. The company produces real beers and ales.

When Oglethorpe returned to England late in 1736 to raise more money and troops for Georgia, he left Horton in charge of Frederica. New to both military and civil management, Horton had more problems with the colonists than he ever did in supervising the troops. Every day at Frederica brought new complaints from the settlers, who were well aware that their location near Spanish Florida put them at great risk of attack. They panicked every time a strange sail appeared on the horizon. Rumors circulated; gossip passed as gospel. Many times, Horton had to call the colonists from their fields to guard Frederica when a possible attack seemed imminent, making it difficult for them to grow enough food to feed themselves, as Oglethorpe and the trustees expected them to do.

Charles Wesley had a difficult time at Frederica because of intractable colonists and his own inexperience. After just five months in coastal Georgia, he sailed back to England in defeat. His brother, John, traveled to St. Simons from Savannah on several occasions as Charles's replacement, but fared no better. Horton blamed John Wesley for some of his problems with the colonists, believing that the reverend had written letters criticizing him. Furious, Horton informed John Wesley that neither he nor any other colonists would listen to him preach in the future because he satirized and abused them in his sermons. Besides, Horton said, nobody at Frederica had ever heard of the Wesleys' "brand of religion," which later developed into Methodism.

Life was hard for everyone on St. Simons and Jekyll. The colonists and indentured servants, all from cooler climes in Europe, had been plunged into a sweltering, semitropical wilderness swarming with insects, poisonous snakes, and alligators. Horton once killed five alligators in a single day. Oglethorpe had built Frederica on the west side of St. Simons for sound military reasons, but the island's bulk blocked the refreshing sea breezes of summer from reaching the town, which lay exposed to the cold winter winds that blew east from the mainland. Many colonists were Londoners, accustomed to the conveniences and attractions of a big city. To them, St. Simons and Jekyll must have seemed like the ends of the earth. They chafed under Horton's leadership, which was heavy-handed at times. Horton persuaded a colonist to accuse one of Horton's main critics of rape, a charge he knew to be untrue. The man was acquitted by a jury in Savannah but became Horton's lifelong enemy. Another vengeful colonist reported that Horton had stolen a boat, also a false accusation. Horton had to appear

The evangelical brothers John and Charles Wesley. The pair came to Georgia from England with General Oglethorpe and William Horton. After the pious Wesleys had one of Horton's indentured servants put off the boat for bawdy behavior, Horton retaliated by dancing on the deck over the sleeping Wesleys' cabin at midnight. The Wesleys later returned to England and founded the Methodist movement. (*left*: Engraving by J. Thomson after J. Jackson, Wikimedia Commons)

in court to prove the charges baseless. Rebellious colonists threatened to lock up all of Frederica's guns, seize the boats, and put the storekeepers in chains because of a food shortage in town, even though the shortage had been caused by mismanagement in Savannah. Horton, whose temper must have matched his fiery hair, finally threatened to have one disagreeable colonist shot through the head, another chained to an oar in a scout boat, and a third starved to death. Oglethorpe, who had had similar problems managing civilians, turned an unsympathetic ear to their complaints. He instead praised Horton for his efforts: "The people [of Frederica] might have starved or abandoned the place had not Mr. Horton given them his own cattle and corn to eat."

Frederica had been in existence for only three years when Great Britain and Spain declared war on each other in 1739. It was at first called the War of Jenkins' Ear but was later merged with the War of the Austrian Succession. Soon afterward, clashes between the British and Spanish, and between their Native American allies, erupted along the St. Marys River, which forms part of the present-day Georgia-Florida border. Expecting a full-scale Spanish attack, Oglethorpe sent Horton to England in March 1740 to lobby for more troops and equipment for Frederica. Without waiting

Tabby ruins marking the entrance to the wooden barracks, long since lost to time, of Fort Frederica on St. Simons. Major Horton was in charge of the soldiers stationed there.

for Horton's return, Oglethorpe attacked St. Augustine in late spring. The attack was a disaster. The Castillo de San Marcos proved impervious to cannonballs, although British ships bombarded it for almost a month before the ship captains, fearing the approaching hurricane season, sailed back north. The black soldiers and families occupying Fort Mosé, the African outpost and town, were pulled into the stronger Castillo at the beginning of the siege. Some of Oglethorpe's troops moved into the abandoned Fort Mosé, which the British called Fort Moosa. The troops at the small fort grew complacent, sleeping late and failing to post sentries. African troops from Fort Mosé, along with Spanish soldiers and Native American allies, slipped out of the Castillo and attacked the outpost before dawn, killing more than sixty British soldiers and capturing the rest. Some of the British troops were scalped and otherwise mutilated, perhaps by indigenous warriors, who often took arms, legs, and genitals as trophies, as well as scalps. Oglethorpe retreated to St. Simons in defeat. He was criticized on both sides of the Atlantic for losing so many British soldiers in such a dreadful manner. Critics charged him with incompetence and demanded his replacement. The general, ill with fever and depressed by his failure, withdrew to his tabby home near Frederica and stayed there for several months. Adding to his humiliation, British soldiers began referring to the slaughter as the Battle of Bloody Moosa.

Horton's mission to England was successful. He met with a number of British officials, including Sir Robert Walpole, the first de facto prime minister of Great Britain, and with aristocratic members of the Board of Trustees. Among other things, Horton told the 1st Earl of Egmont, John Perceval, that the Georgia land grants should have been larger, since five hundred acres would accommodate no more than twenty head of cattle on sea islands such as Jekyll and St. Simons. Horton got what he asked for, including a company of grenadiers—soldiers armed with grenades—plus permission to bring women and children to Georgia. It is almost certain that his own wife and sons traveled with him on the voyage back. They arrived in June 1742, just a few weeks before the Spanish launched a full-scale attack on St. Simons. Rebecca Horton may have gotten a brief look at the Jekyll plantation and the first frame house her husband and their servants had built, but she and the boys would have been rushed to Fort Frederica before the first shots were fired. Horton remained on Jekyll with his grenadiers to intercept the enemy.

While traveling north to St. Simons, the Spanish ships ran into a storm, forcing some of the smaller craft to take refuge in the sound south of Cumberland Island. Oglethorpe, thinking his two small forts on Cumberland were under attack, rushed

Major Horton took a message to the governor of Spanish Florida, assuring him that General Oglethorpe had no plans to attack St. Augustine. Oglethorpe later attacked the city but retreated after his cannons failed to breach the coquina and tabby walls of the Castillo de San Marco. Original map created in 1740.

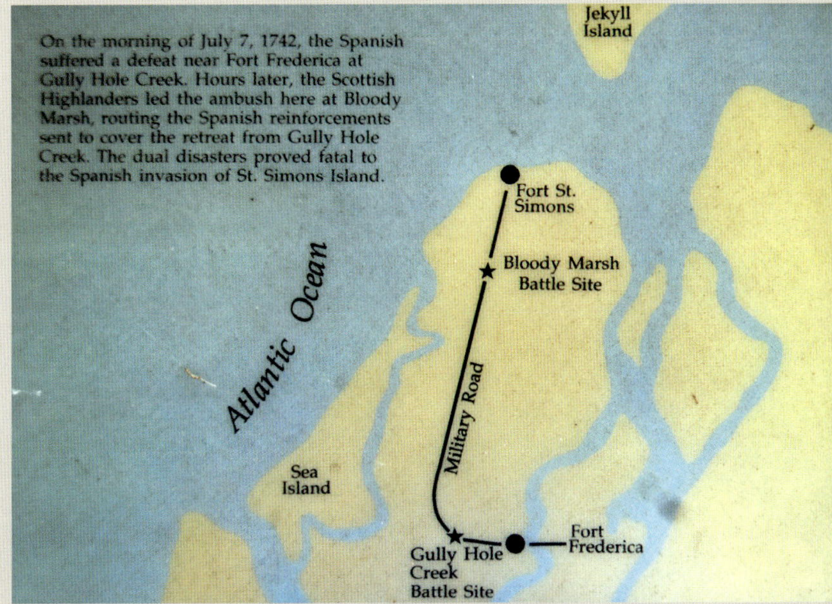

Route of retreating Spanish troops after Oglethorpe defeated their attempt to invade Jekyll in 1742. The soldiers burned the Horton Plantation as they left.

down by boat with reinforcements. He was almost captured by a Spanish warship but managed to reach Cumberland. When the expected attack on the island was not forthcoming, he hurried back to Frederica, leaving Horton on Jekyll in command of soldiers from two companies as well as his newly recruited grenadiers. Although a fort had been designed for Jekyll, it had never been built. Before the Spanish attack, Horton probably erected some sort of defenses to protect himself and his men.

With the bulk of their fleet of more than fifty ships undamaged, the Spanish headed north toward St. Simons with about three thousand troops, including two independent companies from Fort Mosé. One source claims that five hundred African and mulatto Spanish soldiers were involved in the Georgia attack. The ships ran the guns of Fort St. Simons, an earthen battery on the south end of the island, and landed at Gascoigne Bluff on the western shore, named for the captain of the *Hawk*. The Spanish overran Fort St. Simons, burning the houses occupied by British soldiers and their families, who had been moved to the stronger Fort Frederica. Horton tried to move his troops across the sound to aid his comrades, but Spanish control of the south end of St. Simons made it difficult. The young, inexperienced British soldiers manning the guns of Fort St. Simons did not sink a single Spanish ship sailing through the sound, though all were well in range of the British cannons.

The governor of Florida, Don Manuel de Montiano, commanded the Spanish troops. He sent a small contingent of soldiers to find the narrow Military Road, which ran between Fort St. Simons and Frederica on the western side of the island. A handful of British and Spanish soldiers engaged in the Battle of Gully Hole Creek, where Oglethorpe captured two prisoners in hand-to-hand combat. Later on the same day, the British and Spanish met in a high marsh on the east side of St. Simons in the well-known Battle of Bloody Marsh. Both battles were little more than skirmishes. Oglethorpe's forces, outnumbered almost four to one, turned back the enemy almost by accident during the Battle of Bloody Marsh. Some of his troops were in retreat when the Spanish, out of ammunition, retreated, too.

For centuries, historians and others reported that the battle on St. Simons was named the Battle of Bloody Marsh because the marshes ran red with the blood of Spaniards killed in the conflict. Oglethorpe himself claimed more than two hundred Spanish casualties. It was a gross exaggeration. Only about a dozen Spanish grenadiers died in the battle, which was first called the Battle of the Spanish Grenadiers. Soon afterward, however, the skirmish was renamed the Battle of Bloody Marsh. One

A monument on St. Simons Island commemorating the approximate site of the Battle of Bloody Marsh.

modern expert at the Fort Frederica National Monument thinks that British soldiers, or perhaps Oglethorpe himself, were embellishing to counteract their humiliating defeat two years earlier at the Battle of Bloody Moosa in St. Augustine.

Three days after the battles were fought, Horton made a risky move. He sailed his troops across the sound in broad daylight, in full view of Spanish forces, and reached Frederica. Don Manuel, on the south end of St. Simons, was pondering his next move, and Horton's reinforcements must have given the Spanish leader second thoughts about attempting another attack. In addition, Oglethorpe had engineered a bit of counterintelligence, arranging for the Spanish to capture a letter reporting that British reinforcements were on the way from Charleston. When three British ships appeared on the horizon, Don Manuel was convinced. He ordered his forces to retreat.

On their way back to St. Augustine, some of the Spanish troops stopped on Jekyll long enough to burn Horton's house and other plantation buildings, kill his livestock, and destroy his crops. His property was targeted because he was Oglethorpe's top aide and because his presence on Jekyll made it an important British military outpost. In addition, Spanish officials may have recalled how Horton had defied their former governor by refusing to answer questions when he and the major were prisoners at St. Augustine.

After reducing Horton's plantation to smoking ruins, the Spanish left Jekyll in a rush. Wounded Spanish soldiers who died after the troops were in retreat were left unburied on Jekyll's south end, along with Spanish cannons and other ordnance. Perhaps the Spanish feared Horton would see the fires on Jekyll and hurry over with troops to defend his home, although nothing in the record suggests that he did. Horton must have had mixed emotions on the day of the Spanish retreat. He would have been both overjoyed by the British victory and devastated by the destruction of the plantation he had worked so hard to build.

He was not the sort to grieve for long. By the following year, William and Rebecca had rebuilt their house and outbuildings, replanted crops, and replaced the slaughtered cattle and sheep. Their two boys, still young, would have helped, perhaps by weeding Rebecca's herb and vegetable gardens near the house or by gathering firewood in Jekyll's lush forest. In their free time, William Jr. and Thomas would have loved swinging on Jekyll's wild grapevines, hunting for turtle eggs on the beach, and searching for arrowheads and spear points at the edges of the marsh. Horton's status with Oglethorpe brought a variety of interesting visitors to Jekyll. Native Americans paddled over in dugout canoes with gifts of venison and wild turkeys, which earlier French explorers had called "Indian peacocks" because their feathers were richly colored and iridescent. Important people who came to Frederica were always invited to tour Horton's plantation. One of them, William Logan, a Philadelphia Quaker, visited Jekyll while on a business trip to St. Simons. Logan later reported that the Hortons dealt "genteely" with their guests and that Horton was "very fine in conversation" and "very much the gentleman." Logan was likewise impressed with the work Horton had done on the plantation.

Aside from the pleasure of visitors, the family probably had a hard time on Jekyll. The Spanish had retreated, but Horton knew that they might return for another attack at any time. Everyone on Jekyll stayed alert for any hint of an invasion. Horton traveled often on Oglethorpe's behalf, and it must have been frightening for Rebecca and the boys to stay on Jekyll without him. She might have taken them to Frederica during his absences, for company as well as protection.

Horton's business often took him to South Carolina, where he made a favorable impression. The people of St. Helena's Parish, which includes coastal Beaufort, elected him as their representative to the Sixteenth Royal Assembly, which convened in

Charleston in 1747. South Carolina's governor, James Glenn, recommended Horton to another state official as a man experienced in dealing with Native Americans.

In South Carolina, Horton might have met an unusual teenager named Eliza Lucas. There is no doubt that he had heard of her success at growing indigo and processing the dye on her grandfather's plantations near Charleston. In 1746, Horton planted indigo on Jekyll, one of the first indigo crops grown in Georgia.

After defeating the Spanish on St. Simons in 1742, Oglethorpe left again for England in the following year, once more putting Horton in charge of the soldiers and colonists at Frederica. Oglethorpe intended to return to Georgia, but never did. Horton continued to serve in his stead while, at the same time, trying to run his plantation on Jekyll. Four years later, he announced that his Jekyll acreage was "totally unfit for cultivation," and asked the trustees to grant his son Thomas five hundred acres on the Ogeechee River in modern Greene County, which offered much better farmland. There is no record of what became of Horton's elder son, William, who may have died or returned to England as an adult. An epidemic of fever struck Frederica in 1747, and Horton, then in his early forties, was one of the victims. Rebecca's nursing helped him recover, but he never fully regained his strength.

In the following year, Horton attended a Savannah meeting to speak in favor of legalizing slavery in Georgia, although he had been one of its major opponents in Oglethorpe's day. Perhaps he thought slave labor could rescue his Jekyll plantation. While in Savannah in late 1748, he caught a "malignant fever" and died. Thomas inherited his father's property on Jekyll but never farmed it, preferring to work his inland Georgia acreage on the Ogeechee. Rebecca may have left Jekyll after her husband's death and moved away from the coast to be with her son.

Oglethorpe's regiment at Fort Frederica was deactivated in 1749. The war between Spain and Great Britain was over, and the British military presence was no longer needed on St. Simons. Without the soldiers to support Frederica's economy, the town died. Most of the soldiers and settlers moved elsewhere, but a handful of troops joined a new independent company and a few of them stayed behind. Among them were the brothers Captain Raymond Demeré (DEM-ree) and Lieutenant Paul Demeré, French Huguenots who had been recruited by Horton as grenadiers. Great Britain decided to maintain a small outpost on Jekyll after Horton's death, and Paul Demeré was sent to the island to command about a dozen soldiers and two noncommissioned officers. Captain Raymond Demeré took command of the troops on Jekyll the following year

Indigo Blues

Courtesy of Sten Porse, Wikimedia Commons

FROM START TO FINISH, dealing with indigo was an unpleasant proposition involving slimy, rotting foliage, reeking indigo vats, clouds of insects, and stale human urine. After Eliza Lucas learned how to grow the plants and process them into the deep blue dye prized in Great Britain, indigo became one of the most profitable crops in colonial America. In the Carolinas and Florida, the work was done by slaves. In Georgia, slavery was banned until 1751, so Horton's indigo workers were either hired or indentured. In 1746, a Jekyll visitor reported that Horton had eight acres of indigo growing on the island, tended by a Spaniard and an Englishman who boasted that Jekyll's indigo was as good as any from the West Indies.

As soon as the indigo budded, the plants went into the first of a series of large vats used to make dye. While the plants steeped—for as long as twenty hours—they had to be watched around the clock until they fermented. The smell of the fermenting plants drew flies and other insects to the vats, which Horton would have located far from his home and pastures so that he, his family, and his livestock would not be plagued by bugs and vile odors.

Like moonshiners, the best dye makers learned to read the mixture, judging its readiness by the vigor of the bubbles, the color of the froth, and the noxiousness of the odor. When the time was right, they drew the liquid into a second vat called the beater and pounded it with paddles to cause the particles to settle to the bottom as indigo mud. The liquid was then drained into a third vat, and the mud was packed into cloth bags and hung to drain. The damp mud was molded, cut into small cakes, and air-dried. Horton's workers had to protect the drying cakes from flies, which laid eggs in the mud and caused it to rot, and direct sunlight, which made the cakes crack. Because indigo is not water soluble, dyers often dissolved the cakes in stale human urine; male urine was said to be best. There is no record that Horton ever sold indigo dye produced on Jekyll, although his wife or servants may have used it to dye cotton grown on the island or wool sheared from their sheep.

Eliza Lucas pioneered the colonial indigo industry in America. She was just fifteen when she took charge of her grandfather's three large plantations near Charleston. Her mother was an invalid, and her father was involved in political and military affairs in Antigua. Her father sent her seeds from the West Indies, and she settled on indigo as the most promising. After she shipped the first six pounds of indigo dye to England in 1744, the British began offering a generous subsidy to encourage others to follow her lead. Eliza shared her seeds and knowledge with other planters, Horton perhaps among them. Indigo became a mainstay of the colonial economy, second in value only to rice, and ten times more valuable per pound. The colonies exported large quantities to Great Britain until the start of the Revolutionary War, when the British stopped paying subsidies to the rebellious Americans. Indigo dye was made in the new republic after the war. It colored the first flags of the United States, the bonny blue flag of the Confederacy, and Levi Strauss's iconic jeans.

and kept the Horton plantation in operation, although he lived at Harrington Hall, his plantation on St. Simons. He petitioned the Royal Council for a life estate on Horton's land and requested six hundred additional acres on the island. He was granted the extra acreage but denied the life estate, although Demeré continued to graze cattle on Horton property for the rest of his life.

Jekyll passed through several more hands before 1800. It was owned by Clement Martin Sr., who moved his family into the Horton house; by Richard Leake, who married Martin's daughter, Jane; and by a group of French noblemen who fled the guillotine in France and purchased several islands on the Georgia coast. One of the Frenchmen had acquired all of Jekyll by 1800. He and his descendants owned the island for most of the nineteenth century.

Christophe Anne Poulain du Bignon

BORN IN 1739 on the rugged coast of Brittany to a noble but impoverished French family, Christophe du Bignon was sent to sea at age ten. His parents knew the mortality rate for cabin boys was high, but they believed there was no other option for their eldest son. There was no money to send the boy to school to become a lawyer, a minister, or a military officer, which were acceptable professions for the nobility. Only commoners engaged in trade; aristocrats who did so lowered their status in society, which the proud du Bignon family, with noble roots dating back to the fifteenth century, was not willing to do. There was only one other avenue that a nobleman—or noble boy—might pursue and still retain his standing in the community: a career in maritime commerce with the respected French East India Company's private navy.

More than half the company's cabin boys were between the ages of nine and fourteen. Martha L. Keber, an expert on du Bignon, notes that a cabin boy's first duty was to survive, especially in parts of the world, such as Africa, where tropical fevers were endemic. During du Bignon's first voyage to West Africa, his ship picked up a load of 500 slaves on Gorée Island, off the coast of Senegal. There was a small French garrison on the island and about 250 people, all of whom were engaged, in one way or another, in the slave trade. After the captives were loaded aboard and crammed below decks, the ship traveled around the Cape of Good Hope, crossed the equator, and eventually delivered its miserable human cargo to the tropical island of Mauritius. The island, located in the Indian Ocean more than a thousand miles off Africa's southeastern coast, was also called the Isle de France. On the three-and-a-half-month journey, almost 150 slaves died of scurvy, and the rest were desperately ill of the same disease when the ship docked. Du Bignon may have been shocked, at least at first, by the deaths. If so, it is likely that he soon toughened up and adopted the attitude of the captain, the crew members, and the older cabin boys: dead slaves represented a financial loss but nothing more. For the rest of his life, du Bignon saw slaves as a business asset, although he fathered at least one child by a slave on Jekyll and made sure that mother and child were cared for after his death.

Du Bignon survived his maiden voyage to Africa and made many trips to India, Spain, Madagascar, and other ports of call. By the time he turned twenty-one, he had achieved the rank of officer. He continued to climb the ship's ladder of success. When

Great Britain and France became embroiled in the Seven Years' War, du Bignon became a privateer, helping his shipmates capture British vessels and sharing in the spoils, some of which were substantial. Although privateers attacked ships, they were not outlaws. Unlike pirates, which preyed on ships from any country, privateers had letters of marque from their governments, which allowed them to capture enemy ships. Du Bignon later captained many of his own vessels, doing work that was always demanding, sometimes rewarding, and often dangerous. During the American Revolution, France joined the side of the Patriots, and du Bignon again became a privateer attacking British ships.

He was thirty-six when he met a young widow, Marguerite Lossieux, on Mauritius. Marguerite had a son and daughter by her first marriage. After she married du Bignon, they moved to his home parish in coastal Brittany. Du Bignon, whose career as a mariner had made him financially secure, searched for a small estate and found a historic property not far from his childhood home. It was a dignified fifteenth-century manor house suitable for an aristocratic family. The house was surrounded by twelve thousand acres of land, complete with a pond and a dovecote. Du Bignon bought other property in the area. While he was at sea, Marguerite managed the properties and reared her children. Tenant farmers worked the land and provided a steady income for the family.

Because du Bignon was so often away, he spent little time with his two stepchildren when they were small. He did pay off the sizable debts they had inherited from their father, as well as some of the debts they incurred later as adults. By the time du Bignon made his move to Georgia years later, he and Marguerite had started another family. His stepchildren were grown and gone by then. None of them joined their mother and du Bignon in Georgia, although four of her son's children later came to live with them on Jekyll. Although he had helped his stepchildren financially, du Bignon considered Marguerite's grandchildren greedy and grasping. The perception, real or imagined, cost him his relationship with his own eldest son, Joseph.

In 1791, with a revolution brewing in France, du Bignon joined a partnership called the Société de Sapelo. It was formed by a group of aristocratic French expatriates who purchased all or part of six Georgia sea islands, including Jekyll, intending to exploit them and make their fortunes. Like the du Bignons, thousands of other aristocrats came to the United States to escape the revolution. A number of French planters from the

Caribbean island of Santo Domingo also sought refuge in the United States after the Haitian slave uprising of 1791.

Du Bignon invested in the Sapelo Company after hearing one of the partners describe the giant live oaks that grew on the sea islands. As an experienced seaman, he knew that live oak was prized by shipbuilders all over the world. He and his five-year-old son Joseph traveled with some of the partners to America. Marguerite, then pregnant with their third child, stayed in Brittany with Henri Charles, Joseph's three-year-old brother. Du Bignon was fifty-one when he bought shares in the Sapelo Company. He had faced challenges and danger since he was ten. He knew how to work hard to achieve his goals. If the other partners had been anything like him, the Sapelo Company might have succeeded.

Instead, the partners, most much younger than du Bignon, were convinced that the sea islands would make them rich with very little effort on their part. In addition to selling live oak timber, they planned to profit from annual sales of domestic livestock and the feral hogs that ran free on the sea islands and multiplied in the marshes and maritime forests. They planned to buy slaves and grow money-making crops such as indigo, sea island cotton, and rice. Until the partners could build their own houses, they would share a large but modest frame house on Sapelo Island's north end, which had once been home to an indigenous Guale settlement called Chucalate, a name later corrupted to Chocolate. When the company was up and running, each partner would select land on Sapelo and build a plantation where he and his family would enjoy lives of elegance and ease. The partners purchased fifteen slaves to do the hard labor of cutting and dressing timber, wrangling livestock and wild hogs, building the communal house and outbuildings, and growing crops.

Du Bignon's youthful partners had no concept of what it would take to accomplish their grandiose plans. Neither did the oldest partner, who was sixty-three and had

always lived a French nobleman's life of leisure. Nicolas-François Magon de La Villehuchet of Brittany even bragged about spending his time "vegetating" on the sea islands after he joined the partnership. When he left one of his young partners, ill with fever, stranded on Sapelo for almost a month, Villehuchet made a bitter enemy. The younger partner labeled him a good-for-nothing drunk and began calling him the Old Codfish. Villehuchet had come to Georgia to escape a dangerous situation in France. When a mob of vengeful peasants broke into his chateau, Villehuchet shot and killed one of them. He was tried and acquitted, but the revolutionaries were outraged, convinced he had gotten preferential treatment because of his aristocratic status. It would be another year before the Terror officially began and the guillotine commenced its bloody work, but Villehuchet, fearing a successful appeal of his acquittal and a second trial with a negative outcome, fled to Georgia.

He may have thought coastal Georgia could provide a haven for himself and his family from the escalating turmoil in France, which was on the brink of revolution. Poverty-stricken commoners were rising up against the well-fed nobility and the clergy. Angry mobs had burned chateaus to the ground and attacked aristocrats in their homes.

After spending a few months inspecting Sapelo and the other sea islands, du Bignon returned to France to take care of business and to bring his wife and two younger boys to Georgia. He left his eldest son, Joseph, in the care of one of his partners on the island. Back in France, du Bignon realized how dangerous conditions had become for the aristocracy. The country was in an economic death spiral because of government mismanagement, debt from several wars, and extravagant spending on the part of the royal family. King Louis XVI, his wife, and their children were apprehended while trying to flee the country. Crop failures over several years had led to food shortages so serious that starving people rioted over the price of bread. Peasants boiled over with resentment against the nobility, including aristocratic members of the clergy, especially since the working class paid taxes but the nobility and clergy did not.

Du Bignon bought a ship he renamed *Le Sappello* to sail back to Georgia with Marguerite and their two younger sons. The youngest boy, born while the captain was inspecting his American holdings, died early, probably before he turned five. His name has not been found in historic records, and very little is known about him.

There were many conflicts among the partners. They depended on the labor of slaves but had no idea how to deal with them. The partners had not anticipated the expense of feeding and clothing slaves, or providing them with housing and rudimentary medical care. Nor had they expected them to be rebellious. One partner had all the company's slaves marked with inventory numbers burned into their chests, which made it easier for authorities to identify and return runaways but would not have endeared him to the Africans so branded. The partners did not spare the lash, and the backs of many island slaves bore permanent scars. Some were subjected to even more draconian punishments. They were forced to wear iron leg shackles and iron collars, which rubbed their skin raw. In the hot, humid climate, the wounds would have become infected almost overnight, in large part because of the shortage of sanitation in the slave quarters. A few slaves were banished to neighboring Blackbeard Island, a deserted sandspit east of Sapelo covered with palmetto thickets and six-foot-long rattlesnakes. It is remarkable that some of the Sapelo slaves later found the courage to retaliate against their owners. They burned down the Sapelo stable and hay barn and destroyed an entire year's corn crop.

The partners were overwhelmed by problems. Their livestock sickened and died, including a whole flock of sheep that expired after eating sandspurs. Crops were washed away by floods, eaten by insects, whipped to rags by strong winds, and parched by drought. Debts mounted and profits dwindled. Bickering soon escalated into outright hostility. Some of the partners were convinced that the others were conspiring to cheat them. Lawsuits and countersuits were filed. When du Bignon returned to Sapelo, he realized that the partnership was imploding. Over the next two years, he managed to trade his shares in the Sapelo Company for a majority interest in Jekyll. Six years later, he owned the entire island.

CHAPTER IV Jekyll's French Accent

[1801–1857]

The Sapelo partnership was dissolved in 1794. Later that same year, three of du Bignon's former partners died, two by violence. One was shot to death by his uncle, a partner in the company, during an argument on Sapelo Island. Villehuchet, the Old Codfish, was the other victim of violence. He missed his family in France, hated the isolation of the sea islands, and loathed some of his partners. He also missed his old way of life, where his title had won him automatic respect and deference. Villehuchet remained in Georgia for less than two years before returning to France. By then, the mood of the country had changed, and not in his favor. He was retried for the murder of the man who had broken into his chateau. This time the Old Codfish was convicted, sentenced to death, and lost his head to the guillotine.

By the time Marguerite du Bignon arrived in Georgia, she was approaching her midforties and might have passed her childbearing years. At any rate, she bore the captain no more children. Du Bignon probably fathered another child by Maria Theresa, a mulatto slave whom he purchased for a high price. Her child was named Margueritta, a name oddly similar to that of du Bignon's wife. In his will, du Bignon left the then-elderly Maria Theresa a lifetime income and the services of a slave. He also left Margueritta a lifetime income and recommended that both mother and daughter be set free, although at the time, manumission, or the freeing of slaves, was illegal in Georgia. Marguerite du Bignon probably knew about her husband's longtime relationship with Maria Theresa, but she also knew it was unlikely to affect her position as his legal wife or that of their two sons.

Although du Bignon owned other property in Georgia, including 1,200 acres on the Glynn County mainland and houses in Savannah and on St. Simons, he and Marguerite always made their permanent home on Jekyll. They moved into the old Horton house with their boys in 1794; two female servants shared it with them. The two-bedroom place must have been crowded, with four adults and at least two children in residence. The family later enlarged and refurbished the old tabby house, but during their early years on the island, the du Bignons lived frugally. Marguerite had managed her husband's affairs in Brittany while he was away at sea, and she may have played a leading role in handling his plantation business on Jekyll.

Unlike his former partners, du Bignon understood that his aristocratic birth was no guarantee of success or financial security. He had worked hard since he was ten years old, and he was prepared to work hard for the rest of his life. Most of his assets, including the family's fine furniture, silver, china, and other trappings of wealth were still tied up in Brittany, where they were difficult to retrieve during the upheaval in France. Because he was a nobleman, du Bignon's French estate had already been targeted for confiscation. His agent saved the property by producing a document that listed the captain as a citizen of the United States and a permanent immigrant rather than as an aristocrat who had fled the country just to escape the revolution. Despite his limited funds in Georgia, du Bignon must have been happy about the move to Jekyll, away from the turmoil in France and on Sapelo. On the island, he was once again the captain of his own ship, in command of his own destiny.

The early 1800s were golden years for du Bignon on his private Golden Isle. Once the French Revolution ended, he began selling off assets in Brittany or transferring them to Georgia and using them to finance his Jekyll operation. After the American Revolution, coastal planters had begun planting sea island cotton on a large scale. It fetched high prices in European markets because its long fibers and silky texture were perfect for making fine cloth and lace. Sea island cotton was more delicate and harder to grow than upland varieties of cotton. It thrived only within thirty miles of

Old botanical print of the Sea Island cotton once grown on Jekyll Island. (From Franz Eugen Köhler, *Köhler's Medizinal-Pflanzen* [1897])

the Atlantic, and the best cotton of all was said to grow in range of ocean spray. Given decent market prices, island planters like du Bignon could make a make a small fortune on just one harvest. They could also lose a year's income overnight to bad weather or bugs, both of which regularly ravaged the islands.

Sea island cotton was du Bignon's main crop on Jekyll, but he knew the danger of relying on a single crop. He diversified, growing barley, hay, corn, potatoes, and a variety of vegetables. He raised livestock: cattle, sheep, and pigs for food, and horses to breed so that he could sell the foals. Like many of the sea islands, Jekyll had its own citrus grove, orange trees planted more than a century earlier by Spanish friars. The grove produced until 1835, when the trees were killed by a hard freeze. During his long career at sea, du Bignon had witnessed many deaths due to scurvy, including those of about 150 slaves on his first voyage as a cabin boy. Although vitamin C would not be known as the cure for scurvy until the 1930s, mariners had long observed that citrus fruits prevented the disease, so he may have valued his orange grove on Jekyll more than most.

Du Bignon believed slaves were key to the success of his Jekyll plantation. By the time he owned the whole island, he also owned sixteen slaves. He had acquired several during the dissolution of the partnership, and he spent most of his available funds buying more. Unlike slaves on the isolated sea island plantations who spoke the lilting Gullah Geechee creole, a combination of English and dozens of different African languages, the du Bignon slaves spoke French. The captain may have selected them, at least in part, for that reason, or it may have resulted from his preference for doing business with men from his native country. Du Bignon recruited other Frenchmen to rent or work land on the island. Even though he rented property to a few English speakers, French was the dominant language on Jekyll for decades.

The du Bignons, like the other sea island planters, were noted for their hospitality. They often entertained visitors, especially other aristocratic French expatriates. Captain du Bignon had a number of French friends and business associates in Savannah, where he owned a townhouse. He also bought a tabby house on neighboring St. Simons in the old town of

Carriage rides around the island, a pleasure enjoyed by the northern millionaires who once wintered on Jekyll as well as visitors today.

Frederica, which had been almost abandoned after Oglethorpe disbanded the regiment in 1748. A fire destroyed many of the buildings about a decade later. Du Bignon's closest friend on St. Simons was John Couper, a convivial Scotsman who owned Cannon's Point, one of the finest of all the coastal plantations. Couper's dry sense of humor must have baffled the captain at times, but du Bignon was probably fascinated by the agricultural experiments Couper conducted on his plantation, including growing olives and producing olive oil at the behest of Thomas Jefferson. The house at Frederica might have made it easier for du Bignon to take Marguerite and the children to the larger island for weddings, dances, boat races, picnics, and other festive events that were a regular part of St. Simons society. Although the du Bignons were devout Catholics, du Bignon donated money toward the construction of a sanctuary for Christ Church, the Episcopal church at Frederica, whose congregation dated back to the days of General Oglethorpe and the Wesley brothers.

The St. Simons planters were a close-knit group. They founded the St. Clair Club, which met in an unoccupied plantation house that they rented as their clubhouse. Once a month, the members—all male, even though one of the island's finest planters was a woman—gathered for gourmet suppers, conversation, and entertainment. Du Bignon was invited to one of the club suppers—an honor, since only three guests were permitted at a time. Years later, a member's son described the night in November when du Bignon attended.

He and the others arrived on horseback at sunset, since the planters considered it unmanly to require the comfort of carriages for trips around the island. The clubhouse sat in a grove of live oak trees. Since the prospect of harvesting live oak for shipbuilding was what had prompted du Bignon to invest in the Sapelo Company in the first place, he would have cast an expert's appraising eye over the trees. One of the live oaks near the club was a giant specimen that the planters had named "Old England."

As the men entered the clubhouse, they were greeted by John Couper, their host for the evening. Each of the club members took turns acting as host, providing all the food, imported wine and spirits, entertainment, and servants for the evening. Johnny, one of Couper's slaves, played the fiddle and helped other slaves serve supper. Couper's French-trained African chef, a freeman named Sans Foix, prepared a memorable meal for the fourteen men. They were first served clam broth and chicken mulligatawny soup, followed by fresh-caught fish, shrimp pies, crab in the shell, roasted meats, and vegetables. Tartlets of dried fruits, nuts, and orange marmalade made from citrus grown on the island were offered for dessert. Almost every morsel du Bignon and the others consumed that night had been harvested on St. Simons or Jekyll, or in the nearby marshes and waterways. Even the candles that gave the men's faces a mellow glow were made from the fragrant berries of wax myrtle trees that grow wild on the sea islands.

After dinner, the table was cleared of its cobalt and white Chinese porcelain, and slaves brought in a giant punch bowl. The punch was a potent mixture of rum, brandy, sugar, lemon juice, and lemon zest. The rum and brandy were imported, but the sugar and lemons came from sugar cane and citrus grown on the island or nearby. The members and guests began by toasting President James Monroe. After additional toasts, the well-lubricated diners began to sing. In a voice described as husky, du Bignon offered "Cheer Up, My Lads, Cheer Up!" The song, an appropriate choice for a former sea captain, tells the rousing but tragic tale of an American ship chased and sunk by a British man-of-war.

After several more hours of singing, toasting, and storytelling while the servants enjoyed leftover food and drink in the back rooms, it was time for the men to go home. They stood, joined hands, sang "Auld Lang Syne," and then started their rides through the dark island woods. Each man was accompanied by a mounted slave ready to render aid if necessary.

Unlike many of the sea island planters, who left their low-lying properties during warm weather, when mosquitoes swarmed and malaria ran rampant on the coast, du Bignon and his family stayed on Jekyll year-round. The captain had no desire to relinquish control over his plantation, even at the risk of his family's health. He did emulate other sea island planters who worked their slaves on the task system rather than in gangs that labored from dawn until dusk, the standard practice on upland plantations. Under the task system, each field hand was given a specific task to complete in a day. The strongest slaves, the full hands, were given the hardest jobs, while half hands and quarter hands, often women and children, were assigned less demanding work. After the slaves finished their tasks, they were usually allowed to spend the rest of the day hunting or fishing, tending their gardens, and caring for their chickens. As a result, they provided much of their own food, which saved the planters money. Work on Jekyll was managed by an overseer and, in the fields, by a driver called Big Peter, a slave whom du Bignon trusted and considered competent. Du Bignon knew the capabilities of each of his sixty slaves, and may have worked them harder than most sea island planters. He boasted yields of cotton on Jekyll that were unmatched even by the finest plantations on the coast. Although du Bignon considered himself a benevolent slave owner, he regarded his slaves as a business asset to be bought and sold, worked hard, and punished when he thought they needed it. Big Peter administered the harsh punishments ordered by du Bignon. Perhaps as a consequence, the slaves on Jekyll had a long history of attempted escapes.

Four of Marguerite du Bignon's grandchildren came to live with the family on Jekyll, three of them shortly before the War of 1812, because their father, Marguerite's son by her first husband, was too poor to support them. The grandchildren were young: Melanie was in her early teens; her brother, Louis, was eleven; their little sister, Clemence, was nine. An even younger sister, Eleanore, joined them on Jekyll later. Marguerite sent the girls to expensive boarding schools in Charleston and Savannah to be tutored in French. For additional fees, they could also study drawing, dancing, penmanship, music, and other subjects appropriate for well-bred young ladies. After he married Marguerite, du Bignon feared that his stepchildren, whose father the captain considered a ne'er-do-well, would claim a share of the estate he planned to leave to his own children. Before leaving France for Georgia, Marguerite signed a document agreeing that du Bignon's stepchildren had no right to inherit anything from their stepfather. Du Bignon always seemed to believe his stepchildren were after his money, and later extended that belief to his stepgrandchildren, as well.

The stepgrandchildren no doubt resented du Bignon's attitude. Louis left Jekyll for Savannah as soon as he was old enough. He lived on his own in rented rooms and died there alone of fever when he was eighteen. When Melanie, the oldest of the girls, married in Savannah, du Bignon did not attend the wedding. Worst of all, du Bignon's eldest son, Joseph, secretly married one of Marguerite's granddaughters, Clemence. At the time, Joseph was in his midthirties. Du Bignon vehemently opposed the marriage, perhaps more because he thought Clemence wanted to get her hands on his money than because she was Joseph's biological half niece. The Catholic Church did not approve of cosanguination, marriages involving shared bloodlines.

Even before his marriage, Joseph had not lived up to his father's expectations. He showed no interest in the Jekyll plantation. After Joseph and Clemence married, they moved to the Glynn County mainland, since there was no chance that they would be welcome or even tolerated on Jekyll. Joseph did well during his service in the militia, but afterward he never seemed to find his footing. Christophe du Bignon saw Joseph only once after the marriage, when both father and son were giving court depositions regarding du Bignon's losses in the War of 1812. Du Bignon never forgave his oldest son for marrying Clemence, and it is unlikely that he ever met Joseph's children. When Christophe du Bignon died, he left Joseph a token sum in his will, almost as an insult.

Boat Rides to Freedom

The burning of Washington, D.C., during the War of 1812. George Cockburn commanded the British troops responsible for the destruction. He later raided the du Bignon home on Jekyll. Troops made off with many of the family valuables, slaughtered livestock, and destroyed personal property, including the clothing of a du Bignon grandchild. (Courtesy of the Library of Congress)

A SLAVE NAMED Alexis or Alik was one of the repeat offenders. When du Bignon offered a ten-dollar reward for his return, he remarked that Alexis's description had been printed so often in runaway slave notices that it would be useless to repeat it. He repeated it anyway. Alexis, he reported, was in his midforties, short, stout, bilingual in French and English, and pitted with pockmarks, perhaps from smallpox. According to the notice, Alexis had escaped by stealing the yawl boat of du Bignon's sloop on the night he was released from jail, where he had been locked up after being captured during a previous escape attempt.

Tom was another slave determined to flee Jekyll. He had been shot in the shoulder during an earlier escape attempt, which cost him the use of his right arm. In spite of his disability, Tom paddled away from the island in a stolen fishing canoe. According to du Bignon's agent, who placed a runaway-slave notice in a Savannah newspaper, Tom was "very artful" in staging his escapes. Tom once circulated rumors of his own death after he fled Jekyll, perhaps with help from fellow slaves. After he was reported drowned, news of his mainland burial reached the island. Du Bignon's notice proclaimed that the ten-dollar reward would be paid "on [Tom's] being apprehended, dug or fished up" and delivered either to the captain or to jail.

During the War of 1812, du Bignon and other sea island planters lost slaves en masse to the British after Admiral George Cockburn was ordered to destroy sites on the Atlantic Seaboard. Cockburn, described as a ruthless and fiery old sea dog, was the British officer responsible for destroying the nation's capital. When word reached Washington, DC, that Cockburn was on his way, panicked residents piled furniture and other valuables on carts and fled, along with President James Madison and his wife, Dolley. The president and first lady left behind a banquet just prepared for forty White House guests who had been invited to celebrate America's victory over Great Britain—prematurely, as it turned out. British troops not only enjoyed the food but also raided Madison's closet for clean clothes before burning down the White House, along with the rest of the city. Cockburn was labeled an "infamous scoundrel and notorious incendiary" by the Americans who offered a reward for him, dead or alive, plus $500 each for his ears.

The British admiral led a nighttime attack on Fort McHenry, near Baltimore. The bombs bursting in air, as well as the fact that the United States repulsed the British attack, prompted the amateur poet Francis Scott Key to write "The Star-Spangled Banner." Cockburn then sailed south to stir up trouble on the southern coast and divert American troops from an impending British attack on New Orleans. In November 1814, one of Cockburn's frigates landed on Jekyll.

The British mariners made their way to the du Bignon house and began to loot the place and destroy the captain's property as he watched, furious and humiliated but helpless to stop them. The British troops stripped the house of valuables, including silver plate, gold and silver jewelry, cash, personal papers, and gold-framed miniatures of Christophe and Marguerite, the only known portraits of the couple. They left the place in shambles, even destroying the clothing of du Bignon's three-month-old grandson. The Horton house had by then been enlarged with wooden wings to accommodate the du Bignons' son Henri, his wife, and their children.

The assault on the house was a severe blow to the family, but it was minor compared to the loss of almost half the plantation's slaves. Twenty-eight slaves fled Jekyll with the British, including Big Peter, du Bignon's trusted driver, as well as a carpenter, a cook, a seamstress, and other skilled slaves. Alexis and Tom, who had tried and failed to escape so many times before, probably found freedom at last on a British boat.

The British staged other raids on Jekyll, including one after the war officially ended in mid-February 1815. The news did not reach coastal Georgia in time to prevent the final raid, when British troops took anything of value that remained in the du Bignon home. By then, the family had taken refuge on the mainland. During the raids, the British destroyed du Bignon's cotton house and gin and his entire crop of sea island cotton. The troops shot most of the Jekyll cattle, made off with all of du Bignon's rice, and confiscated a thousand pounds of salted meat earmarked for feeding the family and slaves until the spring crops came in.

By the time the war ended, Cockburn had liberated thousands of slaves up and down the Georgia coast, which represented the largest nineteenth-century diaspora of African slaves from the United States. They were relocated to the British colonies of Canada, Trinidad, and Bermuda. Hundreds of slaves who escaped to the British belonged to du Bignon's wealthy planter friends on St. Simons. John Couper joined a small contingent of planters who traveled to Bermuda, where some of the sea island escapees were waiting aboard ships for transport to British colonies, to try to persuade them to return to their island plantations. Fredrick, a du Bignon slave, recognized Couper and commented that he wished his own master were in Couper's place so he could "shove him down into the sea." Couper, recalling an earlier claim by du Bignon that Frederick was one of his favorites, was shocked by the slave's comment. The Scotsman probably had no idea how slaves were treated on Jekyll. Although some of the slaves did go back to Couper's plantation, not one of du Bignon's returned to Jekyll.

Ann Amelia Nicolau of Bordeaux, France, came to coastal Georgia to be with her brothers after their parents were killed in slave uprisings on the Caribbean island of Santo Domingo. Henri du Bignon, one of the sons of Christophe du Bignon, married the young woman in 1808. She was the mother of nine of Henri's children; his mistresses and second wife added a dozen more offspring. (Courtesy of the Jekyll Island Museum Archives)

Henri, the son who pleased his father, inherited the bulk of Jekyll and the rest of his father's estate.

Du Bignon was delighted with the choices Henri made, especially his choice of a wife. Years before Joseph and Clemence were married, a seventeen-year-old orphaned Frenchwoman named Amelia Nicolau came to live in Georgia with her brother, Bernard. Their parents had been killed during the slave uprising in Haiti, and their older brother insisted that they join him in Georgia. He drowned not long after they arrived, and Bernard was stricken with a serious illness. Amelia was left on her own. John Couper and his wife, Rebecca, well-known for their generous hospitality, insisted the teenager stay with them at Cannon's Point until Bernard recovered. Amelia was still mourning for her parents and the brother who drowned, so the Coupers did not tell her that Bernard might not survive.

Probably because Amelia was French and her plight stirred his sympathy, du Bignon traveled to St. Simons to pay her a courtesy call. Once he saw Amelia, he decided on the spot that one of his sons should marry her. He informed the young woman that one of his sons was "good and stupid" and the other was "clever but wicked." Henri was no doubt the good but stupid son. Amelia was shy, charming, and beautiful, with long dark hair and expressive dark eyes. She was also smart. Once she knew even a little about the du Bignon family, Amelia realized her future would be bright with Henri, who was even then his father's favorite.

In spite of Henri's youth—he was only seventeen—the du Bignons encouraged him to court Amelia. A complicated marriage contract was negotiated and signed. Bernard survived his illness in time to help hammer out the document on behalf of his sister. Henri and Amelia married when they were both nineteen. Du Bignon gave them ten slaves, forty acres of sea island cotton land on Jekyll, and other things of value. Their first child, a daughter named Louisa, was born in February 1808. Du Bignon, then sixty-eight, fell head over heels in love with the little girl. Louisa remained her grandfather's favorite and became the darling of coastal society because of her kindness and charm.

Even before inheriting his father's estate, Henri du Bignon had expanded his interests beyond Jekyll. He was a member and a secretary of the Savannah-based Aquatic Club of Georgia and often raced his four-oared canoe boat, the *Lizard*, in coastal regattas. Slaves rowed the boats during the competitions, which were accompanied by heavy betting by planters and slaves alike. Unlike his father, Henri was involved in

Ann Amelia Nicolau du Bignon was buried in the du Bignon family cemetery on Jekyll.

civic affairs. He worked on behalf of Glynn Academy, the county's public school in Brunswick. The school, chartered by the Georgia Legislature in 1788, is the second-oldest public school in the state and is still a high school. Henri served as Glynn Academy's treasurer and on the school board. He was a member of the Brunswick city commission, an inferior court judge, and the first president of the Bank of Brunswick, organized in 1838. For several years, Henri was a district militia officer. Elected captain by the men in his company, he later became a colonel. The title followed him for the rest of his life, just as the title of captain had followed his father.

Christophe du Bignon, the family patriarch, did not age gracefully. He became a bitter old man, convinced that people were out to swindle him. He was depressed by crop failures and low prices for sea island cotton. His eyesight failed. Louisa, his favorite grandchild, died when she was sixteen. Her death broke his heart. He cried every day for months afterward. In September 1825, at age eighty-six, du Bignon died. His wife, Marguerite, followed three months later. She was sixty-three. They were both buried on Jekyll, the captain under a live oak tree by Du Bignon Creek near the Horton house. The du Bignon family plot, surrounded by a low wall, is near the house and creek. Three of the people buried there were family members; two were servants.

A marble slab marking the grave of a du Bignon family member.

After Christophe du Bignon's death, Henri was left to carry on his father's legacy on Jekyll. The elder du Bignon might have reconsidered his opinion of his "good" son had he known the direction Henri's life would take later.

Henri gave his youngest daughter, Eugenia, a slave named Julia, who was born in 1826, the year after Eugenia's birth. The girls grew up together on Jekyll and played together almost every day, becoming close friends. Henri sold Julia's father away when she was a year old, so she had no memories of him. She did recall her childhood years on Jekyll as happy ones. Interviewed as an elderly woman many years later, Julia remembered that all she had to do as a little girl was to "play from morning till night." When she was older, she worked in the du Bignon's kitchen. As a house slave, she would have been more privileged than the field hands, but for unknown reasons, she later worked in the fields with her mother and sisters. As an elderly woman, she bragged to her interviewer that she could outplow any man. If she or the other slaves did not complete their assigned tasks, she reported, they were whipped. Otherwise, the slaves were treated reasonably well by Henri du Bignon, Julia reported.

Henri's Progeny

HENRI DU BIGNON sired at least twenty children by wives and mistresses: eleven by his first wife, Amelia; five by his second wife; three by his longtime lover; one by a free woman of color; and another by a Jekyll slave. Many du Bignon descendants today, black and white, trace their ancestry to Henri. Around the same time he was courting Amelia, or shortly after they married, Henri probably fathered a daughter by an island slave. The child's name was Harriot. From the time of her birth, Christophe and Marguerite showed unusual concern for Harriot's welfare, suggesting that they knew she was their granddaughter. They had her baptized on Jekyll in 1811—three years after Henri and Amelia married—and made it clear they intended to help her in life. Harriot's baptismal certificate, entered in the official records of the Catholic church in Savannah, noted that she was a freeborn mulatto. Henri fathered another child, a girl named Charlotte, by a free black woman. Her baptismal record identifies her as Henri's illegitimate daughter.

Henri had a long-term affair with a woman on Jekyll that began in the late 1830s, more than a decade after his father's death. The du Bignons hired a widow named Sarah Aust to tutor their children. She moved to Jekyll with her daughters, Mary and Margaret, and soon became Henri's mistress, bearing him three children: Leonidas, William, and Rosalia Elizabeth. Amelia certainly knew about her husband's affair with Sarah Aust, since it was conducted right under her nose on a very small island. She would have known about Henri's other out-of-wedlock children as well. Like her mother-in-law, Marguerite du Bignon, Amelia probably turned a blind eye to her husband's infidelities, knowing her status as his wife made her position and that of her own children secure. The affairs, however, were probably painful and possibly embarrassing for both Marguerite and Amelia. Planters' wives often retaliated against slave women who became their husbands' mistresses, even though the slave women had little or no choice in the matter. After Amelia's death in 1850, Henri gave her an elaborate funeral in Brunswick, followed by a boat cortege from the mainland to Jekyll. The boat carrying Amelia's coffin led the procession, and a long line of boats filled with relatives and friends followed. The crew of the leading boat was dressed in mourning clothes and sang spirituals during the journey. Amelia was buried in the family plot on Jekyll, next to her adult son who had died the week before.

After Amelia's death, everyone expected Henri to marry Sarah Aust after a decent period of mourning, since he had already fathered three of her children. Instead, the good son again shocked the coastal community by impregnating Mary, one of Sarah's daughters by her first marriage. Mary was twenty; Henri was sixty-three. Their first child was born just a year after Amelia's death. Henri and Mary married the following year, moved to Brunswick, and built a home at Ellis Point on Yellow Bluff Creek, where they had four more daughters. Leonidas and William, two of the sons Henri fathered by Sarah Aust, now his mother-in-law, came to live with him and their half-sister, Henri's wife, Mary. Amelia's children probably felt uncomfortable with their father and young stepmother living on Jekyll. They might even have felt sympathy for Sarah Aust. Although she had been their father's mistress, she had also been their tutor, and they probably cared about her.

Before leaving the island with Mary, Henri divided his slaves among his surviving children and left the Jekyll plantation to be cared for by his two unmarried sons, John Couper and Henry Jr.

When Eugenia married Archibald Burke and moved to Carrollton in northwestern Georgia, Julia was sent along with her. Perhaps fearing, with reason, that her husband had eyes for Julia, Eugenia made her former playmate's life miserable. Julia said Eugenia made her sleep under the house, cut off her long, straight hair, and made her husband whip her bare back. Julia was rented out several times to other planters in the area, which, she said, she preferred to staying with the Burkes. They sold her several times, but Archibald Burke always bought her back, suggesting that his wife's suspicions might not have been baseless. For months after the Civil War ended, the Burkes refused to let Julia go. After several unsuccessful attempts, she escaped and moved to the Atlanta area. She married a man named Rush, had a number of children, and lived to be well over one hundred years old.

When Henry Jr. and John took over the management of Jekyll after their father's marriage to his former lover's daughter, they started with a handicap. Henri's division of the island slaves among his children left the brothers shorthanded on the plantation. They had fewer than half as many slaves as before, not nearly enough to keep the plantation in full production. The island's agricultural land had long since been exhausted by heavy planting. To support the raising of sea island cotton, the sandy soil had to be manured every year, with livestock waste and rich alluvial mud from the marshes. Digging and hauling the material to the fields and turning it into the soil was hard, dirty work, requiring a full contingent of slaves. Henri would have expected his sons to purchase additional slaves with their first few cotton crops, especially since prices for sea island cotton at the time were excellent. But in 1854, just two years after Henry Jr. and John took over, a hurricane destroyed all the cotton on Jekyll and left the fields and pastures a soggy mess.

Although their financial situation was precarious, the du Bignon brothers were still solid members of the upper echelon of society on the Georgia coast. Their father and grandfather had been respected planters on Jekyll Island for as long as most people could remember. The brothers had many influential friends, including one of the wealthiest men in the South: Charles Augustus Lafayette Lamar of Savannah. One of Lamar's given names came from the Marquis de Lafayette, the French nobleman who supported George Washington and Thomas Jefferson during the American Revolution. When Charles Lamar was baptized at Christ Church in Savannah, Lafayette stood as his godfather and held the infant in his arms during the ceremony.

Charles Augustus Lafayette Lamar, the scion of a prominent and wealthy Savannah family, was a southern firebrand who conspired to bring African captives illegally to Jekyll Island in 1858. The captives traveled for six weeks across the Atlantic in appalling conditions aboard the converted racing yacht *Wanderer*; many died on the voyage. Two du Bignon brothers were coconspirators, but neither they nor Lamar were ever convicted of the crime. *Wanderer* descendants still live in the area. (Courtesy of the Georgia Historical Society)

Charles Lamar, the eldest of six children, was the son of Gazaway Bugg Lamar, one of the South's wealthiest and most prominent citizens. When Charles was fourteen, Gazaway commissioned the building of an innovative iron steamship, the *Pulaski*, to carry freight and passengers from Savannah to Baltimore. After the *Pulaski* had made three successful round-trips, Gazaway arranged for his wife, his children, his sister Rebecca, and a number of prominent friends to accompany him on a *Pulaski* outing. The trip began on a balmy June morning in 1838, but turned into tragedy the following night off the coast of North Carolina. The boiler exploded, blowing a hole in the ship's side and scalding many of the passengers and crew. The *Pulaski* began sinking. Charles led his two younger brothers through listing companionways filled with smoke and panicked passengers to his parents' stateroom. When the ship broke apart, the family was separated. Charles clung to flotsam for the rest of the night before drifting near a large section of the wreckage where his father, his Aunt Rebecca, his brothers, and about twenty other victims were huddled, barely above water. His mother and sisters were gone. Fifty years later, Charles's aunt, Rebecca Lamar, wrote a moving account of the ordeal. She, her nephew Charles, and his father were the only family members who survived the tragedy.

Although Charles later became a prosperous businessman like his father, his personal life was marked by more devastating losses. All five of his sons and one of his daughters died in childhood. The tragedies may help explain why a man who was wealthy, secure, and successful joined forces with a small but vocal group of radical

The steamship *Pulaski*, destroyed by an explosion off the North Carolina coast in 1838. Charles Lamar was aboard the ship, which his father owned. The explosion killed Lamar's mother and his six siblings. (From S. A. Howland, *Steamboat Disasters and Railroad Accidents in the United States* [Worcester: Dorr, Howland, and Company, 1840], 46)

southerners called the fire-eaters. They included politicians, planters, and preachers, all proslavery and anti-North to the point of obsession. They resented the fact that northern states were prospering while the South, heavily dependent on agriculture, was struggling. Southerners purchased goods from the North, exported their cotton on northern ships, bought insurance from northern companies, and borrowed money at high interest rates from northern banks. The fire-eaters believed the North was bleeding the South dry.

Slavery was another major issue. There were three million slaves in the South, representing a huge part of the region's wealth. If slavery were outlawed, as many in the north thought it should be, the southern economy would collapse. Importing slaves directly from Africa to the United States had been banned since 1808 by federal law. Most southerners, even slave owners, supported the ban on the slave trade, as well as another law passed later that made the offense punishable by death. Charles Lamar and the fire-eaters were openly contemptuous of northerners who lobbied for banning slavery but had no qualms about making money themselves from slaves. When northern businessmen acquired plantations in bankruptcy, they did not usually free the slaves, but sold them and pocketed the profits. Northerners also made fortunes from shipping southern cotton produced by slave labor. Ironically, the heart of the illegal slave trade was not the Deep South but New York City. Ships left New York ports every day for Africa, where they would pick up boatloads of slaves and sell them for huge profits in Cuba and elsewhere, enriching the accounts of northern investors.

Charles's father, Gazaway Lamar, had moved to Virginia after the *Pulaski* tragedy, where he remarried and started a second family. Instead of resenting the North for its success, he saw it as a land of opportunity. He relocated to New York and founded the Bank of the Republic on the corner of Wall Street and Broadway. He was soon involved in a major insurance company and other lucrative businesses. Distressed by Charles's radical views, Gazaway tried to reason with him, without success. He wrote to his brother, John, that Charles was "so crazy on the Negro question—that I can make no impression on him."

Charles Lamar was convinced that the laws banning the Atlantic slave trade should be repealed. He believed that if he imported slaves from Africa, no jury in the South would convict him. Acquittal, he thought, would nullify the law and provoke its repeal. He attempted several times to send ships he owned to Africa to pick up slaves, but each time his efforts were thwarted. In 1858, Lamar and a small group of

like-minded men purchased a luxury yacht to use as a slaver. He then conspired with his good friends on Jekyll, the bachelor brothers John and Henry du Bignon, to land a load of slaves on the remote island. Lamar, who was already rich, participated because of his radical political beliefs. The du Bignons, who probably shared Lamar's views on slavery, needed the fifteen thousand dollars he offered to pay them. They needed to buy more slaves to save the family plantation.

A few months earlier, Henry and Charles had gotten into an argument at the Savannah horse track. Both might have been drinking; Henry was probably drunk. In the course of the disagreement, he drew a knife and threatened Charles and later threw a heavy glass inkwell at his friend. Charles drew his pistol and shot Henry in the face. The bullet lodged below Henry's right eye. It was successfully removed, but he lost the sight in that eye. By the next day, Henry and Charles were friends again. They may have chalked up the incident to the fact that both were high-spirited southern gentlemen settling their differences in a time-honored way.

Charles Lamar was an ardent secessionist who believed the southern states needed to leave the Union in order to prosper. As it turned out, his beliefs and actions may have helped provoke the first shot fired in the Civil War.

The Last American Slave Ship

AS SLEEK AND GRACEFUL as a bottlenose dolphin, the luxury racing yacht *Wanderer* was a marvel of the shipbuilder's art. Slightly more than one hundred feet long, depending on whether she was measured from bow to stern or along her keel, she was built at a Long Island boatyard during the winter of 1857–58 for a wealthy Louisiana sugar planter who belonged to the prestigious New York Yacht Club. The *Wanderer* was a rich man's toy. Her main cabin and the captain's stateroom were decorated with mirrors in gilt frames, damask and lace curtains, satinwood cabinets, fine carpets woven in Brussels, ornate rattan furnishings, a library of leather-bound books, and etchings worthy of a serious collector. Most of all, the *Wanderer* was designed for speed. The sugar baron who had her built was an admirer of the schooner *America*, which then held the title as the fastest ocean-racing yacht in the world. In 1851, the *America*, representing the New York Yacht Club, won the first international match race around the Isle of Wight against a bevy of British racing yachts, finishing eight minutes ahead of its closest competitor. The famed America's Cup trophy was named in her honor. The New York Yacht Club held the trophy for more than a century, from 1857 until 1983, when the *Australia II*, racing for the Royal Perth Yacht Club, beat the New York club's defender, ending the longest winning streak in international sports history.

The *Wanderer*, a luxurious racing yacht built for speed. It was converted to a slave ship by a group of conspirators who used it to import African captives illegally into the United States by way of Jekyll Island. (Courtesy of the Jekyll Island Museum Archives)

The sterling silver cup awarded to the winner of the America's Cup. The *Wanderer* was designed along the same lines as the *America*, first recipient of the trophy—the oldest one given for an international sporting event—in 1841. (Courtesy of the Library of Congress)

The *Wanderer* was designed along the same lines as the *America*. Under sail in a good wind, the sugar baron's yacht could achieve a speed of twenty knots, almost unheard of at the time. Because of a pointed bow and sharply incurving hull, it had almost no cargo space below decks, not that a racing yacht needed any. The proud owner, eager to show the *Wanderer* off in New Orleans, had it provisioned in New York for the voyage home with such delicacies as shrimp, crabs, lobsters, soft clams, and other fresh local seafood, as well as imported cheeses, dates, coffee, tea, brandy, and ginger, a time-honored cure for seasickness. On the journey, the *Wanderer* stopped in Charleston, Savannah, and Brunswick. It had been written about in all the major newspapers and magazines of the day and was famous the length of the Atlantic Seaboard. At every port of call, it was met with cheers from admiring crowds along the waterfront. Charles Lamar almost certainly turned out to greet the boat in Savannah; the du Bignon brothers and their father probably welcomed it in Brunswick. Considering the social status of Charles Lamar and Henri du Bignon Sr., the du Bignon brothers might have been invited aboard to admire the boat's amenities and enjoy a glass of port with its owner. While the *Wanderer* was in Brunswick, it raced in a local regatta against dozens of other boats. It danced away from the competition, beating the next-fastest yacht in a short race by three hundred yards. Brunswick mayor Carey Wentworth Styles, a close friend of Charles Lamar, presented the loving cup to the *Wanderer*'s owner. Styles later was a founder of the *Atlanta Constitution*, which became one of the nation's largest newspapers and, for a time, one of the South's most liberal news organs. Just four months after showing off his new yacht in New Orleans and Cuba, the sugar baron—claiming that his wife wanted a beamy, comfortable boat instead of a sleek racing yacht with limited cabin space that heeled over under sail—took the *Wanderer* back to New York and sold it.

Captain William C. Corrie, the scion of an old Charleston family, was one of the buyers, as was Corrie's friend J. Egbert Farnum. Corrie lived in Washington, DC, where he worked as a congressional lobbyist, although he bragged more about bribing congressmen than lobbying them. He enjoyed telling stories about how much he had paid to put each politician in his pocket. Farnum was a dashing, hard-drinking soldier of fortune who served as a commander in a well-known mercenary army. He loved

Off Jekyll, a fisherman casting his line near one of the Intracoastal Waterway day markers designed to guide boats past area shallows.

recounting his adventures to an admiring crowd, describing how he had hacked his way through snake-infested jungles, rafted down piranha-ridden rivers, and braved wild and dangerous outposts of the world. Charles Lamar was also among the *Wanderer*'s new owners, but he made sure his name was omitted from the bill of sale. He had been so vocal about his intent to import slaves into the United States from Africa, in violation of federal and state laws, that if authorities learned he was among the yacht's new owners, the boat might never have been allowed to leave the United States.

Over the next several months, Lamar and his partners had the *Wanderer* secretly modified into a slave ship. They had fifteen-thousand-gallon water tanks installed. Observers noted that the tanks held enough water to supply the yacht's regular crew and passengers for two years. When authorities in New York questioned Corrie about the size of the tanks, he wined and dined them in the captain's cabin and convinced them the tanks were needed as ballast when a racing yacht of the *Wanderer*'s caliber was competing. Corrie took the boat to Charleston, where he took on rough pine lumber that would be used to build a slave deck in the cramped hold after the yacht reached Africa. He stocked up on trade items to use when purchasing slaves.

Many historians believe the *Wanderer*, which arrived in Georgia in late November 1858, was the last ship to import a large cargo of slaves from Africa into the United States. Others, including the famed writer-folklorist Zora Neale Hurston, claimed the *Clotilde* held that dubious distinction. A 1944 article by Hurston recounts her interview with an elderly former slave who told her that he had arrived in Mobile Bay on the *Clotilde* in the summer of 1859 or 1860. Hurston claimed the *Clotilde*'s hull was still visible at low tide in the marshes of Bayou Corne, near where the schooner was said to have been scuttled on a summer night. She reported that 110 men, women, and children were shuttled ashore in Alabama and sold. After emancipation, the freed slaves settled in a community long known as Africa Town, which is home even now to people believed to be their descendants.

There is still debate about whether the *Clotilde* landed slaves from Africa in the United States. After controversy exploded over the *Wanderer*'s landing, reports began surfacing of other slave ships discharging illegal cargo on the southern coast. President James Buchanan sent an undercover investigator to check out the rumors. The investigator spent several months interviewing planters, state and federal authorities, and others before concluding that the reports were all false, "founded upon the movements of the *Wanderer* negroes, or else they were mere fabrications, manufactured and circulated for political effect, or to fill a column in a sensation newspaper." It was, of course, in the Buchanan administration's best interest to refute the reports of other slave ship landings. At any rate, the *Wanderer* is usually billed as the last *documented* ship to import captives from Africa directly into the United States. It is also the only slave ship whose name was permanently linked to the Africans it transported. They were always known as *Wanderer* slaves.

In part, the *Wanderer*'s notoriety was due to timing. The southern states were threatening to secede from the still-young and fragile union. More and more southerners were beginning to support the idea of secession, even though most had never owned slaves. One of many points of contention leading up to the Civil War was southerners' deep resentment that northerners were trying to tell them what to do.

After landing its cargo on Jekyll, the by then notorious *Wanderer* changed hands several times. At one point, it was stolen by pirates and taken to Africa on another slaving mission. The first mate and crew mutinied off the coast and set the pirate captain adrift in a small boat. The mutineers then brought the yacht back to the United States and turned it over to authorities. During the Civil War, the *Wanderer* was confiscated by the U.S. government; it served as a vessel in the U.S. Navy until the end of the war. It was then sold for commercial purposes and operated until 1871, when it ran aground and broke up off the coast of Cuba. It was a sad ending for a once-lovely racing yacht whose reputation was forever tarnished by the conspirators who involved it in the world's ugliest trade.

CHAPTER V From Africa to Jekyll

[1858–1885]

When the *Wanderer* arrived in west Africa in September 1858, the coast was patrolled by the African Squadron, composed of navy ships from both Britain and the United States. Charged with intercepting slave ships, the squadron was never very effective, primarily because only twenty-eight ships were assigned to patrol the three-thousand-mile-long slave coast. The squadron's ships were old and slow, and the captains were usually servicemen whose careers had stalled. The African Squadron was regarded as a dreadful duty station, not only because of the quality of the ships and the men involved, but also because of the unhealthy conditions on the western coast of Africa. More often than not, men aboard squadron boats were sick with fevers.

Captain William C. Corrie and J. Egbert Farnum sailed on the *Wanderer* to Africa, but the person at the helm was a man named Dennis Brown—or was it Seth Briggs? The captain used both names, and others as well. His crew was a mix of rough-cut Greek and Portuguese seamen who seemed out of place on a luxury vessel like the graceful *Wanderer*. They would have looked far more natural sailing under the skull and crossbones than the burgee of the exclusive New York Yacht Club.

The mouth of the Congo, where the slave ship *Wanderer* idled as its captain waited to pick up an illegal cargo of slaves. (Courtesy of MONUSCO/Myriam Asmani, Wikimedia Commons)

Brown headed for the mouth of the Congo River. There, two more men joined the crew: tattooed Africans with teeth filed to points, in the style of their culture. They paddled alongside in a canoe and boarded the *Wanderer* to guide it upriver. The yacht passed several small villages before reaching the trading center, a haphazard compound of crooked buildings teetering on stilts over the river. Corrie and Farnum went ashore and arranged to purchase a load of slaves, using rum, cutlasses, muskets, and gunpowder as currency. They paid the equivalent of fifty dollars a captive. In the United States, they could expect each captive to bring five hundred dollars in hard cash. After the preliminary negotiations were complete, a slave deck was built just below the *Wanderer*'s main deck. Then it sailed back toward the open sea to wait for the captives to be assembled. While the yacht sailed up and down the coast for a week or more, Corrie and Farnum enjoyed views of native villages, lush foliage, and exotic animals, all perfumed with the fragrance of African wildflowers blooming in the hot tropical sunshine.

When the *Wanderer* returned to the Congo River, one of the African Squadron ships, the heavily armed *Medusa* of the Royal Navy, was lying at anchor near the river

mouth, on the lookout for slave ships. Corrie brazenly ordered Brown—or was it Briggs?—to drop anchor alongside the *Medusa*. He invited the British commander to come aboard for drinks and, later, dinner. Corrie and Farnum spent several weeks entertaining officers of the *Medusa*, who were happy to be convinced that the *Wanderer* was a luxury yacht taking a couple of wealthy gentlemen on an adventure cruise. When another yacht arrived at the river mouth, her captain challenged the *Wanderer* to a race. Corrie and Farnum accepted. Their yacht again ran away with the competition, passing her opponent "like the wind," according to a note Corrie scribbled in the ship's log. When the *Medusa* finally departed to take care of squadron business elsewhere, Brown sailed the *Wanderer* south for several days and dropped anchor along a remote stretch of coast. The crew signaled with a lantern; there was an answering signal from the jungle.

The slave trader had assembled about five hundred Africans, most of them teenage boys, to make the crossing to America. Each captive had been branded on the chest with a hot iron shaped like the letter *W*, possibly a reference to the yacht's name. The burns were still fresh and painful as the captives were paddled by canoe out to board the yacht. They were led below to the cramped space that would be their fetid prison for the next six weeks. Each captive was made to lie on his side in the fetal position, facing the bow. The captives were so crowded that the chest of the person behind touched the back of the person ahead. Each had a space about twelve inches wide, eighteen inches high, and fewer than five feet long. There was not enough room for anyone to sit upright, and only the shorter captives could stretch to their full length. One of the few women aboard was pregnant and nearing her delivery date. Her two teenage sons were brought aboard with her. The family would have tried to stay together as the hold slowly filled with terrified people. In slave-trading parlance, the *Wanderer* was "tight-packed," a practice condemned by many traders as too brutal, or at least too costly, since many slaves on tight-packed ships died before reaching their destination. Buyers did not pay for dead slaves. As the last load of ten or fifteen captives was being paddled through the surf and out to the yacht, a lookout on the *Wanderer* spotted an African Squadron ship approaching. It was the USS *Vincennes*, an aging navy vessel with a long and honorable history of missions all over the world. By the time she joined the African Squadron, she was long past her prime, with a leaky hull, sagging sails, and creaking timbers. Her commander was an incompetent petty tyrant loathed by his 150-man crew. The *Vincennes* was not looking for the

The Wanderer Memorial on the south end of Jekyll Island, where 409 captive Africans were offloaded in secret after their perilous journey across the Atlantic Ocean. The dedication was made in 2008, on the 150th anniversary of the *Wanderer* landing. The memorial has since deteriorated and needs replacing.

Wanderer when she chanced upon her. But even a bumbling commander could recognize the signs of a slave ship being loaded.

Corrie and Farnum had two choices: run or surrender. If they surrendered, they would be arrested and charged with piracy, an offense punishable by death. They would also lose their cargo, representing thousands of dollars, and the *Wanderer* would be confiscated. As the *Vincennes* maneuvered to intercept the yacht by blocking the deep, narrow channel that led through shoal waters to the open sea, Corrie and Farnum opted to run. Brown hauled the *Wanderer*'s sails tight. The boat heeled over, put its lee rail in the water, and flew straight toward the *Vincennes*. Moments before the ships would have collided, Brown pulled the *Wanderer*'s sails even tighter, pointing her bow almost straight into the wind. A lesser ship would have fallen into irons, which the writer Erik Colonius, an expert on the *Wanderer*, calls "the nautical equivalent of a nervous breakdown." In irons, a ship's sails no longer catch wind, and it stalls, dead in the water, the main boom swaying back and forth over the deck. The *Wanderer*, however, was no ordinary ship. It brazened past the bow of the *Vincennes* with fifty feet to spare. The crew of the navy vessel later admitted they could have stopped the *Wanderer* with a cannonball through her rigging, but they were all too awed by the yacht's speed

The Middle Passage

ON THE SLAVE DECK BELOW, conditions were awful from the outset. As the ship heeled over to run, the chained and near-naked captives slid along the rough, splintery boards. Any that were seasick had to vomit in place, since they could move no more than a few inches. There were no sanitary facilities of any kind. No water was available to wash away their vomit or other wastes, so they lay in them and shared them with their neighbors. It was dark in the hold, especially after the crew locked down the hatches for the night. Hatch vents were left open to funnel air below, but the vents could not move enough air to cool 487 people packed together like sardines. The stench and the temperature rose to unbearable levels. By the following morning, all the captives were gasping for air. Half a dozen were dead. Their bodies were hauled to the main deck and thrown with casual callousness overboard. One account of the *Wanderer* claims the crew threw living captives overboard while it was being chased by the *Vincennes*. A period painting depicts the captives being tossed into shark-infested waters. The report and the painting are most likely inaccurate, although there were reports of live captives being thrown overboard when slave ships were in danger of being caught by authorities. Once the *Wanderer* passed the *Vincennes*, it was in no danger from the squadron vessel, which could have caught the racing yacht only by sprouting wings. After the first captives died, the crew began bringing the others up on deck in groups, where they were fed cornmeal gruel and hard biscuits and allowed to enjoy the fresh breeze for an hour or so before the next group of captives was led up, blinking and disoriented, into the sunlight. On deck, the Africans were encouraged to play drums and tambourines and dance, not only to entertain the crew but also to keep their muscles from deteriorating. After several days, the crew rigged up a pump and sprayed seawater over the captives to clean them up before returning them to the hold. One captive rigged a piece of iron to keep a hatch vent open. After being caught, he was whipped repeatedly and had his back sliced multiple times with a knife. The man bore the torture in silence until the crew doused him with seawater. As the salty water hit his open wounds, the captive screamed and passed out.

On the tenth day of the crossing, the wind died. Clouds massed, promising a heavy blow. The captain reefed the sails before the storm attacked with high winds, torrential rain, and rough seas. Thunder boomed like cannon fire, and lightning blazed, seeming to aim for the ship's tall masts. Waves crashed over the bow and foamed along the deck. Afraid the ship would sink, Brown ordered the hatches closed and the air vents covered. The captives screamed and moaned as they struggled to breathe in the airless hold. The storm continued through

Jekyll's south beach, where more than 400 African captives were offloaded from the Wanderer in November 1858.

the night. The *Wanderer* plunged, pitched, and rolled; the captives chained on the slave deck plunged, pitched, and rolled along with her. In the morning, the crew opened the hatches to find the captives covered with vomit, bodily wastes, and blood. Skin had been rubbed from their bodies as they skidded around on the rough boards during the storm. The dead were dumped overboard. The rest were brought to the main deck in groups to be hosed off and fed. By the time the *Wanderer* finally reached the entrance to St. Andrews Sound, six weeks after leaving the African coast, eighty captives had died and their bodies had been tossed into the Atlantic. No record exists of any of their names.

Corrie and Farnum got a replacement for one of the dead captives. A baby was born during the voyage to the woman whose teenage sons came aboard with her. She cannot have given birth on the slave deck, where she had no room even to part her legs. Perhaps the crew allowed her the privacy of a cabin and a female captive to help her, since there was no doctor aboard. If not, the woman would have given birth alone on the main deck in the glare of sun or the chill of night. Perhaps the new mother was given extra rations of food and allowed to stay topside with her infant for the rest of the voyage. At any rate, she and her daughter both survived. The baby was later named Clementine du Bignon, indicating she was purchased by or given to someone in the du Bignon family, perhaps Henri, who still owned Jekyll but lived in Brunswick while his sons managed the island plantation. One of Clementine's older brothers, Mazinga—later named Tom Floyd—was purchased by a planter in Camden County. After the Civil War, Tom Floyd moved to St. Simons Island. His great-grandson, born on the island in 1936, was Jim Brown, one of the greatest running backs in National Football League history.

and the skill of the helmsman to react. As the *Vincennes* wallowed in her wake, the *Wanderer* raced into the first night of what would be a dreadful journey for the captives packed below.

A few days before the *Wanderer* arrived on the Georgia coast, the du Bignon brothers sent a notice to the *Savannah Daily Morning News*. It warned that anyone landing on Jekyll to cut wood, hunt, or look for shipwrecks—or for any other reason—would be prosecuted. Had it been posted at some other time, the advertisement would have been viewed as a straightforward "no trespassing" notice. On the eve of the *Wanderer*'s landing, however, it was obviously designed to keep the slave ship's arrival secret, and prosecutors later used the notice as evidence during the trials of the conspirators. Brown steered the battered yacht toward shore, but anchored outside St. Andrews Sound. Even such a skilled and experienced a captain was unwilling to navigate the sound's treacherous shoalwaters without a local guide.

James Clubb, the lighthouse keeper on Little Cumberland Island and a harbor pilot, was such a guide. He was supposed to board the *Wanderer* and steer it to an anchorage near Jekyll. The crew signaled for Clubb, but after waiting most of the day, Corrie and Brown rowed ashore to look for him. They met a young man who seemed shocked to see two sunburned men in tattered clothing with unkempt hair and beards. Corrie introduced himself as Captain Cook and Farnum as Mr. Brookstone. The young man was not the harbor pilot, he explained, but only the assistant light keeper. Clubb had gone to Jekyll to tend a beacon on the north end of that island. The assistant followed them in his boat back to the *Wanderer*, then rowed Corrie to Jekyll, commenting that he hoped the *Wanderer* was not a slaver. Corrie laughed off the comment.

The two men trekked to the north end of Jekyll, stopping at a house occupied by John Couper du Bignon. After Corrie and du Bignon talked privately, du Bignon informed the assistant of Captain Cook's real identity and explained that they were old friends. The *Wanderer*, he said, had 407 *apprentices*, not slaves, aboard, who were in immediate need of food, water, and medical treatment. It was legal to bring apprentices into the United States from other countries, but only under certain strict conditions. Corrie and du Bignon would have been hard pressed to explain why they needed to land more than four hundred African apprentices in secret on a remote island instead of off-loading them openly at a coastal port. The young assistant keeper knew his place, however, and did not ask the gentlemen for an explanation.

The three men found Clubb tending a small Jekyll beacon that overlooked St. Simons Sound. Du Bignon tried the apprentice story on the older man. Clubb scoffed, saying he knew the *Wanderer* was a "damned slaver." He usually charged fifty dollars to bring a ship into St. Andrews Sound. For the *Wanderer*, his fee would be ten times that. Corrie protested, shocked by the high price, but du Bignon agreed. He, like Clubb, knew they had no other option.

At dawn, Clubb rowed to the *Wanderer* and boarded the once-lovely yacht. The stench from below almost knocked him to his knees. He took the helm and guided it into the sound as the rising sun gilded his wake. He anchored a hundred yards from Jekyll's south end. The *Wanderer*'s crew began shuttling the captives to the beach in two of the yacht's boats and in a boat owned by the du Bignons. One captive died moments after reaching shore and was buried in a shallow grave. The others fell to their knees, weeping and laughing, grateful to be on dry land in the fresh air. Although it was the end of November, the weather might still have been balmy, as it often is on the sea islands in late fall. Several du Bignon slaves were brought to the beach to attend to the newcomers. The half-starved, half-naked captives and the fully dressed, well-fed du Bignon slaves stared at each other in amazement. When one of the captives spoke, an elderly du Bignon slave named Jack burst into tears. He had not heard his native language spoken for seventy years. As the unloading continued, the *Wanderer*'s iron mess kettle was brought ashore and filled with cornmeal. After the captives had eaten a meal of hot gruel, many fell asleep on the warm sand or on beds of fragrant pine needles in the woods fringing the beach. Perhaps the resinous scent of the pines helped to drive away the horrible smell of the *Wanderer*'s hold.

When the coastal steamer *St. Johns* passed through Jekyll Creek that evening on a regular run between Fernandina and Savannah, it was intercepted by a rowboat from Jekyll. The steamer stopped long enough to take Farnum aboard. He signed the ship's register as Mr. Wilson. When the boat reached Savannah the following day, Farnum-Wilson headed straight for the elegant downtown residence of Charles Lamar. After they talked, Charles hired the steamer *Lamar*, which had once been owned by his family, to make a run south that night. He hired his own captain, but when the man did not show up on time, Lamar was forced to use the *Lamar*'s regular captain, Luke Christie. Several prominent men boarded the steamship for the trip, including a

Large trees felled by erosion on Jekyll's north end.

well-known slave trader, a member of the Savannah city council, and Charles Lamar himself. The steamer reached Jekyll after dark the following day. Henry du Bignon rowed out to show Captain Christie where to anchor and where to drop the gangplank on the riverbank. Lamar, Corrie, and the other men hurried into the woods, leaving Christie behind, with instructions to wait on the boat.

Before the *Lamar* arrived, the captives on Jekyll had been given blankets and scraps of clothing and examined by a Brunswick doctor, the husband of one of the du Bignons' sisters. The captives were again encouraged to dance to keep their muscles strong. About two hundred were loaded onto the steamship. Some balked in terror at the gangplank, fearing another ocean voyage, but were finally persuaded to board. While the slave trader stayed on Jekyll to market the remainder of the captives, the *Lamar* headed up the coast with Charles Lamar on board. It entered the Savannah River after dark and slipped passed the coastal city. Lamar returned to his house in downtown Savannah before the captives were unloaded near a plantation in South Carolina about fifteen miles upriver. When they were released in a cornfield rattling with dry, winter stalks, the famished captives found ears of corn overlooked by the harvesters and gobbled the hard kernels. They also made hand traps for field mice, which the protein-starved captives devoured. About ten days later, another boat arrived to take some of the captives farther upriver. The captain of the second boat was given a young captive as payment. He took the boy to his home in Augusta, but so many people came to see the "wild African boy" that the captain pronounced him a nuisance and gave him back.

A month or so after the *Wanderer*'s landing, a group of thirty-eight Africans arrived by train in Montgomery, Alabama. They were off-loaded in chains and transferred to hay wagons that took them to slave lodgings in the city. The residents of Montgomery flocked to see people they considered wild Africans, with their tattooed faces and filed teeth. Because of the laws banning slave importation, most slaves in the South by the late 1850s had been born in the United State, as had many of their parents and grandparents. The newly arrived captives were as alien to the domestic slaves as they were to Montgomery's white residents. The *Wanderer* captives were also excellent mimics, a skill that amazed everyone. Anything said to them, even complicated phrases and complex words, was repeated back perfectly.

The following day, the Africans were taken to the Alabama River and loaded on a steamboat bound for the Gulf of Mexico. It is this group of captives, according to

During the Spanish-American War, the filibuster tug *Dauntless* docked at night in the Satilla River west of Jekyll to pick up an illegal cargo of Cuban freedom fighters and armaments.

some scholars, that settled Africa Town near Mobile Bay after the Civil War and provoked reports that an illegal slave ship named the *Clotilde* had landed slaves in the area.

Corrie had stayed behind on Jekyll with the slave trader, who wasted no time in finding buyers for the rest of the captives. Corrie had the *Wanderer*'s slave deck ripped out and then sent her up the Little Satilla River to be cleaned and fumigated.

The yacht was scrubbed with lye and doused with vinegar to counteract the rank smell. After the boat was sanitized, deodorized, and made reasonably free of the rats and roaches that had proliferated during the Atlantic crossing, Corrie hired a man to sail it to the nearby port of Brunswick. Corrie showed up soon afterward at the port collector's office, asking for clearance papers to take the *Wanderer* to Charleston, its home port. He claimed that the papers had not been stamped at the last port of call because the port official was absent that day. He explained that the *Wanderer* had been caught in a violent storm offshore, no doubt to justify the yacht's bedraggled appearance. A cleaning, no matter how thorough, could not remove all the ravages of the voyage.

Within a day of the *Wanderer*'s landing, rumors that a large cargo of slaves had been off-loaded on Jekyll swept along the coast like a summer thunderstorm. The port collector, who was one of the last to hear the gossip, stamped Corrie's paperwork, but Corrie did not depart with the yacht right away. By the next morning, even the port collector had heard rumors of a slave ship that were impossible to ignore. He rowed out to the *Wanderer*, checked it out, and found nothing amiss. But when he reexamined its papers, he discovered a forged stamp. He sent a message to the assistant U.S. Attorney in Savannah, informing him of his discoveries and suspicions. Just as he finished writing the note, the steamboat *Lamar* arrived to tow the *Wanderer* away. When Corrie saw the port collector approaching the yacht, he fled, leaving behind a trunkful of personal items, notebooks, and even the ship's logs.

The *Wanderer* captives were sold all over the Southeast, some to planters in Glynn and Camden Counties, although the conspirators tried to move as many as possible to more distant locations. Some of those taken up the Savannah River were sold to area planters. More than one hundred were sold in South Carolina's old Edgefield District, just across the Savannah River from Augusta. Some were put to work in the famed Edgefield potteries.

The *Savannah Republican* newspaper broke the story of the *Wanderer*'s landing, reporting that the yacht had off-loaded a large cargo of slaves near Brunswick. The story appeared a day later in all major U.S. newspapers, in the *London Times*, and in other international publications. The *New York Times* ran the story, but editorialized that the report of the incident might have been started as a joke by Corrie and Farnum. The *Times* noted that claims of the *Wanderer* off-loading as many as four hundred slaves were absurd, considering the racing yacht's cramped space below decks. Earlier in the year, the *Times* had cited similar reasons in articles chastising authorities for suspecting the *Wanderer* of being a slaver. Another newspaper, citing an interview with Farnum after he arrived home in New York, likewise debunked the story, noting that Corrie and Farnum had entertained the African Squadron officers of the HMS *Medusa* in the Congo River and had been wined and dined by Royal Navy officers in return. The reporter described the yacht race off the African coast as further evidence that the *Wanderer* was on a pleasure excursion, noting that the yacht beat its competition "as easily as a race horse would beat a common roadster."

Roadsters, high-stepping steeds bred for trotting competitions, were popular as gentlemen's carriage horses, but were not noted for speed.

Yet it soon became evident, even to skeptics, that the story of the *Wanderer*'s exploits was true. Planters around the Southeast bragged openly about owning *Wanderer* slaves. There were confirmed sightings, in Georgia and elsewhere in the region, of groups of Africans with tattooed faces and filed teeth, whose presence could be explained only by their having arrived on the racing yacht. Charles Lamar was arrogant enough to drive a young African through the streets of Savannah in his carriage, proclaiming to everyone, even to a federal official, that the boy was a genuine "live African" brought to the United States on the *Wanderer*. Lamar boasted that he was an owner of the racing yacht and had sent her to Africa to engage in the transatlantic slave trade in order to prove that the laws against it were unconstitutional. Once northern newspapers were persuaded that the stories were true, they began howling for prosecutions. The *Times* targeted Charles Lamar in particular, calling him a kidnapper, a felon, a spineless coward, and a scofflaw, and urging authorities to bring him to trial.

But to prove their case, prosecutors first had to produce evidence: namely, the captives themselves. A couple of federal officials slipped onto Jekyll one night not long after the *Wanderer* off-loaded its captives and sneaked through the woods, following the sound of drums and tambourines. They saw Africans dancing, but were spotted before they could capture anyone. The musicians and dancers scattered into the woods. The agents managed to nab a teenage boy who had been injured on the voyage and was unable to run away. They took him back to Savannah and gave him medical care at a slave facility. About five hundred people came to get a look at the wild African boy, who amazed the visitors with his ability to mimic them. One night, three men showed up and took the boy with them. It is not known who they were and where they took him.

Another group of about three dozen *Wanderer* captives were detained by a deputy federal marshal in Middle Georgia's Telfair County. They were released on the advice of a federal official in Savannah after he wired his superiors in Washington, DC, asking for advice. He never received a reply.

In April 1859, the first *Wanderer* indictments were handed down. They named John Couper du Bignon and Henry du Bignon as conspirators. John was found not guilty thirteen months later. Henry's case was never prosecuted, apparently because he was not living on Jekyll when the captives were landed, even though witnesses placed him

Face Jugs

THE EDGEFIELD DISTRICT, which now embraces all or part of South Carolina's Aiken, Edgefield, and Greenwood Counties, was home to potteries that produced the country's first alkaline-glazed stoneware. Before 1820, when alkaline glazes were introduced into the United States, ceramic glazes were lead based. If they were poorly fired—and many were—lead could leach out, poisoning anything stored in the vessels. Glazes made with lead, still popular today, are safe as long as they are properly fired.

Some experts say *Wanderer* captives who worked at the potteries were the creators of the face jugs that are now considered art treasures. The newly imported slaves brought traditions and religious beliefs from Africa to the Edgefield District, where most or all of the resident slaves had been born in the United States. Some were third- and fourth-generation Americans who had adopted, however reluctantly, the customs and religions of the country in which they lived. For years, *Wanderer* captives were identified with the notorious slave ship and were viewed, by whites and even by American-born blacks, as wild, exotic, and fascinating. At the Edgefield potteries, slaves used scraps of clay to make small jugs and then decorated the jugs with faces. The potters used white kaolin river clay mined in the district to form facial features that would stand out against the darker stoneware. In Africa, traditional masks were often inlaid with bits of white shell or clay to represent eyes and teeth; in parts of West Africa, kaolin was considered a sacred material. The faces on the Edgefield jugs had large, sometimes bulging eyes and prominent teeth. The pointed teeth featured on some of the jugs probably represented the filed teeth then common in parts of Africa.

Many of the *Wanderer* captives came from the widespread Kongolese culture of west-central Africa, where a belief in magic and the ability to contact spirits was strong. The Kongo people believed that spirits, including those of their dead ancestors, could be caught in containers called *nkisi*, which were often decorated with humanlike faces and forms. In Kongo villages, a diviner would activate the *nkisi* by filling it with magical material such as kaolin river clay to trap the spirits inside, where they could be petitioned by the jug's owner for help or to assist the owner in casting magical spells, both good and evil.

It may be impossible to determine whether any of the *Wanderer* slaves made face jugs at the Edgefield potteries, because the jugs were not signed or marked by individual craftsmen. One face jug bears the words "Squire Pofu," which, in Swahili, means the "Blind Squire." Scholars speculate that the jug, which features unique black eyes, may have been used to conjure an enemy in order to make him go blind. Another expert suggests the jug might have been made by a potter to honor a blind ancestor.

Art experts, archaeologists, and historians still debate the function and meaning of the face jugs. At the time they were made, the jugs were considered unattractive by many white people and acculturated blacks; in fact, they were often called ugly jugs or monkey jars. Many of the faces are distorted and disturbing. Scholars speculate that the scary faces might have been used for jugs designed to hold whiskey, to discourage children from imbibing. Others say the faces may have alerted children and illiterate adults to the contents of jugs used to store substances such as turpentine or kerosene.

Face jugs have been found in cemeteries, where slaves and poor blacks were often buried in unmarked graves. There is speculation that the jugs served as gravestones and were given ugly faces to scare the devil away. Recent research indicates that the jugs probably served multipurpose functions and might have been deliberately designed to be misinterpreted by white people.

Although other cultures around the world have crafted ceramics decorated with facial features, the face jugs from the Edgefield potteries are considered unique. Dale L. Couch, curator of decorative arts at the Georgia Museum of Art, in Athens, said he believes the jugs were created as "acts of dignity and defiance" by enslaved potters. Original face jugs have been found far from the old Edgefield District, including at stops along the Underground Railroad.

Face jugs. (From the collection of Carl and Marian Mullis of Atlanta, on extended loan to the Georgia Museum of Art; images © Georgia Museum of Art, University of Georgia)

The possibility that *Wanderer* slaves crafted face jugs at the Edgefield potteries came to light in recent years when a genealogist named April L. Hynes of New York discovered a jug unearthed by her grandfather in 1950 on a construction site in Philadelphia. She traced its origin to the Edgefield potteries, learned about the arrival of slaves from the *Wanderer* in the district, and began searching for descendants of people brought over on the yacht turned slaver. Hynes and her coresearcher, Mark Newell, an archaeologist and writer at Armstrong Atlantic University in Savannah, participated in a PBS documentary series, *History Detectives*, that featured interviews with a number of *Wanderer* descendants. Hynes and researchers at the Jekyll Island Museum continue to search for other descendants of those captives.

When white potters began making face jugs in about 1880, slave potters apparently abandoned the craft, at least at the Edgefield potteries. After the Civil War, the black potters may have drifted away from the district or found other work in the area. Early face jugs are treasured today as art pieces, sought by museums and collectors. In recent years, a jug sold for almost $70,000.

on the island at the time the yacht was unloaded. Charles Lamar and others were also indicted. All those who were tried were acquitted. Lamar, the chief instigator, was never even brought to trial. The *Wanderer* was confiscated and sold at auction. Charles bought her back for four thousand dollars, considerably more than he had intended to pay, but another man had bid against him. After the bidding closed, a furious Lamar attacked the rival bidder and knocked him down.

When Abraham Lincoln was elected in 1860, there was little doubt the South would secede. Talk of secession had been going on for several years. Lincoln had never proposed a ban on slavery, but he did oppose extending it to new states entering the Union. Charles Lamar and his cohorts were spoiling for secession and eager for war. Charles wrote to his father a few weeks after Lincoln's election, explaining his desire for the South to take action: "We do not care for what the world may approve of—We know we are right & we'll act regardless of consequences." John and Henry du Bignon, like Lamar, were also avid—or rather, rabid—secessionists.

In December, the southern states began to secede. In January 1861, Georgia became the fifth one to leave. In the next month, Jefferson Davis was elected president of the Confederate States of America. One of the fire-eaters, a close associate of Charles Lamar, is said to have fired the first shot at Fort Sumter, a federal fort located on an island in Charleston harbor. The shot marked the start of the Civil War. Like most sea island planters, John and Henry du Bignon moved their slaves to the mainland during the war to keep them from being liberated by Union forces. Confederate batteries were erected on St. Simons and Jekyll to guard the entrance to Brunswick harbor, one of Georgia's two ports at the time. By a strange coincidence, the lieutenant colonel assigned to build the battery on Jekyll was Charles Lamar, who joined the Confederate army shortly after the conflict began.

Lamar took issue with the engineers who were sent to Jekyll and wrote a letter of complaint to his superior officer. The head engineer was so offended by Lamar's comments that he refused to return to the island. Lamar shouldered the task himself, but was driven to distraction by the late arrival of vital supplies and by what he claimed was incompetence on the part of his commanding general in Brunswick, who seemed not to grasp the importance of the Jekyll batteries. In addition, Lamar did not have a boat on Jekyll. The boat that brought over supplies, including food for the troops, was often so late that the food spoiled before it arrived. The troops had to wait for their pay too, which hurt morale and caused so many problems for Lamar that he told his father he was thinking of resigning his commission.

The attack on Fort Sumter, in Charleston harbor, April 1861. The assault by Confederate firebrands launched the Civil War. (Currier and Ives lithograph; Courtesy of the Library of Congress)

In January 1862, Lamar must have been pleased when General Robert E. Lee and other high-ranking Confederate officers arrived to inspect the progress on Jekyll. Lee was pleased with the batteries, which were still under construction, but he was critical of Lamar's men, whom he described as ragged, dirty, and undrilled. Lamar was no doubt so focused on getting the batteries built to his exacting standards that he had put everything else on hold. Confederate officers who later saw Lamar's completed batteries were impressed: one said they were the finest on the coast, and another pronounced them stronger than the batteries at Fort Pulaski near Savannah. As it turned out, the Jekyll and St. Simons batteries were never used. Lee pulled Lamar and his troops from Jekyll to help defend Savannah, which was in danger of being captured by Union forces. Additional guns intended for Jekyll were diverted to Savannah. Guns already placed on the island were moved to Brunswick. Before the Confederate troops withdrew from the area, they burned strategic sites in Brunswick, including the railroad station and the docks, to make them useless to Union forces. On St. Simons, Confederates blew up the lighthouse that had overlooked St. Simons Sound since 1810. The day after the Confederates left the Glynn County islands, Union forces moved in. A few Confederate soldiers who stayed behind in Brunswick ambushed five or six

Union troops who came ashore in search of cattle. The skirmish is sometimes referred to rather grandly as the Battle of Brunswick.

When Union forces arrived on Jekyll, they began dismantling the batteries on the island's north end. Some were former slaves who had helped construct the fortifications. One Union officer reported that the black workers cheered every time they recovered a section of iron from the sand, as though they had scored a personal victory against their former owners. Lamar had constructed another battery on the south end of the island to guard the entrance to Jekyll Creek, but the northern troops never found it. A Union commander praised Lamar's batteries, saying they were of "much greater strength" than the ones he had seen on larger St. Simons.

Lamar resigned his commission in mid-1862 after not being granted the additional troops he requested. Union ships had established a blockade around the southern coast, from Charleston to the Mississippi River. Lamar and his father commissioned a small fleet of fast, side-wheel steamships designed to run the blockade, and were no doubt delighted to call the effort the Georgia Importing and Exporting Company. The governor, at Charles Lamar's request, appointed him the official agent to "charge and conduct" such activities for the state. The blockade-running fleet was a great success. One ship made it through eight times. The Union was winning more battles, however, and the South was struggling to assemble enough men and supplies to continue the fight. Lamar rejoined the Confederate army after his home city of Savannah fell to the Union. His elegant downtown house was occupied by northern troops; so were the leafy green squares laid out in Oglethorpe's time. General William T. Sherman captured the city but did not torch it, since it had no military value. He instead presented it to President Lincoln as a Christmas gift.

General Lee surrendered to General Ulysses S. Grant on April 9, 1865. Jefferson Davis, the president of the Confederacy, did not accept the surrender and encouraged southern troops to continue to fight. Lamar by then was in Columbus, the only Georgia city that had not fallen to the North. About a week after Lee's surrender, Lamar was killed while Confederate troops were making a last stand in Columbus. He never saw his baby daughter, born while he was gone to war. The Lamar family and the du Bignons were linked by a final thread: one of Lamar's daughters later married a nephew of John Couper du Bignon and Henry du Bignon.

From Riches to Ruin to Riches

Henri du Bignon, the father of Henry and John Couper du Bignon of *Wanderer* notoriety, died the year after the Civil War ended. He was seventy-nine. His wife, Mary, was thirty-six. Henri left everything to her and their five daughters, the youngest of whom was only two, except for small bequests to Mary's mother, Sarah Aust, his former mistress, and the children Henri fathered by Sarah. There is no record whether Mary and Sarah ever reconciled after Mary married her mother's lover and became stepmother to her own half-brothers, her mother's three children by Henri. Henri's children by Amelia, his first wife, were not mentioned in his will, probably because he had given them slaves before the Civil War and property on Jekyll during the conflict. Henri did not will anything to the offspring he fathered by an island slave and a free black woman.

His sons, Henry and John Couper du Bignon, returned to Jekyll after the war to the plantation established some seventy years earlier by their grandfather, Christophe du Bignon. The place was in ruins. Fields were overgrown, the tabby Horton house had been damaged by Union cannon fire, their slaves were freed and gone, and they had no money to hire help to work the land. Like many other once-wealthy southern planters, they became poor almost overnight. Anything they might have saved, including the fifteen thousand dollars they were paid for the use of Jekyll as the *Wanderer*'s off-loading site, was in worthless Confederate money.

The brothers had to mortgage their shares of the island in order to survive. Henry was subsequently sued by his heirs and creditors, but managed to retain ownership of his property on Jekyll by declaring bankruptcy. After he became ill, he left Jekyll and stayed at the Brunswick house of his elder sister Eliza until his death, in 1885.

Although neither Henry nor John Couper du Bignon ever married, John Couper's longtime relationship with Sylvia, a slave on Jekyll, lasted for more than twenty-five years. He and Sylvia had six children: five born into slavery before the Civil War, and one into freedom afterward. Robert, their eldest son, was born when Sylvia was about fifteen and John was in his thirties. After the war ended, she returned to Jekyll as a free woman, took the surname "du Bignon," and lived with John Couper and their children on the island for years, according to June Hall McCash, who wrote about the couple in her book *Jekyll Island's Early Years*. Separated from the mainland by miles

of salt marsh and tidal creeks and accessible only by boat, Jekyll was among the few places in the Deep South at the time where a white man and a black woman could live openly as husband and wife. John, Sylvia, and the six children were still living together on Jekyll in 1870, according to census records, which list John as head of household.

John acknowledged paternity of his children by Sylvia, at least in a way. In 1872, he signed a legal document agreeing to educate and care for them financially until they turned eighteen. Sylvia signed the document with an *X*. Her name does not appear again in public records, although some of her descendants still live in the area, as do many other du Bignon descendants, black and white. By 1880, John was probably living alone on Jekyll, since Sylvia is not mentioned in that year's census. She may have died in the interim. Robert, John's oldest son, was married and working for him as a sharecropper on the island. Robert later purchased land from his father on one of the marsh hammocks between Jekyll and the mainland.

John Couper du Bignon died in 1890 on Jekyll, a few years after the island was sold to the members of a millionaires' club. They allowed him to remain on Jekyll until his death. He built a tiny shack in a sea island cotton field on the west end of Wylly Road, a good distance south of the Horton House, where he and his family had lived for so many years. After he died, the little shack was torn down.

A new generation of du Bignons flexed their financial muscles after the war. Starting in 1879, John Eugene du Bignon, a nephew of John Couper and Henry, began buying property on Jekyll from du Bignon heirs and creditors. John Eugene was the grandson of Henri and Amelia du Bignon, the child of their son Joseph, who died before Henri divided his property among his children. Because his father died young, John Eugene did not inherit property on the island. But he was a go-getter, as determined to make his fortune as his great-grandfather Christophe had been. He was involved in banking, publishing, manufacturing—including a company that made stones from cement—railroads, steamboats, and numerous other enterprises, including the Oglethorpe House in Brunswick, which later became the elegant Oglethorpe Hotel. Although he attempted to raise cattle on Jekyll, he realized that the island's future would not be rooted in agriculture. John Eugene had noticed that wealthy northerners were beginning to discover what one national publication referred to as the "tender beauty" of the Georgia sea islands. Andrew Carnegie's brother, Thomas, had paid a high price for land on neighboring Cumberland Island, where the Carnegies were already building a family mansion called Dungeness. John Eugene, along with his brother-in-law, decided that their best option for making a profit on Jekyll was to market the island to rich Yankees as an exclusive hunting enclave.

Du Bignon's brother-in-law, Newton Finney, lived in New York and was a member of the upscale Union Club, which included some of the wealthiest and most powerful businessmen of the day. Finney thought some of his fellow club members would pay top dollar to hunt on Jekyll, but they would need a place to stay. John Eugene built a large, comfortable house on Jekyll in 1884 where he could entertain Union Club members whom Finney invited to the island for several days of hunting. In publications in which he owned an interest, John Eugene touted Jekyll as "the finest hunting ground in Georgia," and made sure that the visiting hunters saw the articles raving about the abundance of deer, wild turkey, and other game on the island. One Union Club member who attended a hunt was so charmed by Jekyll that he offered to buy it outright if John Eugene could get title to the whole island. By then, several other Union Club members had stayed at John du Bignon's island house, and more were eager to hunt on the secluded island and enjoy its wild bounty.

Instead of selling Jekyll to a single buyer, Finney and John Eugene realized they could make more money by selling it to a group of wealthy people. They formed the Jekyll Island Club as a hunting organization and offered a total of one hundred shares for sale, targeting members of the Union Club in New York. Finney aimed to recruit fifty members who each would buy a minimum of two shares of stock in the club for $600 a share, which included two building lots. Members could resell one of their shares to anyone approved by the other members, or to members who wanted additional lots. Finney exceed his own expectations and sold shares to fifty-three members. John Eugene had paid $13,000 for the entire island; he sold it for $125,000 to the newly formed club. He and Finney split the profits. As a founding member of the Jekyll Island Club, John Eugene could retain his house on Jekyll. It was a win-win deal for everyone involved.

CHAPTER VI The Jekyll Island Club

[1886–1947]

THE MEMBERS of the Jekyll Island Club were wealthy, powerful men, celebrated as captains of industry and cursed as robber barons. Although they were said at the time to control an astonishing one-sixth of the world's wealth, experts today say their economic power was probably underestimated.

Their wealth and fame put them on a permanent red carpet; every detail of their public and private lives was reported and scrutinized. Their names, like those of film and rock stars today, were instantly recognizable: Astor, Goodyear, Rockefeller, Vanderbilt, Morgan, Pulitzer. They saw opportunity in the inventions of their time—gas lighting, the telephone, electricity, structural steel—and used those inventions to help create new industries. They built the first cross-country railroads, ran the first transcontinental telephone lines, and built New York's first steel-framed skyscrapers. During the later 1800s and early 1900s, they founded, financed, and operated the first of the world's giant conglomerates as well as other large and lucrative businesses: Standard Oil, U.S. Steel, AT&T, International Harvester, the Singer Manufacturing Company, General Electric, Lorillard Tobacco, Marshall Field & Company, and a host of other successful concerns. In the process, they created an age of unprecedented

A formal dinner at the Jekyll Island Club attended by the Thomas Carnegies of neighboring Cumberland Island. It was rumored that Carnegie had been turned down for club membership because of brutal conditions in his steel mills, but he had bought Cumberland as his private hunting club and retreat before the Jekyll Island Club was founded. (Courtesy of the Jekyll Island Museum Archives)

growth and prosperity—and committed some of the worst corporate crimes in American history. Mark Twain nicknamed the period the Gilded Age because its glittering façade covered a multitude of social and economic sins.

The new industrialists were cutthroat businessmen. They bribed politicians, threatened competitors, worked their employees (including children) for long hours at low wages, and hired violent thugs to break up labor unions and strikes. Their workplaces were unhealthy and often downright dangerous. For many years, politicians declined to pass laws establishing a minimum wage, outlawing child labor, or mandating safety regulations, claiming that business should operate with a minimum of government interference. Many of the legislators were motivated by under-the-table money instead of moral conviction. The new industrialists tried to blunt public criticism of their shady business practices with high-profile acts of philanthropy. They endowed hospitals, libraries, universities, museums, and other institutions that continue to benefit society today.

The new industrialists built glorious mansions in the best neighborhoods in New York, Chicago, Philadelphia, and Boston. Their vacation homes in Newport, Rhode Island, and other upscale resorts were only slightly less lavish than their primary

The Jekyll Island Club. (Courtesy of the Jekyll Island Museum Archives)

residences. They entertained on a grand scale and attended the opera, the ballet, and other cultural events. They were seen at all the right places, including the most exclusive European spas. Everywhere they went, they were pursued relentlessly by the press. A need for privacy was one of the reasons the millionaires clamored to join an exclusive club on a small, out-of-the-way sea island off the Georgia coast. On Jekyll, they created a world of their own, and like exotic birds, they migrated south to winter there for more than fifty years.

Originally planned as a hunting club for a handful of wealthy men, the Jekyll Island Club evolved into something much more impressive. Within two decades of its founding in 1886, the club was described by a national magazine as "the richest, the most exclusive, the most inaccessible club in the world." Surrounded by a moat of marshes and tidewaters seven miles from the mainland, the island was a natural fortress, easy to protect from the press and other intruders. A popular claim of the time was that no unwanted foot ever stepped onto Jekyll when the millionaires were in residence.

Club members found the island's semitropical winter climate ideal. Daytime temperatures seldom dropped below the freezing point, and snow was a rarity. For people accustomed to the bitter cold, heavy snows, and gray skies of northern and midwestern winters, Jekyll's weather was delightful during the months the club was officially open, from January 1 until around Easter. Some members arrived early enough to celebrate Christmas on Jekyll, holding holiday parties for island employees and their children and treating them all to gifts. One wealthy family celebrated by decorating their Christmas tree with seashells gathered on the island's beach. The effect was charming until the sea creatures inside the shells died, flooding the cottage with the odor of rotting seafood.

Several club members traveled back and forth to Jekyll aboard their luxurious oceangoing yachts. J. Pierpont Morgan, one of the most important bankers and financiers of the era, owned a series of yachts, all named *Corsair*. The largest, *Corsair IV*, was 343 feet long, the size of a cruise ship. A crew of seventy-six ran the yacht and pampered Morgan and his guests. The *Corsair IV* was too large to dock at the Jekyll wharf or even in Jekyll Creek, so the captain had to anchor out in St. Simons Sound. Whenever the yacht arrived off the island, a small cannon was fired to launch the flotilla of smaller boats needed to transport club members, their guests, and their luggage from the yacht to Jekyll. When the boat carrying Morgan reached the wharf, uniformed staff stood at attention on either side of the structure as the great man walked onto the island.

Most club members and their families traveled by train to Brunswick, the small mainland city closest to Jekyll, in elegant private railway cars. In addition to sitting rooms and bedrooms, the cars included observation platforms, fully equipped kitchens, dining rooms, and rooms for the owners' valets, assistants, secretaries, chefs, and maids, plus tutors and nannies for the club members' children. The cars were works of art. Paneled with mahogany, fitted with polished brass, sparkling with crystal light fixtures, and decorated with sumptuous silks and velvets, the private railway cars were known as "mansions on rails." When the train reached Brunswick, the millionaires and their servants boarded the club's yacht for the thirty-minute trip to the island. Local newspapers covered every detail of the club members' comings and goings while they were on the mainland, but once they reached the island, the spotlight was switched off.

When the club purchased Jekyll, there were only a few structures on the island, and none was suitable to accommodate people accustomed to the best of everything. The members' first order of business was to build a place to stay, socialize, and dine. The ornate Queen Anne style, with its wraparound porches, towers, decorative chimneys, and large windows, had just come into vogue in the United States. Charles A. Alexander, a Chicago architect, adopted it for the graceful four-story clubhouse—five

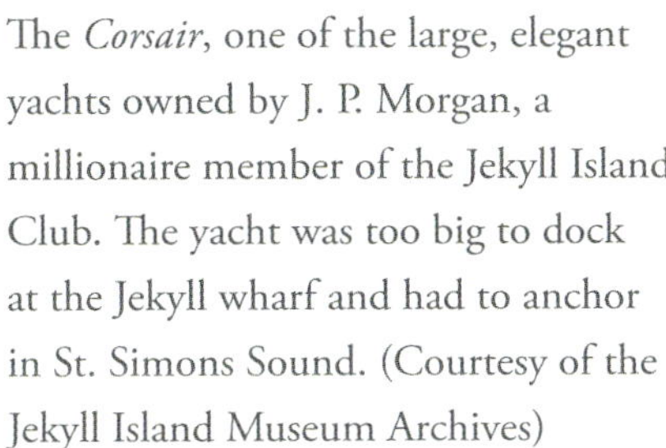

The *Corsair*, one of the large, elegant yachts owned by J. P. Morgan, a millionaire member of the Jekyll Island Club. The yacht was too big to dock at the Jekyll wharf and had to anchor in St. Simons Sound. (Courtesy of the Jekyll Island Museum Archives)

stories if the sole tower room is counted—to which was soon added a large annex to accommodate all the members and guests. Alexander managed to make the Jekyll Island clubhouse casual, cozy, and elegant. The original clubhouse boasted sixty guest rooms; leaded art-glass windows; rooms for card games, reading, and billiards; a grand dining room with high ceilings; oak wainscoting; Ionic columns; and wide, shady verandahs. It was the perfect building for Jekyll, its wide windows offering views of the well-groomed grounds, Jekyll Creek, and the long stretch of marsh between the island and the Glynn County mainland. The marshes had been immortalized just a decade earlier by the popular Georgia poet Sidney Lanier in his poem "The Marshes of Glynn." Lanier cemented his fame by dying young of tuberculosis.

Like the island's earliest indigenous inhabitants, the clubhouse's builders were forced to adapt to the lack of natural stone on the sea island. They constructed the building's foundations of cement mixed with oyster shells, a modern takeoff on the oyster-shell tabby used by the island's first European residents. Club members hired one of the nation's most prominent landscape architects, Horace William Shaler Cleveland, because they liked his natural approach to landscape design. Cleveland also designed the famed Sleepy Hollow Cemetery in downtown Concord, Massachusetts, where

A tabby pathway under the limb of a giant live oak. The path meanders through Jekyll's National Historic Landmark District.

Nathaniel Hawthorne, Henry David Thoreau, and Ralph Waldo Emerson are buried. His other projects included Roger William Park in Providence, Rhode Island, and St. Anthony Park in St. Paul, Minnesota. On Jekyll, he called for roads no wider than necessary and plantings that complemented the island's native tangle of live oaks, magnolias, cabbage palms, and palmetto thickets, all intertwined with wild grape vines, purple wisteria, and Cherokee roses, the state flower of Georgia (although it is not native to the state). Yellow jessamine perfumed the air when it bloomed, obligingly, in early spring, while the millionaires were still in residence. Cleveland decided that most of Jekyll should remain as it was, believing that natural surroundings would help club members relax and unwind from the pressures of the outside world. His plantings around the clubhouse were admired by everyone, especially the island's native white-tailed deer. To discourage the deer from eating the landscaping, members had a fence built around the clubhouse compound, and employees resorted to pouring whale oil on the plants as a deer repellent.

The Jekyll Island Club Hotel faces west across the famed Marshes of Glynn, with the Atlantic Ocean stretching to the horizon in the background.

To prepare the club for its maiden season, which opened officially in mid-January 1888, one of the members, Richard L. Ogden, agreed to act as superintendent. Ogden, the cofounder of a carriage and car manufacturing company in San Francisco, once served a term as commodore of the prestigious San Francisco Yacht Club and was considered the best yachtsman on the bay. He sold one of his yachts, the *Peerless*, to the king of Samoa, and it constituted the country's entire navy. Ogden's business had suffered financial problems because of the failure of a bank that backed his company, and he needed the $2,500 annual salary, equivalent now to about $70,000, offered by the Jekyll Island Club. Ogden, a popular, outgoing man, spent well over a year dealing with club concerns before the official opening and almost lost his mind because of all the problems that cropped up. One involved Jekyll's nonnative wildlife. The small island was overrun with feral hogs, cattle, and horses, most probably descended from stock brought to the island during the plantation era, although it is possible that the ancestry of some of the pigs dated back to Spanish occupation of the coast. The mares were purchased by Thomas Carnegie, who owned most of neighboring Cumberland Island, and the cattle and stallions were sold on the mainland.

Thomas Carnegie, the brother of the millionaire industrialist Andrew Carnegie, and Thomas's wife, Lucy, were sometimes guests at the Jekyll Island Club for social events and dinners. They traveled between the neighboring islands on their private launch, just as club members sometimes took the Jekyll boat on excursions to explore nearby sea islands. It was rumored that the Carnegies had been denied membership in the Jekyll Island Club because Andrew Carnegie, the cofounder and owner of U.S. Steel, treated his mill employees so badly. Because Carnegie provided no safety gear, his workers wore two pairs of woolen underwear for protection against the cauldrons of molten metal, which sometimes tipped over and splashed steel-mill napalm over the workers or pelted them with hot chunks of slag. Their families dreaded the sound of the mill's whistle because it notified them that yet another worker had been maimed or killed. Carnegie was no doubt a ruthless businessman, as were many of his ilk, but the rumor that he had been blackballed by the Jekyll club was untrue. Well before the club was organized, the Carnegies had bought land on Cumberland Island and were building Dungeness, their fifty-nine-room version of a Scottish castle.

The hogs on Jekyll proved impossible to eradicate. The superintendent reported that the animals were fast and tricky, with almost-human intelligence. The island's superintendent hired a professional to reduce Jekyll's pig population, but after many of

The ruins of Dungeness, the mansion built by Thomas Carnegie on Cumberland Island on the site of a hunting lodge built in 1736 by Georgia's founder, James Oglethorpe. Fire, possibly set by an arsonist, destroyed the fifty-nine-room mansion in 1958.

the hunter's dogs were killed by aggressive porkers, the man resigned. The millionaires were encouraged to hunt what were billed as "wild boar," nomenclature that had real meaning after the king of Italy, Victor Emmanuel III, contributed stock to the island. The monarch shipped a pair of wild Italian boars to an American diplomat in 1909 as a gift. When they arrived in New York, dock officials demanded their immediate removal. The frantic diplomat appealed to his resourceful friend J. P. Morgan to deal with the animals. Morgan had them sent to Jekyll, where the king's wild boars interbred with the island's more pedestrian pigs.

Managers of undeveloped Georgia sea islands today still battle the problem of feral horses and hogs, which trample and eat dune-stabilizing sea oats, marsh plants, and the seedlings of live oaks, the longest-lived and largest trees of the southern coast. Feral hogs also eat the eggs of endangered sea turtles that nest on island beaches.

When the clubhouse opened in January 1888, it was just what the millionaires had ordered. A Brunswick reporter pronounced the place comfortable and substantial but not gaudy. That was true, at least by the standards of the new industrialists, whose properties elsewhere were extravagant monuments to their wealth and social standing. Among the glitterati who arrived for the first season were the William A. Rockefellers, the Marshall Fields, and the William K. Vanderbilts. Vanderbilt and a party of seven traveled to the island aboard his luxurious steam yacht *Alva*, named for his wife. A few years later, Alva Vanderbilt scandalized club members and society at large by divorcing her husband and soon afterward marrying a guest who had traveled with them on their first voyage to Jekyll. Alva Vanderbilt, who received a settlement from her former husband reported to be in excess of $10 million, alleged as grounds for divorce that her husband had committed adultery.

Guests, referred to as strangers on the island, were allowed to visit no longer than two weeks at a stretch. They also had to pay 20 percent more than members for everything at the club: rooms, meals, horseback rides, and other amenities. During busier parts of the season, the clubhouse became so crowded that strangers were banned outright after February 20 in order to make room for all the members.

In an era when women were routinely excluded from prestigious social clubs, they and their families were encouraged not only to spend time on Jekyll but also to participate in all the club's activities. Like their powerful husbands, most of the Jekyll wives, as well as their daughters and other female relatives, were a spirited lot, delighted to defy the old rules of society. The fact that they were on a secluded island, out of the public's critical eye, gave them even more leeway to kick up their heels. On Jekyll, they enjoyed swimming, tennis, lawn croquet, and golf. During the club's early years, hunting was the most popular pastime with men and women, but after the first golf course was built near the clubhouse, golf claimed the title with both sexes. Women enjoyed traditionally male pursuits such as fishing, skeet shooting, camping, and horseback riding. Bicycling, a sport once considered dangerous and suitable only for daring young men, caught on with women in the late 1800s after safer bikes were developed. For a time, bicycles remained so expensive that only well-off people could afford them. After prices dropped, the bicycle came to symbolize the liberated woman of the late nineteenth century. The famed suffragette Susan B. Anthony credited bicycles with doing more to emancipate women "than anything else in the world," by giving them a sense of freedom and self-reliance.

A new fad during the era of the Jekyll Island Club. Bicycles were considered too dangerous for women to ride. The women of the club were adventurous, however, and took to the sport with great enthusiasm. (Courtesy of the Jekyll Island Museum Archives)

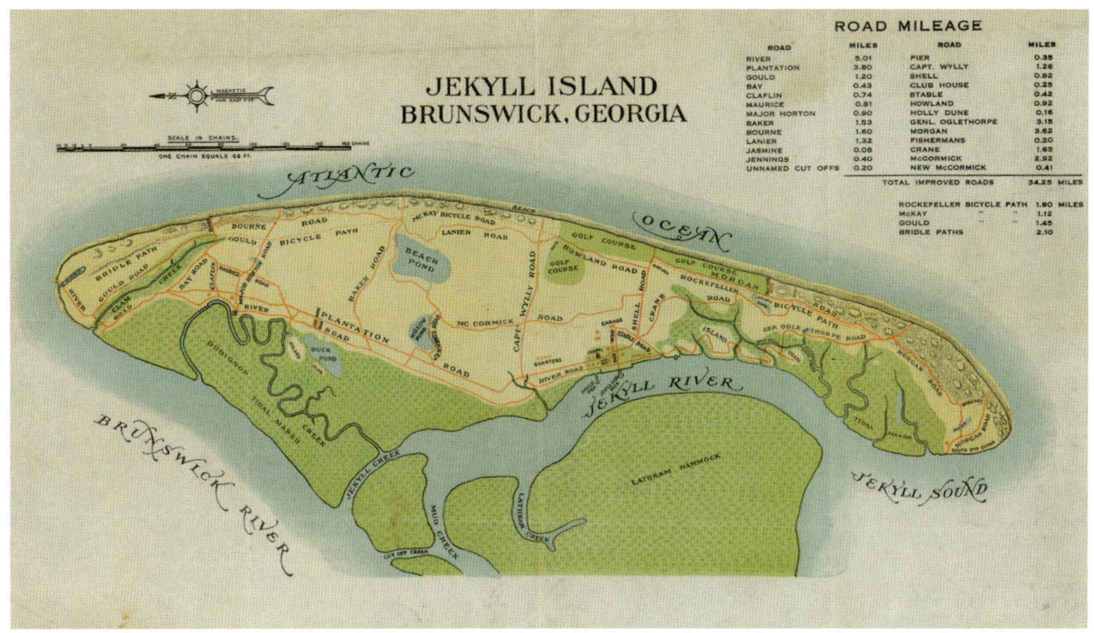

1930s bike map. (Courtesy of the Jekyll Island Museum Archives)

Another popular sport was Red Bug racing. Red Bugs were low-slung, open-air vehicles powered by gasoline or electric engines. They resembled oversized snow sleds with wheels: one for steering, the other four for running the roads, including the rough oyster-shell-paved roads of Jekyll. The gas-powered models could reach speeds of twenty five miles per hour, and club members, who even on vacation liked to engage in cutthroat competitions, often staged races on the beach. Red Bugs were first manufactured by the Briggs and Stratton Company, which painted them bright red and called them Flyers. The name may have been changed at the suggestion of a Jekyll club member familiar with the ubiquitous island variety of red bugs: tiny red mites whose bites itch for weeks.

Some of the sports enjoyed by women at the Jekyll Island Club were controversial enough to make news off the island. When they began chalking cues and sinking balls alongside the men in the club's billiards parlor, the activity was reported, with verbal arched eyebrows, by the *New York Times*. The venerable newspaper noted that "the ladies play billiards in the common billiards hall and go anywhere they choose." A few

Red Bugs, small vehicles imported by members of the Jekyll Island Club to drive around the island and on the beach. Powered by electricity or gasoline, the vehicles, originally called Flyers, were renamed by club members in honor of the tiny biting insects of the same name, which are ubiquitous on the island. (Courtesy of the Jekyll Island Museum Archives)

disgruntled male club members launched a plot to have women banned from the main parlor, where the men gathered after supper to trade investment tips, discuss international affairs, smoke cigars, and talk about club concerns. The effort to ban women was unsuccessful, no doubt because the millionaires' wives and other female relatives were just as determined as their husbands to enjoy the freedom afforded them on the island. In 1893, Kate Papin became the first full-fledged female club member when she took over a membership share from her father after he retired from the club. Other women were later elected board members, and two served as vice presidents.

During the club's first year of operation, everything that could go wrong did. The experienced servants that Ogden had planned to hire from the upscale Oglethorpe Hotel in Brunswick turned out to be otherwise occupied, and he had to make do with unskilled staff. There was not enough hot water to supply the kitchen, guest rooms, and laundry at the same time. Members complained that the gas lighting was too dim. The club's stable, built before the first season, turned out to be inadequate to accommodate all the horses the millionaires shipped to the island. Ogden had a second, twenty-stall facility built. A dozen club members joined forces in 1897 to build the

The Jekyll Island Museum, housed in the building where horses were stabled for members of the Jekyll Island Club.

Ernest Grob, the longtime superintendent of the Jekyll Island Club, was a genius at meeting the needs—and wants—of wealthy club members. (Courtesy of the Jekyll Island Museum Archives)

Club Stable, the only one still standing. It featured forty-six stalls, all spoken for by the Stable Associates. The expensive wines provided for the dining room by one supplier were pronounced undrinkable by the guests, who sent them straight back to the kitchen. Ogden was overwhelmed, not only by the problems but also by all the advice offered by the other take-charge club members, each of whom had a different suggestion for how the superintendent should handle things. Ogden was more than happy to tender his resignation at the end of the first season.

The club hired another superintendent. During his brief tenure, the club retained Ernest Grob, who had clerked during the first season, to manage the clubhouse, work as cashier, and keep accounts. By the end of the second season, Grob, a young Swiss immigrant, had proved to be so valuable that he was elevated to the superintendent's position. Grob held the post from 1889 to 1930. He was the perfect man for the job, according June Hall McCash and her late husband, William Barton McCash, former college professors whose books about Jekyll and the millionaires' club are classics—well researched and richly detailed. The McCashes noted that Grob's "old-world charm, deference to the wealthy members, and constant attention to their every need became as much a part of the club's fabric as its island setting." Grob himself often commented that the club was run more like a large European country house than a hotel, albeit a country house with hundreds of guests who stayed for months instead of weekends. Grob was accustomed to accommodating wealthy people. During summers, he managed the Malvern Hotel in Bar Harbor, Maine, where the Vanderbilt family had several vacation mansions on so-called millionaires' row and sometimes stayed at the Malvern, as did many other socialites. Grob brought many of the Malvern's staff to Jekyll with him for the winter season.

Because the clubhouse operated on a first-come, first-served basis, members often had difficulty finding accommodations, especially in late winter and early spring, when the weather on Jekyll was usually at its finest. The house that John Eugene du Bignon had built as a hunting lodge to lure prospective investors to Jekyll was conscripted to handle some of the overflow. The rustic property rented for $15 a day, the equivalent of more than $360 now. Grob began urging members to build private houses so that they could be sure of having a place to stay and bring their guests. Taking his advice, fifteen members built, over a period of years, what they called cottages, most in the vicinity of the clubhouse.

Compared to the millionaires' homes and other properties elsewhere, their Jekyll houses *were* cottages. By any other standards, they were mansions, not just in size but

in furnishings and appointments. The largest, built in the Italian Renaissance style in 1918 by William Teller Crane Jr., featured seventeen bathrooms and a formal sunken garden. Crane's father had made his fortune in plumbing fixtures and supplies. When Crane built his cottage, he was criticized by club members who considered it ostentatious, especially after the *Brunswick News* billed the structure as a winter palace and reported that it cost $100,000—more than $1.5 million today. A club member's daughter commented that Crane's was the only house on the island that the other club members never referred to as a cottage.

A young woman named Kate Brown from Worcester, Massachusetts, was hired as a personal secretary to Edith Macy, the wife of the industrialist and club member Valentine Everit Macy, and as a tutor for their children during their time on the

The Crane Cottage, built in 1917 by the plumbing magnate Richard Teller Crane, Jr. It was the largest cottage constructed by any member of the Jekyll Island Club. Other members considered it ostentatious.

island. Macy's wealth was inherited; his father left him more than $20 million when he was still a boy. The amiable Macys treated Kate as one of the family, inviting her to dine with them at the clubhouse instead of with the servants, treating her to golf lessons, and involving her in other island social events. Kate was once invited to a well-attended afternoon tea at the Crane Cottage. In a letter to her mother after the event, the young woman wrote that when she stepped inside the huge house, she was "announced by a perfectly trained man in perfectly fitting plum-colored livery." Kate Brown's letters are filled with such humorous details about what the millionaires considered their simple lifestyles on Jekyll.

The other cottages were not as well supplied with bathrooms as Crane's, but they were all large and comfortable, and offered an extraordinary range of amenities tailored to their owner's tastes and interests:

- David H. King Jr., the New York contractor who built Madison Square Garden and the base for the Statue of Liberty, was the only club member to build a one-story cottage, which he named **Chichota**. It boasted a swimming pool, one of the first private pools constructed in Georgia.

A stone lion still standing guard at the entrance to a Jekyll Island Club cottage lost to time.

The entrance to Gould's casino, to which club members had an open invitation. (Courtesy of the Jekyll Island Museum Archives)

- Edwin Gould was so charmed with Jekyll Island that he purchased Chichota Cottage during the first week he visited in 1900. Gould purchased other lots and built **Cherokee Cottage** for his in-laws and a separate playhouse, called the casino, for his two sons. The casino featured an indoor tennis court, a bowling alley, a game room, a greenhouse, and an indoor shooting range. Club members and their families had an open invitation to enjoy the casino whenever they liked. Gould inherited his fortune from his father, Jason "Jay" Gould, who became one of the richest men in American history by building railroads and speculating. Jay Gould became notorious for his association with "Boss" Tweed, the man who headed Tammany Hall, a powerful New York City political machine known for flagrant graft and corruption.
- Charles Stewart Maurice, a co-owner of the world's biggest bridge-building company, insisted that bridge-building techniques be used for his **Hollybourne Cottage** on Jekyll. Bridges built by Maurice's company included the Niagara Cantilever Bridge in New York and the Hawkesbury River Railway Bridge in New South Wales, Australia. He chose tabby as the building material for his Jekyll cottage. Hollybourne was the only club cottage built of tabby.

Hollybourne Cottage, built by the engineer Charles Stewart Maurice in 1890. It was the only cottage at the Jekyll Island Club built of coastal tabby.

Cottage owned by the famed newspaper publisher Joseph Pulitzer, who retreated to Jekyll for peace and quiet in his declining years. He is said to have paid a boat captain a $100 a day not to sound his boat's horn as he passed through Jekyll Creek. (Courtesy of the Jekyll Island Museum Archives)

- The **Pulitzer Cottage**, owned by the noted editor and publisher Joseph Pulitzer, was soundproofed because Pulitzer was so sensitive to noise. He is rumored to have paid a boat captain one hundred dollars a day not to blow his vessel's horn when he passed through Jekyll Creek near Pulitzer's cottage. Pulitzer owned the *New York World* and the *St. Louis Post-Dispatch*, major newspapers of the era. Although his reporters were known for hard-hitting investigative reporting, Pulitzer also used the lurid tactics of yellow journalism: screaming headlines and sensationalized stories. The renowned Pulitzer Prize for excellence in journalism is named for him. Pulitzer died aboard his yacht *Liberty* on his way to Jekyll in 1911.
- **Indian Mound Cottage**, originally built for Gordon McKay, was later remodeled for William A. Rockefeller, who added an elevator, a walk-in safe lined with cedar, and hot and cold salt water piped into the master bath. In Victorian times, salt baths, known as *sool-baths*, were believed to stimulate the central nervous system and promote good health. William cofounded the Standard Oil Company with his brother John D. Rockefeller, one of the richest and most successful businessmen in history.

A gray-shingled cottage built in 1891 and later owned by William Rockefeller, a cofounder of the Standard Oil Company.

Sans Souci, one of the country's earliest condominium complexes. Apartments were owned by such wealthy luminaries as J. P. Morgan.

- Henry Hyde, whose Equitable Life Assurance Society became the world's largest life insurance company, led the effort to build a luxurious six-unit apartment complex. He named it **Sans Souci**, French for "without care." It was next door to the clubhouse, the undisputed center of social life on the island. Sans Souci was one of the nation's first condominiums. All but one of the units were quickly sold. Although J. Pierpont Morgan is often credited with having the complex built, he was a latecomer who purchased the last available unit. In addition to the owners' units, there were twelve rooms for servants, who helped ensure that the members' visits to Sans Souci were indeed without care.

By 1898, the Jekyll Island Club was running smoothly enough for Cornelius Bliss, a club member and the U.S. secretary of the interior, to invite President William McKinley and the first lady to visit. The president planned to come to Jekyll in February or March, but had to postpone the trip when the battleship *Maine* blew up

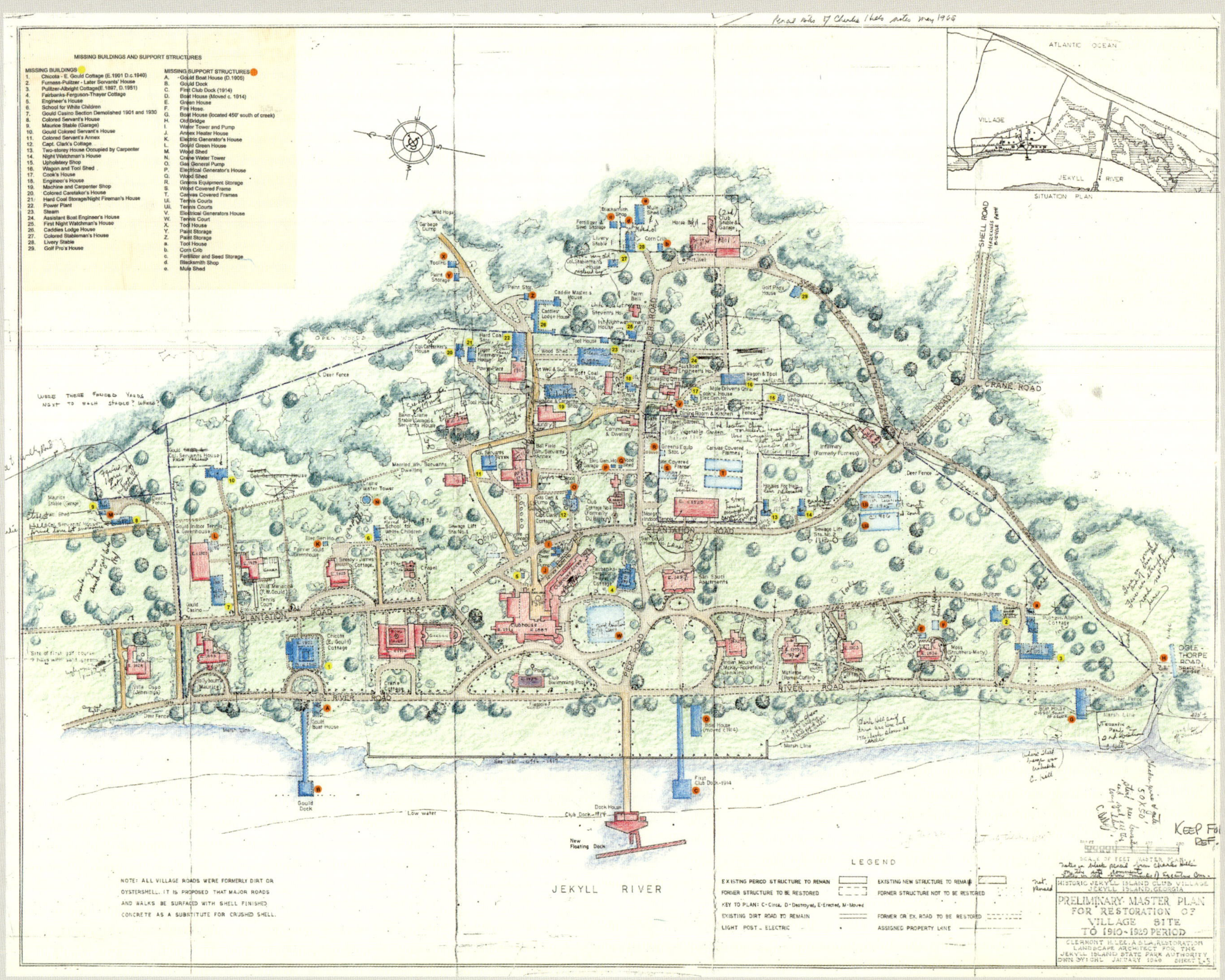

Map of the cottage colony. (Courtesy of the Jekyll Island Museum Archives)

in Havana Harbor on February 15 while Cuban rebels were fighting to achieve independence from Spain.

Gun carriages that held cannons designed to protect Jekyll Island from an invasion by the Spanish Armada during the short-lived Spanish-American War of 1898. The old carriage and its auxiliary parts now rest quietly in a wooded area on the south end of Jekyll.

Even before the Spanish-American War began, members of the Jekyll Island Club were nervous about the situation in Cuba. Newspapers, including Pulitzer's, and war hawks in Congress had been whipping up a frenzy of fear by reporting that the Atlantic and Gulf Coasts were vulnerable to attack by the infamous Armada Española, or Spanish Armada. The Spanish Armada is among the world's oldest active naval forces and was once a major one. During the Spanish-American War, it was not nearly as formidable as it once had been, although its reputation still frightened people. With access to powerful governmental officials, including President McKinley, the club members demanded and got cannon batteries installed on both ends of Jekyll, equipped with large parrot guns left over from the Civil War. A Brunswick newspaper reported that the club members wanted their "pretty cottages" protected in case of an enemy invasion. The parrot cannons were removed after the brief war ended, but the carriage for the south battery still stands on Jekyll, hidden by foliage and sand dunes that have grown over the past century.

President McKinley's resolve to stay out of the Cuban revolution crumbled when the *Maine* exploded and sank in Havana Harbor on February 15, 1898, killing more than 250 American sailors. Newspapers and politicians blamed the Spanish and inflamed the public with screaming headlines and sensationalized reporting, even though the explosion may have been an accident. Some have even suggested the explosion was contrived as a covert operation by hawks in the U.S. government to force McKinley to declare war. Whatever the cause, the sinking of the battleship provoked a national push for the country to join the conflict. "Remember the *Maine*, to hell with Spain!" became a popular rallying cry all over the United States. Two months later, McKinley asked Congress for a declaration of war. The Spanish-American War lasted only three months, and the Spanish Armada never came close to Jekyll; American warships destroyed it in Manila Bay in the Philippines.

The Club Member and the Cuban Conflict

The *Dauntless*. (Courtesy of the Library of Congress)

DURING THE 1890s, a great deal of sympathy built up in the United States for Cuban freedom fighters, especially in Florida, where cigar factories employed a number of workers from the Caribbean island. John Eugene du Bignon, who retained membership in the Jekyll Island Club when he sold the island to the millionaires, defied federal law and helped smuggle arms and men to Cuba. He purchased an interest in the oceangoing tugboat *Dauntless*, which was docked in Brunswick and reputed to be the fastest tugboat in the South, and found a daring captain to run it. The ship was soon dubbed the "Artful Dodger" by the press because it made so many successful smuggling trips and eluded authorities from both Cuba and the United States.

President McKinley, who was trying to keep the country out of war, ordered authorities to intercept so-called filibuster vessels like the *Dauntless*, which were attempting to violate federal neutrality statutes. "Filibuster," which ultimately comes from a Dutch word meaning "freebooter" and originally referred to adventurers or pirates, has acquired different meanings over time, including the supplying of military aid to revolutionaries and, today, the obstruction of legislative proceedings.

Du Bignon, who was probably proud of his uncles' involvement in the *Wanderer* conspiracy, must have been excited by the notion of participating in another illicit seagoing venture. Perhaps he was also tempted by the money: owners of filibuster ships were paid $6,000 to $8,000 per trip, the equivalent of about $165,000 to $220,500 today. He became the managing owner of the *Dauntless* and hired one of the most colorful of the filibuster captains to make smuggling runs to Cuba: "Dynamite Johnny" O'Brien, who earned his nickname by transporting sixty tons of dynamite to the rebels to blow up railroad bridges and other structures essential to the Spanish military effort.

O'Brien made so many successful runs to aid the rebels that the Spanish commander in Cuba threatened to hang him in full view of the entrance to Havana Harbor as a warning to other filibuster captains. O'Brien responded that he would capture the Spanish leader instead, chop him into small pieces, and "feed him to the fires of the *Dauntless*." Such braggadocio made O'Brien and other filibuster captains folk heroes in the United States and the Caribbean.

On one of Dynamite Johnny's filibuster runs on the *Dauntless*, he was scheduled to carry about seventy-five freedom fighters to Cuba, plus a load of arms and ammunition. In Charleston, the freedom fighters boarded the rear car of a train bound for Jacksonville, a cigar-making center known to authorities as a popular departure point for filibuster boats. About

Docking site of the filibuster ship *Dauntless*, on the banks of the Satilla River. There it would pick up men and arms bound for Cuba.

fifty government detectives tried to board the same car but were told it was private, so they traveled in railcars farther forward. During the journey, the train stopped briefly after dark at the junction of two rail lines about twenty miles west of Jacksonville. A Cuban-born railroad employee quietly uncoupled the rear car. As the bulk of the train proceeded toward the Florida city, another engine picked up the freedom fighters' car, plus two more rail cars parked on a blind siding and packed with armaments. That short train traveled back across the Georgia-Florida line and later stopped at a trestle on the Satilla River, which empties into St. Andrews Sound south of Jekyll. The *Dauntless* was docked beside the trestle, waiting to load the men and cargo. At dawn, Dynamite Johnny navigated the Satilla and the shoal waters of St. Andrews Sound before making another successful run to Cuba. A Brunswick newspaper quickly reported the expedition: "Beyond reasonable doubt, Brunswick's tug *Dauntless* is en route to Cuban waters on a filibustering operation." Although du Bignon denied the allegation, the newspaper reported that he had been in Jacksonville on the night the *Dauntless* departed. It is possible that du Bignon was instead at the Satilla River trestle just for the thrill of being involved with the illicit operation. Du Bignon was tried in Brunswick in September 1896, along with the tug's minority owners, for violating federal neutrality statutes. All were convicted of participating in filibustering and fined. A month later, the *Dauntless* was captured by a U.S. warship and confiscated by the federal government. Soon after, du Bignon sold his shares of stock in the Jekyll Island Club to pay off debts. He had almost no other involvement with the club thereafter.

The U.S. battleship *Maine*, destroyed by an explosion in Havana harbor during the Spanish-American War. (Courtesy of Naval History and Heritage Command)

Jekyll was safe from the Spanish, but nothing could protect the island from Mother Nature. Before they bought shares in the Jekyll Island Club, prospective members had been assured that "no destructive storms or cyclones have ever been experienced" on the island. John Eugene du Bignon must have known the assertion was untrue. Although Jekyll, because of favorable natural factors, has endured fewer hurricanes than many places on the Atlantic and Gulf Coasts, it was hit by at least two major storms during the 1800s. In 1804, a few years after Christophe Poulain du Bignon acquired the whole island, a hurricane destroyed his entire cotton crop and ruined plantation outbuildings. Other storms have swept across Jekyll, but none caused as much damage as the hurricane that hit on October 2, 1898, shortly after the end of the Spanish-American War. Ernest Grob, the superintendent, happened to be vacationing in Germany at the time, but his assistant wrote a letter to the club chairman, describing the damage:

"A severe storm and tidal wave struck us Sunday," the man wrote. He noted that the storm wrecked the wharf; a Brunswick newspaper reported that part of the wharf washed up in the yard of Pulitzer's cottage. The windmill that pumped fresh artesian well water to the elevated storage tank blew down. The bridges, bathhouses, and beach pavilion washed away, as did the houses occupied by fishermen on both ends of the island. The brand-new golf course north of the millionaires' compound was submerged under salt water, and trees were downed all over the island. The Sans Souci apartments were damaged, along with most of the cottages, except for Hollybourne, built of sturdy tabby, and the Fairbank Cottage, situated just south of the clubhouse and in the lee of the giant structure. On neighboring Cumberland Island, the pilot boat *Maud Helen* wound up on a bluff at least twenty feet above mean sea level. The hurricane flooded downtown Brunswick and was ultimately blamed for the deaths of 179 coastal residents. Hurricane experts today rank the 1898 hurricane as a category 4 storm, meaning its winds were between 130 and 156 miles per hour. Tropical cyclones in the Western Hemisphere are ranked on the Saffir-Simpson Hurricane Scale from 1 to 5, based solely on sustained wind speeds. In order to keep the scale simple enough for everyone to understand, it does not measure storm surge or any other indicators of intensity. Storms in category 3, 4, or 5 are considered dangerous only because of their potential to damage structures. Of course, storms that powerful also threaten human life, natural areas, and wildlife. None of the hurricanes that hit coastal Georgia during the twentieth century ranked as a major storm; all were category 2 or below.

Experts with the National Weather Service who reevaluated the 1898 storm in recent years say it followed a more southerly track than earlier records indicated. Their investigation indicates that the hurricane made landfall on Cumberland Island, putting Jekyll in the most dangerous, that is, northeast, quadrant. They estimate that the storm had sustained winds of about 135 miles per hour.

The millionaires' timing was impeccable. They left Jekyll shortly before Congress declared war on Spain, and they missed the most powerful storm known to have hit the Georgia coast. By the time the club reopened in the following January, Grob had made some of the necessary repairs, and employees were cleaning up storm debris and rebuilding every day. Jekyll employees were expected to work hard even when the millionaires were not in residence.

During the season, more than 250 employees took care of the island, the club members, their families, and the guests. Grob hired experienced people, many of them recent immigrants, who worked during the summer at posh northern resorts such as Bar Harbor, Newport, and Saratoga Springs, New York. Most of the Jekyll club's white servants were first- or second-generation Irish or Italian, although employees

Refurbished service buildings from the Jekyll Island Club era, now housing such businesses as a gift shop and a bookstore.

hailed also from France, Germany, England, Greece, and Canada. One Jekyll employee recalled that the first thing young Irish maids were taught was never to slam doors. Grob also hired black workers from the mainland and nearby sea islands, many of whom were kin to one another. When one member of a black family landed a coveted job on the island, he or she tried to get other relatives hired. Although black workers were consistently paid less than white workers, the pay and working conditions were generally far superior to those on the mainland and other sea islands. Even on Jekyll, black workers were rarely given positions requiring special skills and were restricted to roads on the island that were not regularly traveled by the millionaires. Black employees worked in the clubhouse as bellboys, cleaners, and kitchen help; fed and groomed the horses and mucked out stables; caddied on the golf courses; and worked as ditch-diggers, in the laundry, and on construction projects. Unskilled laborers earned $1 to $1.50 a day. White employees were preferred for jobs that brought them into frequent contact with club members. When Grob was searching for a bicycle instructor to teach club members to ride on the island, he expressed his wish that the person not be "colored."

A handful of workers, black and white, lived with their families on Jekyll year-round in housing supplied by the club. Two settlements—one called the Quarters, the other, Red Row—were built for black families. Red Row got its name because the

A row of cottages that housed servants at the Jekyll Island Club. It was known as Red Row because the dwellings were covered in rolled red roofing material. (Courtesy of the Jekyll Island Museum Archives)

small houses were roofed and sided with the same red roofing material, which was sold in large rolls. Workers' children attended segregated schools on Jekyll paid for by the club, and some children were born on the island. A doctor was summoned to deliver white babies; black babies were delivered by a midwife.

Most of the black employees on Jekyll spoke Gullah Geechee, a unique creole that blends words and syntax from many different African languages with English. Researchers say that former sea island slaves and their descendants retained the Gullah Geechee language, culture, and beliefs longer than any other group of black people in the United States because of their long isolation on the southeastern coast. Pockets of Gullah Geechee still exist in some rural parts of coastal Georgia, South Carolina, and northern Florida, but most remnants are on undeveloped sea islands such as Sapelo, where the people of the small Hog Hammock community continue, in many ways, to live their Gullah Geechee heritage.

The creole spoken by black people on and off the island was noted by Susan Albright Reed, the daughter of John J. Albright, a club member. She wrote about hearing barefoot Gullah Geechee children talking as they played around the train depot in Thalman, a rural community in western Glynn County, where the Albrights changed trains for the last stretch of their journey to the coast. The language the children spoke, undoubtedly Gullah Geechee creole, was "unintelligible" to her, Reed noted. She also

reported that Grob thought some of the "New York ladies" were too impatient with their black servants at the club because the employees had difficulty understanding instructions. Reed recalled the superintendent saying that the ladies "forget that [the black employees] have been isolated on the island for so long that they hardly speak the same language." It is likely that Jekyll's black employees, even those who lived on the island for years, had been speaking Gullah Geechee long before they came to work for the club.

There were segregated dormitories and mess halls on the oyster-shell-paved road behind the clubhouse that employees called Feeding Road, since renamed Pier Road. During the club era, more than one hundred service buildings were located along or near the road, including the commissary, laundry, upholstery shop, dairy, stables, woodshed, storage buildings, and housing for the bookkeeper, boat captain, carriage drivers, night watchmen, and many others. Most of the service buildings have since been torn down.

The staff's duties included tending the large vegetable garden and harvesting fish, blue crabs, shrimp, and oysters for the clubhouse chef; grooming the compound grounds; building fires in the ninety-three fireplaces in the clubhouse; emptying chamber pots; carrying hot water to guest rooms; and taking care of chickens, cows, and horses. Carriage drivers were expected to be available at a moment's notice to take the millionaires around the island and out on the beach. Employees on the club's boats hauled a multitude of giant steamer trunks and other luggage. A taxidermist operated a shop where he mounted birds and animals shot by the millionaires on hunting expeditions. The club's gamekeeper restocked Jekyll before each season with imported French pheasants and quail. Local fishermen passing through the Jekyll River sometimes saw the long-tailed, russet-colored pheasants perching in trees along the riverbank. The club employed a full-time gamekeeper, but the tenure of one British gamekeeper was cut short when he was caught killing egrets on and around Jekyll and selling the plumes to northern milliners.

The club built separate schools for the children of black and white employees. In addition, a summer school was conducted for black children and their parents. Many of the older adults probably learned to read and write on Jekyll. Because mosquito-borne diseases such as malaria and yellow fever were still endemic on the southern coast, the club employed a series of doctors, most from the Johns Hopkins University School of Medicine, who remained on the island for the entire winter season. While

the millionaires were in residence, the Jekyll Island Club operated much like a small town, albeit a very wealthy one with better housing for workers than most small towns could afford.

President McKinley and the first lady, along with the vice president, his wife, and the secretary of state, visited Jekyll during the 1899 season, spending two nights on the island in Frederic Baker's elegant cottage, Solterra, which burned to the ground fifteen years later. During the visit, some of the black employees performed an old-fashioned cakewalk, a dance that originated on antebellum plantations. When slaves observed their owners engaging in straitlaced European dances in which men and women danced side by side, bowed, postured, and aligned themselves in rows, circles, and squares, they began mocking the dances. They dressed in castoff formal clothing and promenaded in squares, women on the outside, where their partners could swing them as they rounded the corners. Amused rather than offended at being mimicked by their slaves, planters made the dances into competitions, offering a large cake, often a coconut cake, to the winning couple.

Cottage belonging to John Eugene du Bignon, a descendant of Christophe du Bignon. He bought the entire island in the later part of the nineteenth century in order to sell it to rich northerners. He and his brother-in-law, Newton Finney, instead formed a hunting club that evolved into a winter retreat for some of the world's wealthiest people. Potential club members were entertained at du Bignon's cottage. (Courtesy of the Jekyll Island Museum Archives)

Health Care, Sanitation, and Fever at the Club

IT HAS BEEN REPORTED that prospective members of the Jekyll Island Club paid doctors from Johns Hopkins University School of Medicine in Baltimore to travel the world and recommend the perfect place for their winter retreat. The medical school, however, did not open until 1893, seven years after the founding of the club. The rumor may have surfaced because a succession of more than twenty doctors from Johns Hopkins were hired to care for club members on Jekyll and operate the small infirmary on the island. After his first season on the island, one young doctor made it clear that he expected to be treated more like a club member than an employee. Warfield Firor, a doctor whose tenure as the club physician lasted for many years, once diagnosed a guest on Jekyll with advanced syphilis. Firor, sure the man was near death, advised club officers to summon his wife immediately. A former professor from Columbia University's medical school who happened to be visiting Jekyll agreed to look in on the patient. He opined that the man had eaten bad tuna fish on the train trip to Georgia and advised Firor not to be an alarmist. The young doctor politely but firmly replied that he believed the patient would be dead within forty-eight hours. When Firor's prediction proved true, he said it "raised [his] stock" with the club members, since he had outdiagnosed a medical professor from a respected university. Firor was often called to attend club members at their homes in the North when the club was not in session. He reported that many had "fashionable doctors" in New York who did not take care of them properly.

Typhoid fever broke out on Jekyll several times during the millionaires' era. Family members of the south-end fishermen were stricken repeatedly with the disease and were suspected of being carriers. Grob, the superintendent, speculated that a club member or employee might have transported the disease to the island. He also suspected that the island's dairy cows might be infected or that dirty ice from the mainland brought typhoid germs to Jekyll. The club doctor thought it more likely that the island's method of sewage disposal was the culprit. The pipe emptied into Jekyll Creek not far from the underwater cages where oysters bound for the dining room were stored. The doctor recommended several times that the club correct the sewage problem, but nothing was done until after Charlotte Maurice, the wife of Charles Maurice (a member) and one of the most popular women in the club, contracted typhoid fever shortly after leaving Jekyll in the spring of 1909. She died of the disease at her home in New York at the end of summer. The club hired a bacteriologist to find the source of the typhoid before the club opened for the following season. The expert thought there might be a chronic carrier on the island, possibly the south-end fisherman, and recommended a number of improvements, including adding screens to the clubhouse windows and upgrading the sewage system. For whatever reason, the members again took no action. In 1912, after six club members came down with typhoid fever, the club hired yet another expert to investigate. The new consultant concluded that the oysters served in the dining room were infected with typhoid bacteria from raw sewage. The club finally had the sewage system upgraded, and the outbreaks of typhoid fever ended.

James Weldon Johnson, in his novel *The Autobiography of an Ex-Colored Man*, wrote about watching a group of black dancers perform the cakewalk as it was originally done on southern plantations. Johnson said the men moved with elegant, stately dignity while the women walked gracefully beside them. The couples turned the corners of the square together in precise formation, and individual dancers added artistic flourishes. In the late 1800s, minstrel shows in New York and other large cities presented a different version of the cakewalk, often with white dancers in blackface who hammed up the performances, moving in a stumbling, slapstick way. On Jekyll, where black employees had limited exposure to minstrel shows, they may have performed the cakewalk in a style closer to the original. The winner of the dance performed in honor of the dignitaries was awarded with a lavishly decorated cake and the applause of the president of the United States.

It has often been reported that none of the millionaires' cottages were equipped with kitchens. Some of them were, although most club members usually took their meals and afternoon tea at the clubhouse, where a series of talented chefs and a large kitchen staff prepared multicourse meals. Fine crystal, china, and flatware, all monogrammed with the club's scallop-shell emblem, were used in the elegant dining room. Members and guests often lingered for three hours over the evening meal. Club members frequently enjoyed special-occasion dinners staged to celebrate the birthday of a club official, a famous historical figure, or an event.

During the club era, two significant events took place on Jekyll. One was a top-secret meeting whose outcome is still controversial more than a century later. The other was an event publicized nationwide that is still celebrated for opening the door to long-distance telephony. The first event began on a snowy night in November 1910 when six men traveled separately to a railroad station in New Jersey. If anyone asked, they would say they were bound for Jekyll Island to hunt ducks. Instead, they had planned a secret meeting on the island to design a new banking system for the United States after a series of economic panics had resulted in nationwide bank failures and depressions. The men were determined to make sure that any new system protected their own financial interests; legislators and the general public, had they learned of the meeting, would no doubt have been suspicious of, and likely to oppose, anything they proposed. Most of the six men gathered at the New Jersey railway station represented either J. Pierpont Morgan or John D. Rockefeller Jr. At the time, the Morgan and Rockefeller concerns were the hubs of finance in the United States, each group

controlling a vast array of banks and investment companies. One at a time, the six boarded an opulent private railway car, one of the so-called mansions on rails. The car was owned by Nelson Aldrich, a powerful U.S. senator from Rhode Island who served as the Senate Republican whip and was the main advocate for big business in Congress. Aldrich, who had financial interests in banking, manufacturing, and utilities, was one of Morgan's close associates. Aldrich's daughter was married to John D. Rockefeller Jr. The others who boarded the railcar that night were also powerful figures in national and international banking and finance. One was the assistant secretary of the U.S. Treasury Department. Another was president of the most powerful bank in New York; at the meeting, he represented both William Rockefeller, a Jekyll Island Club member and the brother of John D., and an international investment bank. Another member of the group, a German-born partner in the same international investment bank, represented the Rothschild banking dynasty of Europe; his brother headed a powerful banking consortium in Germany and the Netherlands. The last of the six men was the senior partner in the J. P. Morgan Company who headed Morgan's Bankers Trust Company.

To give credence to their announcement of a duck-hunting expedition, the German carried a borrowed shotgun, although he had never hunted game or even fired a gun. Aldrich and the others were determined that no news of the meeting would reach the press or Wall Street. For that reason, they agreed to call each other by their first names only, although such informality was rare at the time. Two chose the first names Orville and Wilbur, in honor of the Wright brothers, whose recent accomplishments in flight were well known. So powerful were the men who met on Jekyll that not a word about the meeting was published until decades later. One of the men explained then why the participants had wanted the meeting kept secret. Frank Vanderlip, president of the National City Bank of New York, said, "If it were to be exposed publicly that our particular group had got together and written a banking bill, that bill would have no chance whatever of passage by Congress."

Isolated Jekyll, far from Wall Street, offered the perfect place for such a conclave. The club had not yet opened for the season, so no other members were on the island. The ever-discreet Grob had made special preparations by sending many year-round employees off the island on vacation and retaining only

Shy wild turkeys. Locals and visitors sometimes catch glimpses of the birds on Jekyll Island. (Courtesy of D. Gordon E. Robertson, Wikimedia Commons)

a handful of others, who were selected as much for their discretion as for their work skills. For nine or ten days, Aldrich and the other members of the so-called First Name Club discussed ways to reform the U.S. banking system. During their time on the island, they took time off to swim, ride horseback, admire Jekyll's natural beauty, and spend one day actually duck hunting. They greatly enjoyed the meals prepared by the club chef. One of the men commented, "Deer, turkey and quail appeared on the table; there were pans of oysters not an hour old when they were scalloped; there were country hams with that incomparable flavor that is given to them in the South." The man said he and the others were working so hard that they "ate enormously." Their visit to Jekyll spanned the Thanksgiving holiday, so the chef prepared a special feast of wild turkey with oyster stuffing, which they enjoyed before going "right back to work."

At the end of the meeting, the six men had devised a system intended to stabilize the U.S. economy. Named for Senator Aldrich, their plan proposed the creation of a central federal bank that could, among other things, accept business debts as collateral for cash. For example, a bank in need of dollars could make a loan, at an interest rate set by the central bank's national board of directors, to a business or an agricultural interest, and receive the same amount of emergency cash from the central bank. In addition, the federal bank could print money when required. Aldrich introduced a Senate bill outlining the proposal a few months after the Jekyll meeting. Aldrich's bill failed to pass, but it did introduce the concept of a central bank whose control was shared by elected officials, bankers, businesses, and agricultural interests.

After several years of wrangling in Congress, the Federal Reserve Act was passed in December 1913, setting up, instead of one central bank, a system of twelve regional banks around the United States that would guarantee repayment of investors' deposits in member banks, up to a specified amount. The Federal Reserve, or the Fed, as it is often called, is still controversial. Some believe it has been the savior of the country's economy; others think it places too much power in what they call a banking cartel, one designed to enrich its members at the expense of everybody else.

In November 2010, on the one-hundredth anniversary of the First Name Club's meeting on Jekyll, members of the Federal Reserve held a conference on the island to commemorate the place where six powerful men designed the prototype of the system.

In January 1915, another momentous event took place on Jekyll, one that was heralded to the world. Theodore Newton Vail, a club member and the first president of AT&T, was spending time on Jekyll, enjoying the delicious meals, fine wines, and spirits served in the clubhouse dining room. He had planned to participate in the first transcontinental telephone call from his offices in New York, but either while he was on Jekyll or shortly before he arrived, he came down with a medical problem. The problem has long been reported as a leg injury, but a Jekyll expert says it is likely that Vail suffered a painful attack of gout, once called the "king's disease" or the "rich man's disease" because in earlier years only royals and the wealthy could afford to eat the sorts of food and drink known to provoke gout attacks. Older, overweight men are more susceptible, and Vail, then in his sixties and portly, fit the profile. In too much pain to travel back to New York, Vail was still determined not to miss involvement in the historic telephone call, which would involve the telephone's inventor, Alexander Graham Bell, in New York; President Woodrow Wilson in Washington, DC; and Bell's well-known assistant, Thomas Watson, in San Francisco, in addition to Vail himself. Special stretched copper wires were designed and manufactured to carry voices over long distance, and telephone poles were erected across the country. When Vail decided to place the call from Jekyll, the special wires had to be extended south from Savannah to Brunswick and then to the island across miles of marshes and tidal creeks. Jekyll already had telephone lines, but they had never been reliable. Vail was well aware that almost anything could short-circuit the call, such as a tree limb falling across a wire, so he had repair men patrolling every mile of the coastal line, ready to repair any damage that might occur. Once the Jekyll line was in place, a so-called perpetual test was maintained so that any problems could be identified and corrected immediately. On the morning of the call, a tree did fall on the line, but a technician stood ready to make rapid repairs.

Although the call itself was historic, lasting for several hours and featuring speeches by dignitaries, the conversation between Vail and President Wilson was brief and less than memorable. When the president came on the line, Vail asked, "Hello, who is this?" Wilson identified himself as the president and commented that he had been speaking across the continent that afternoon. Vail answered, "Oh, yes." President Wilson offered Vail congratulations on his accomplishment; Vail said, "Thank you." Wilson said he was sorry to hear Vail had been ill. Vail said, "I am getting along very nicely. I am sort of a cripple, that is all." The president commented that he hoped Vail would be well soon; Vail again said, "Thank you." And that was it. The call, though less than scintillating, was a major technological achievement that paved the way for telephone communication around the world.

The first transcontinental telephone call was placed from the Jekyll Island Club in 1915 when Theodore Newton Vail, president of the telephone company and a club member, was recuperating on the island, possibly from an attack of gout. Vail had telephone lines run to Jekyll because he did not want to miss the historic four-way call involving Alexander Graham Bell, Bell's famous assistant Thomas Watson, and President Woodrow Wilson. Club members J. P. Morgan Jr. and William Rockefeller sat in on the historic event. (Courtesy of the Jekyll Island Museum Archives)

The economic crash of 1929 and the Great Depression brought a decline in club membership. Many of the original members had died, and the second and third generations were not as devoted to Jekyll as their parents and grandparents had been. The younger people preferred to spend winters at livelier, less remote playgrounds such as Palm Beach, Florida, and Cannes on the French Riviera. In 1939, the remaining members began selling some of the island's pine timber to raise money for club salaries and maintenance. In January 1942, less than a month after the bombing of Pearl Harbor, the Jekyll Island Club opened as usual for the season. Only a handful of members showed up, and in April the club closed for the season. It did not officially reopen during the war, although a few members visited their cottages on the island.

It was widely rumored that General George Patton had come to Jekyll and forced the millionaires to leave because he feared an enemy attack on the island. It was

A turtle at the Georgia Sea Turtle Center on Jekyll. It is the only facility of its kind in the state and one of the few in the world. Center personnel educate visitors and rehabilitate ill or injured sea turtles.

another rumor with no basis in fact. German submarines were in fact patrolling the Georgia coast as early as the spring of 1942. After the club members departed, three merchant ships were torpedoed just off the coast near Jekyll, killing almost two dozen seamen and littering beaches with supplies intended for Allied troops in Europe.

During the war, military patrols roamed Jekyll's beach and manned an observation tower on the island, searching for enemy ships and aircraft. The troops were housed in buildings formerly occupied by club employees. Some also slept in the teahouse, where millionaires had enjoyed afternoon refreshments. One summer night, a young Coast Guardsman reported seeing what he thought were enemy tank tracks in the sand on Jekyll's beach. He rushed to report the sighting to the island's caretaker, who inspected the tracks and proclaimed them to be those of a giant loggerhead sea turtle that had come ashore to lay her eggs. When the turtle crawled back to the sea, she left parallel tracks in the sand that closely resembled the treads of a tank.

After World War II, the Jekyll Island Club never reopened.

Christmas celebrations with a giant tree on the lawn of the Jekyll Island Club Hotel.

Thompson's White Elephant

M. E. Thompson, who, as governor of Georgia, authorized the purchase of Jekyll Island in 1947. (Wikispaces)

AFTER THE WAR, the remaining club members discussed what to do with the island. Several favored turning Jekyll into a resort for wealthy people, along the lines of neighboring Sea Island. They discussed the idea with Alfred W. "Bill" Jones Sr., the developer of Sea Island and its iconic Cloister Hotel. Meanwhile, Governor Ellis Arnall, who had expressed interest in acquiring a sea island to become Georgia's first oceanfront park, appointed state revenue commissioner M. E. Thompson to chair a committee to find a suitable island. After rejecting Ossabaw and St. Simons, Thompson and his committee members recommended Jekyll. They believed that the clubhouse and cottages could be modified to accommodate overnight visitors and noted that the island already had recreation facilities, such as indoor and outdoor tennis courts and an artesian-fed swimming pool, built in 1927 and still in use today. The golf courses built by the club included the Great Dunes Course along the beach, which was designed and named by the golfing great Walter Travis. The club compound included a number of outbuildings that might prove useful as offices and housing for state employees and equipment. If the club refused to sell the island, the state could exercise its powers of condemnation and buy it anyway. A number of prominent coastal residents, including Jones, endorsed the plan, but Governor Arnall abruptly shelved the proposal, for unknown reasons.

Georgia held its gubernatorial election in 1946. At the time, the two-party system was almost nonexistent in the state, long ruled by conservative Democrats. The election's outcome had consequences for Jekyll Island that continue to affect the state park today. Ellis Arnall had decided not to run again for governor. Eugene Talmadge, a staunch segregationist, colorful figure, and crafty politician who had already served three terms as Georgia's governor, ran for a fourth term. Although he was popular with farmers and other rural residents, his high-handed, racist, and often illegal behavior enraged many other Georgians at a time when the state's population was shifting from rural to urban, illiterate to educated, racist to moderate. Accused once of misappropriating state funds in order to raise the price paid to Georgia farmers for hogs, Talmadge freely admitted his guilt, snapping his signature red suspenders and bragging to the farmers, "I did it for you."

M. E. Thompson, the former revenue commissioner who proposed that the state purchase Jekyll, ran for the newly created post of lieutenant governor and won the Democratic primary, which, in Georgia, was tantamount to winning the race. Eugene Talmadge won the gubernatorial primary. He and Thompson were scheduled to take office in January. But the aging Talmadge was in such poor health that his son, Herman, and his other supporters feared he might not live long enough to be sworn in. They cooked up a plan to have Herman Talmadge run as a secret write-in candidate in the general election in November. If his father died, the General Assembly had the option to choose Eugene Talmadge's successor from the three write-in candidates who polled the most votes. Since Eugene Talmadge had no official opposition on the Democratic ticket, it was almost certain that Herman would garner enough votes to qualify for a legislative appointment. Later, it was discovered that many of the write-in ballots for Herman came from people who had been dead for years.

As his son and supporters had feared, Eugene Talmadge died before taking office, in December 1946. Thompson, the newly elected lieutenant governor, claimed that he was Talmadge's logical successor, but state law did not address the issue of who would succeed a governor-elect who had not yet been sworn in. The legislature, packed with Talmadge supporters, voted to give the governorship to Herman Talmadge. Thompson appealed to the Supreme Court of Georgia, which agreed to decide the issue. Meanwhile, the outgoing governor, Ellis Arnall, refused to vacate his office at the state capitol to anybody but Thompson. The upshot was that three men all claimed to be the governor of Georgia at the same time.

The bizarre controversy aroused strong feelings between the competing political factions. Fistfights erupted under the gold dome and on the streets of Atlanta. A member of the legislature chased an opponent through the capitol with a knife, threatening to kill him. Talmadge began carrying a .38 revolver "for protection," he said. The state and national press had a field day. After the legislature named him governor, Talmadge and his supporters elbowed their way into Governor Arnall's office at the state capitol, and for a day both men shared the space. That night, Talmadge supporters sneaked into the capitol and changed the locks on the governor's office doors. When Arnall arrived the

Thompson's political opponent, Herman Talmadge, who critized Thompson for buying the island, which he nicknamed Thompson's white elephant. (Photo by Warren K. Leffler, U.S. News & World Report Magazine Photograph Collection, Library of Congress)

following morning, he found himself locked out and Talmadge ensconced in the governor's chair. Arnall and Thompson both set up alternate gubernatorial offices nearby.

Ben Fortson, the secretary of state, hid the state seal under the cushions of his wheelchair to prevent any of the gubernatorial claimants from stamping legislation into law until the state supreme court ruled. Fortson said later that he felt like a mother duck sitting on a clutch of eggs, waiting for them to hatch. In the spring of 1947, after Herman Talmadge had served sixty-seven days as the appointed governor, the court named M. E. Thompson as acting governor, but called a special election for September 1948 to allow Georgia voters to choose who would complete Eugene Talmadge's unexpired term. Both Thompson and Talmadge announced they would run in the special election. Talmadge moved out of the governor's offices and Thompson moved in.

While Thompson was serving as acting governor, he lost no time in buying Jekyll, using the state's power of condemnation and paying $675,000 for the island. The sale was completed in September 1947. The club members initially resisted the sale, but when the case came to court, they offered no opposition. Thompson asked the legislature to designate Jekyll an oceanfront park for "the ordinary people of Georgia" and requested that it be kept affordable for public use in perpetuity. That language is written into the law that created the Jekyll Island State Park.

The purchase of Jekyll probably cost Thompson the governorship. Herman Talmadge campaigned against Thompson all through 1947 and 1948, calling Jekyll "Thompson's white elephant" and claiming that his opponent wanted the island to use as his private playground. In stump speeches around the state, Talmadge railed that Georgia needed roads and schools more than "resort" islands for crooked politicians. Every chance he got, Talmadge criticized Thompson for buying the lovely little sea island for what was later recognized as a bargain-basement price. Many years later, the bridge over Jekyll Creek was named for Thompson to honor his foresight in buying the island.

Thompson, eager to open the new state park to the public, worked with the Georgia Parks Department to get the island ready for visitors. During the war years, many of the cottage owners and the owners of the annex had deeded their properties to the club, which had not been able to afford to maintain them adequately. They needed to be refurbished. Some of the island's shell roads were impassable, overgrown with thick, knotty palmetto roots, and other roads had been damaged by military traffic during wartime. The golf courses were overgrown, and other recreation facilities needed to be spruced up.

In March 1948, Jekyll Island State Park opened to the public. Visitors traveled back and forth on boats; a causeway to the island was already on the drawing board. The first summer, under the management of the Georgia Parks Department, thousands of state residents and others enjoyed the island that for sixty-two years had been the exclusive property of the wealthiest people in the world. The new state park was a huge success—until Herman Talmadge defeated Thompson in the special gubernatorial election in September 1948. Since Talmadge had campaigned so stridently against the purchase of Jekyll, he could hardly do an immediate about-face and support the state park. Some experts say that contradictory legislation passed at Talmadge's request during his early years as governor handicapped Jekyll's chances of becoming a successful state park and may still cause problems for the island today.

CHAPTER VII Jekyll Island State Park

[1948–1986]

After acting governor M. E. Thompson purchased Jekyll for the state of Georgia in late 1947, the Georgia Parks Department scrambled to get the island ready for visitors. When the new state park opened in the following March, scores of excited people boarded the picturesque sternwheeler *Robert E. Lee* for the forty-five-minute boat ride from Brunswick to the island. (Jekyll's causeway would not be completed for another seven years.) After docking at the Jekyll wharf, visitors could pay a dime to catch a bus to the beach, where the parks department had built a new bath pavilion with dressing rooms and lockers. For a quarter, visitors could take a bus tour of the whole island. They could also rent Jeeps, motor scooters, bicycles, or horses and explore on their own. That first year, thousands of visitors gave the new island park rave reviews. They swam in the ocean, fished in the tidal creeks, grilled hotdogs and hamburgers at the new picnic area, and gaped at the splendor of the mansion-sized cottages and the castle-like clubhouse built by millionaire members of the Jekyll Island Club. More than fifty high school graduating classes from all over Georgia celebrated on Jekyll that first year, and a number of youth groups, including Boy Scout troops, 4-H clubs, and Future Farmers of America

chapters, traveled to the island for memorable vacations. The only recreational amenity not available at the state park on opening day was the golf courses. They were closed because feral hogs, long a problem on the island, had rooted up the greens and fairways.

The clubhouse, rechristened the Jekyll Island Hotel, along with several of the club-era cottages, provided almost 400 rooms to overnight visitors. The clubhouse furnishings had been included in the island's sale, so guests slept in the same ornate beds, stored their clothes in the same antique dressers, and reclined on the same velvet chaises longues as the millionaires. Visitors could play badminton, horseshoes, and tennis on the hotel grounds, and the staff showed movies on the verandah every night. The parks department even arranged for a theatre troop from Atlanta to present a variety of plays that first summer.

The hotel library was well stocked with books, most bearing labels identifying them as the property of the Jekyll Island Club. Some had bookplates noting which millionaire club member had donated them. During the hotel's first year of operation, a number of books and small decorative items disappeared. A few employees were fired

for theft, but some of the memorabilia was most likely pilfered by hotel guests or park visitors who wandered through the hotel's public rooms. Everyone seemed to want to own something that had once belonged to someone rich and famous. In spite of the thefts, Jekyll's first season as a fledgling state park under the management of the Georgia Parks Department was considered a success.

Had acting governor M. E. Thompson won the special gubernatorial election in September 1948, Jekyll's future as a state park might have been brighter. But when Herman Talmadge won the race and took office in early 1949, the park's prospects took a plunge. During the campaign, Talmadge had repeatedly slammed Thompson for buying the island, referring to Jekyll as "Thompson's white elephant." Not long after taking office, Talmadge announced that Jekyll was bankrupting the parks department, and asked the legislature to appoint a committee to recommend whether Georgia should keep the island. The new governor continued to harp on the costs associated with Jekyll, especially when construction began on the causeway linking the island to the mainland. The route, which had to cross a seven-mile stretch of tidal marsh, was much more expensive to build than a standard dryland highway. The bridge over

Jekyll Creek alone cost almost $1 million. Because the creek is part of the Intracoastal Waterway, the new bridge had to be built to accommodate larger boats. It featured a central lift span that could be raised to allow yachts, shrimp boats, and tugs to pass through.

One year after he took office, Talmadge asked the legislature to remove Jekyll from the auspices of the Georgia Parks Department and form a special authority to oversee island operations. Talmadge made sure the legislation was structured so that he and future governors would appoint all the members of the Jekyll Island State Park Authority, giving himself and some of his successors considerable say-so over Jekyll's fate. The law creating the authority included three unusual provisions not applied to any other state park in Georgia:

- It required Jekyll to be self-supporting.
- It restricted development. For decades, state law required 65 percent of the island lying above water at mean high tide to remain undeveloped.
- It mandated that Jekyll's amenities be offered at the lowest rates "reasonable and possible" for the "ordinary people" of Georgia.

From the beginning, the authority has been pressured to make the park profitable. After funding the initial purchase and the cost of the causeway and bridge, Georgia has provided only a modest amount of money for operations, and only in the early years. Unlike other state parks, Jekyll has never received regular legislative appropriations. Talmadge, who helped write the legislation establishing the park authority, seemed almost eager for the new park to fail, which would have supported his claim that Thompson had made a bad deal by buying Jekyll in the first place. When Thompson ran against Talmadge in the next gubernatorial election, Talmadge again used Thompson's purchase of the island as a campaign issue.

While members of the legislative committee were deciding Jekyll's future, the committee leased the island to Barney Whitaker, an Augusta businessman, at Talmadge's request. Whitaker opened the old millionaires' clubhouse as the Jekyll Island Hotel. To publicize the hotel and the new state park, Whitaker hosted a huge barbecue on the island and invited civic leaders, politicians, and other prominent citizens from all over Georgia to attend. He hired a University of Georgia band to play at the barbecue and a light plane to fly around the state with a banner advertising "Beautiful Jekyll Island." In spite of his efforts over the next couple of years, the enterprise failed. When

Whitaker's lease expired in 1951, he had lost about $30,000 of his own money on the venture. After he returned to Augusta, Whitaker started a popular cafeteria chain and operated the successful Clarendon hotels.

When the special legislative committee recommended that the state retain ownership of Jekyll, Talmadge—still grumbling about costs—sent convicts from Georgia's maximum security prison at Reidsville to the island to work, a politically astute move. Many of Talmadge's conservative constituents believed that performing hard labor was an appropriate method of punishing criminals, and convict labor was unpaid. As many as 150 convicts worked on the island over the next five years; Talmadge closed Jekyll to the public for the first four, citing dangerous conditions at the state park. Under the direction of Talmadge's newly appointed park authority, convicts worked with picks and shovels to smooth Jekyll's rough shell and sand roads, chopped out knotty palmetto roots, filled potholes, and prepared the roads for paving. They harvested Jekyll timber and turned it into finished lumber at the island sawmill so that it could be sold to help fund the park. The convicts helped construct Beachview Drive, the island's perimeter road. They cut firebreaks through the woods, dug drainage ditches,

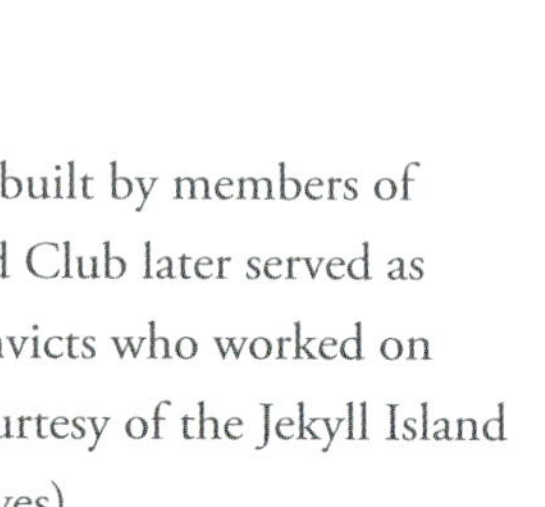

The dairy barn built by members of the Jekyll Island Club later served as housing for convicts who worked on the island. (Courtesy of the Jekyll Island Museum Archives)

and cleared land for ocean-side parks, beachfront motels, restaurants, businesses, and subdivisions. The authority would lease the land to private enterprises and individuals who wanted to build houses on the island; revenue from the leases would help Jekyll meet its mandate to be self-supporting. Working conditions for convicts on the still-wild island were tough. They battled sand gnats, mosquitoes, ticks, red bugs, alligators, and diamondback rattlesnakes, some more than six feet long. They killed the rattlers, skinned them, dried the skins, and used them to make belts and wallets when they returned to their cells at the state prison.

The state revamped the dairy barn once occupied by the millionaires' cows to house the convicts. The camp caused something of a stir in Glynn County. Residents of St. Simons, just a mile away across the sound, were not thrilled to have a prison camp as a neighbor. Although state authorities tried to calm residents' fears by promising that only "white convicts with meritorious conduct records" would be housed on Jekyll, people on St. Simons feared that dangerous felons would be able to escape by swimming over from the neighboring island. At the time, teenage boys who lifeguarded on area beaches swam from St. Simons to Jekyll and back every summer as a rite of passage. Although strong currents and jellyfish were troublesome, it was not a difficult swim, and St. Simons residents, aware of that fact, began locking their doors and windows for the first time. St. Simons children prowled the pier section and south beach every day, scouting for suspicious-looking swimmers coming from Jekyll.

The Price of Gas on Jekyll

WHILE THE CONVICTS were encamped on Jekyll, Erv Davis, an artist on St. Simons, traveled to Little Cumberland Island to spend the day on a friend's yacht, which was anchored in the Cumberland River. Davis borrowed a friend's small boat for the trip. Pete Barnwell, a St. Simons flight instructor, flew a small plane over for the occasion, landing the single-engine craft on Little Cumberland's broad beach, a common practice at the time. Both Big and Little Cumberland were still privately owned and sparsely populated. Davis and Barnwell spent a pleasant day with friends and then headed home when the yacht continued its trip down the Intracoastal Waterway. Davis cranked up the outboard motor, dropped Barnwell off on the beach, and watched him taxi down the strand. As he lifted off, Barnwell misjudged the height of the surf. His fixed landing gear caught a wave tip and flipped the plane upside down in shallow water. Barnwell crawled out, uninjured but fuming. He and Davis tried to right the plane, without success. They boarded Davis's boat for the trek back to St. Simons. They would have to navigate St. Andrews Sound, pass through Jekyll Creek, and cross St. Simons Sound before reaching the dock in the MacKay River, a distance of about fifteen miles. Midway across St. Andrews Sound, the boat ran out of gas. Since it was almost dark, the men rowed to a nearby oyster bank and prepared to spend an uncomfortable night trying to sleep in an open boat. When the mosquitoes and sand gnats found them, they collected driftwood and built a bonfire on top of the oysters. When the superheated shellfish under the fire began exploding like grenades, the men flattened themselves behind a driftwood log to avoid the shrapnel of sharp oyster shells.

The next morning at daylight, tired, thirsty, hungry, and bug bitten, they rowed to the Jekyll wharf, where one of the convicts was working. Davis asked to buy enough gas to get back to St. Simons. The convict offered to give him a full tank in return for a ride off the island. Just then, Davis saw a larger boat heading toward the wharf. It was the owner of the borrowed boat, who was searching for the two missing men. He took them back to St. Simons in his big boat, towing his small boat and leaving the disgruntled convict behind.

An old Jekyll Island bridge, no longer open to vehicles but popular with anglers and bird watchers.

Excited by the prospect of seeing a real convict, the children misidentified many a distant bottlenose dolphin as an escapee.

One prisoner escaped from the work camp while Hal Sigman was on the island visiting a friend whose father was employed on Jekyll. Sigman, who now lives on St. Simons, was a boy at the time. He and his friend were playing in the woods when several helicopters passed overhead, flying low. When a pilot spotted movement among the trees, he dispatched police officers on foot to capture the criminal. Officers instead located the two boys and ordered them to go home and stay there until the convict was located. The man was captured a few hours later, hiding in the woods. There is no record that any prisoner ever made it all the way off Jekyll, although at least one gave it a try.

When Governor Talmadge appointed the members of the first park authority, he named J. D. Compton, then president of the Sea Island Company, to the board. Compton was not the governor's choice. Talmadge had made a deal to include him on the authority in return for the support of Charles Gowen, a popular state representative from St. Simons, in Talmadge's upcoming race for reelection. Gowen, who

The first bridge across Jekyll Creek, now replaced by a high arched span.

A rope swing hidden in the woods, waiting to delight hikers who follow a trail from the St. Andrews picnic area on Jekyll's south end.

had lobbied for the state to buy Jekyll, believed that Compton would be an asset to the board. He was right. Compton is credited with saving the island from the hodgepodge development and carnival atmosphere that plagued so many other beach playgrounds up and down the Eastern Seaboard. He was also probably the only member of Talmadge's authority who knew anything about sea islands in general and Jekyll in particular. Compton had helped to develop tiny Sea Island (just east of St. Simons) and its elegant Cloister Hotel into an upscale resort and residential area. After World War II, when the Jekyll Island Club was pondering its future, Alfred W. Jones, cofounder of the Sea Island Company, considered buying Jekyll and building a similar resort there. After Compton prepared a feasibility study indicating the project would not be profitable, at least not in the early years, Jones decided against the purchase. Nonetheless, the Sea Island Company continued to help with Jekyll's management, and by 1946 it had taken full responsibility for the island. The company continued to manage Jekyll until the following year, when the state bought it.

Compton proved to be Jekyll's best friend during the early years. He persuaded his fellow authority members to hire a respected Atlanta firm, Robert & Co., to prepare a professional plan that would guide development on the island for the next fifty years.

After other firms submitted ideas, Compton convinced his colleagues to approve the Robert & Co. proposal because it focused on the island's natural beauty. Plans favored by some other authority members suggested turning Jekyll into "another Daytona" or "a new Coney Island." The Robert & Co. plan, although advanced for its time, was far from perfect. The company recommended filling in marsh to create land for expansion of the airport, something that would not even be considered today.

Talmadge's second and final term as governor ended just after the long-awaited causeway between the mainland and the island opened in December 1954, with the completion of the lift-span bridge over Jekyll Creek. Talmadge and his handpicked successor, Marvin Griffin, cut the ribbon at the dedication ceremony, although both men had objected to the purchase of the island. Governor Griffin not only adopted Talmadge's "white elephant" terminology in regard to Jekyll, but also, in later addresses to the legislature, referred to the island as a perennial problem and said the state had no business running a beach resort. At one point, he recommended trading Jekyll for an atomic reactor for the Georgia Institute of Technology in Atlanta.

The park suffered during its first decade of state ownership, in part because so few people at the time knew anything about environmental protection or historic preservation. In the 1950s and 1960s, there were no laws guarding Georgia's tidal marshes, freshwater wetlands, beaches, sand dunes, archaeological sites, or historic buildings. At the direction of the park authority, the Pulitzer-Albright Cottage was razed after it suffered minor damage from a small fire. Old documents discovered in the millionaires' clubhouse were burned as trash. Medical and other items from the club's infirmary were consigned to the dump. After Beachview Drive was paved, the authority ordered a stretch of island sand dunes, some of them forty feet high, bulldozed so that visitors driving on the new perimeter road could see the beach and the Atlantic Ocean. Later, the remaining dunes were leveled to accommodate a concrete walkway along the beach between two motels. For many years, the bulldozed beachfront and a giant paved parking lot gave the eastern side of the island a bleak, windswept look. When the dunes were removed, Jekyll's beaches became more vulnerable to erosion. Dunes are important components of the natural sand-sharing system that nourishes coastal beaches eroded by storms and nor'easters. Sand dunes also protect the interior of sea islands from strong winds and flooding.

Hal Sigman of St. Simons, who was caught up in the search for the escaped convict, spent a lot of time on Jekyll as a youth. He remembered that the island's beaches were always pristine, raked every day to remove the piles of dead marsh grass, called marsh

wrack, that wash up on every tide. Secretary of State Ben Fortson, who was then serving on the park authority, preferred clean beaches and ordered the work done. It was not known at the time that marsh wrack helps build dunes by stopping blowing sand.

Although Jekyll's environment has been altered over thousands of years by human occupants, the state probably did the greatest damage, if only by virtue of having powerful equipment such as draglines and bulldozers to work with. The state's road-building projects and new drainage ditches disrupted natural flows to freshwater wetlands and ponds that had offered habitat for hundreds of plants and animals, some of them rare or endangered. The park authority expanded Jekyll's small airport, built during the millionaires' era, by filling in several acres of tidal marsh on the western side of the island. Georgia's marshes, now protected by law, constitute some of the most productive acreage in the world, providing food, shelter, and nursery grounds for thousands of species, including shrimp, fish, blue crabs, and oysters.

The structure now called the historic Jekyll wharf. It was built to accommodate the yachts of millionaires who wintered on the island. (Courtesy of the Jekyll Island Museum Archives)

Probably the greatest environmental damage to the island occurred when the authority built a new boat marina in the late 1960s. Two large basins, one filled with salt water and the other with fresh, were dredged out of a tidal marsh on the island's western shore. The dredged material, called spoil, was used to build dikes around the basins as well as a parking lot and an area for service buildings. The marina was sited adjacent to Jekyll Creek, a short link in the Intracoastal Waterway. In spring and fall, streams of yachts that locals call snowbirds pass through the creek, migrating south for the winter, north for the summer. The authority expected the new marina to generate revenue by enticing the snowbirds to stop for gas, pay to dock overnight, and spend money at Jekyll restaurants, shops, and attractions. Instead, the marina was an embarrassing failure. As soon as dredging was complete, the saltwater basin began silting up. Tidal marshes form in areas of heavy natural siltation, and the site chosen for the new marina was no exception. After dredging the basin again and again at great expense, the authority members finally realized it was futile to fight Mother Nature and abandoned the project. By then, the hydrology of the area had been compromised, and native plant communities wiped out. Invasive plants not indigenous to Jekyll colonized the dredged spoil, which was toxic to many native plants, and established a foothold on the island.

During Griffin's administration, Atlanta newspapers charged that the park authority was spending lavish amounts of money to renovate Cherokee Cottage, a twenty-two-room jewel of Italian Renaissance architecture on Jekyll, to be the governor's "summer mansion by the sea." The cottage had been built for the family of George Shrady, a prominent New York physician who treated Union troops and U.S. presidents, and witnessed the first execution by electrocution, which he found abhorrent. The authority also considered building a private wharf for the gubernatorial boat. Probably because of the negative publicity, Griffin announced he would never stay in Cherokee Cottage. Before he made that statement to the press, however, he quietly had more than two dozen valuable pieces of antique furniture and art from the cottage shipped to the governor's mansion in Atlanta. A Jekyll archivist said furniture and art from other millionaires' cottages was also sent to the governor's mansion during the Griffin era. Nobody is sure whether art and furnishings from Jekyll made the transition from an earlier gubernatorial mansion to the present governor's residence, because descriptions of the pieces were so vague.

The park authority came under fire again during Griffin's administration for granting no-bid contracts and leases on Jekyll and for making purchases without following the guidelines required by state law. Authority member Jim Compton, the Sea Island Company president, tried without success to convince his fellow board members to conduct business legally and ethically. When they did not, Compton resigned in September 1955. When a state senator was charged not long afterward with selling alcohol on Jekyll without a license, the *Atlanta Constitution* ran a series of scathing articles claiming that the authority was to blame for all sorts of political corruption at the state park. In response to the negative publicity, the legislature restructured the authority in 1957, replacing gubernatorial appointees with state elected officials, including the secretary of state, the attorney general, the public services director, the director of the parks department, and the state auditor. At the end of his term in 1959, Griffin left office under a cloud. Several members of his administration had been tried and convicted of crimes, and his brother was reputedly involved in illegal activities. A Fulton County grand jury investigated the governor himself but did not bring charges.

The newly structured park authority hired A. J. "Judge" Hartley, a retired assistant attorney general, to handle the day-to-day operations of Jekyll. Hartley's title was honorary; he had never served as a judge. Under his management, Jekyll at last began to realize its potential as a functioning state park, a moderately priced beach playground, and a thriving residential area. The first motels opened, including the Wanderer, named for the infamous slave ship that landed its sad cargo on Jekyll just before the Civil War. There were other motels with names linked to the island's history, such as

the Buccaneer and the Corsair, the name that Jekyll Island Club member J. P. Morgan chose for his succession of luxury yachts. Like other development on the island in the late 1950s and 1960s, the motels were designed in the midcentury modern style. The authority augmented the dark, ornate Victorian furniture at the Jekyll Island Hotel with modern pieces such as tables shaped like boomerangs and sofas with straight lines and metal feet. The new pieces fought with the hotel's luxurious, albeit old-fashioned, look.

The lease of lots in the residential areas did not get off to a flying start. Leasing land to build a house on was a new concept at the time in Georgia. In addition, Griffin's frequent threats to sell or trade Jekyll probably made some prospective leasees nervous. Larry McDonough was one of the first year-round residents of the island. He moved to Jekyll in 1957 and later built a house there where he and his wife reared their five children. McDonough, born in 1922 and still living on the island in 2014, said Jekyll's neighborhoods have always been quiet and uncrowded, even when the beachfront convention center is packed or thousands of tourists show up for island festivals and annual events such as the Fourth of July celebration. Jekyll long ago ran out of residential lots; the last house was built on the island during the 1970s.

One of McDonough's daughters, Marie Sigman, who now lives on St. Simons, moved to Jekyll as a teenager. There were thirteen school-age children on the island at the time, but no schools. Marie and her four siblings were not eligible to ride the public school bus to Brunswick because they attended Catholic school. McDonough, reluctant to make the round trip twice a day between Jekyll and Brunswick, devised a plan for his offspring to ride the public school bus. The children wore ordinary clothes on the bus and carried their parochial school uniforms. When the bus discharged its passengers, the McDonough children got off, walked the short distance to the Catholic school, changed into their uniforms, and reversed the process for the after-school ride home.

By the 1960s, Jekyll was showing signs of becoming a community. New restaurants offered full menus, including fresh seafood caught in local waters. With the exception of the Jekyll Island Hotel's dining room, the first island eateries were snack bars with limited menus. A grocery store and gas station opened on the island, along with

The Crane Cottage, the largest residence built by a member of the Jekyll Island Club.

The Jekyll Estates Motel, which opened in the 1950s on the island's beachfront. (Courtesy of the Jekyll Island Museum Archives)

Residential subdivisions serving as quiet enclaves on a state-owned island that hosts millions of visitors every year.

The Welcome Center, located on the causeway. It offers the usual array of brochures, books, and souvenirs, plus a tower that provides a great vantage point for viewing the flora and fauna of the vast *Spartina* marshes that flank Jekyll's western shore.

a variety store and clothing shops. A state trooper was assigned to patrol Jekyll and its causeway. A state patrol post was later built adjacent to the causeway, and for some years, patrolmen got extra pay because they worked in such a remote area.

Ever mindful of the need for Jekyll to support itself, the park authority focused on building attractions to keep visitors coming to the island. It constructed a large fishing pier that jutted into the waters of St. Simons Sound on Jekyll's north end. They built a futuristic-looking recreation building that fronted the beach on the east side of the island. The facility was later expanded to include a convention center. Jack Hice, an entrepreneur from St. Simons who was handling publicity for Jekyll at the time, suggested the modern complex be called the Aquarama. Authority members liked the name and adopted it. Island visitors and residents thronged the Aquarama's bowling alleys and heated indoor swimming pool. The pool was billed as "Olympic-size," and the Amateur Athletic Union staged meets there, including several where national swimming records were broken. The hearts of young swimmers who had won the honors were broken when the pool turned out to be smaller than official Olympic size. For that reason, the Aquarama no longer hosted swim meets that required a regulation-size pool, but it continued to be one of the island's most popular attractions for many years.

During the mid-1950s, the island's first museum was opened by Tallu Fish, a recent widow and former journalist. In 1947, during M. E. Thompson's term as governor, Indian Mound Cottage, owned at one time by Standard Oil cofounder William

The iconic Aquarama, considered ultramodern in 1961. It was razed to make way for the $50 million beachfront convention center, which opened in 2012. (Courtesy of the Jekyll Island Museum Archives)

Rockefeller, was designated a museum, but nothing had been done since then. Fish persuaded the park authority to let her organize and publicize the facility. By that time, many of Jekyll's historic treasures had already been lost, many to the state's heavy-handed efforts to improve the new park during its formative years. Two of the millionaires' cottages and many of the club's service buildings had been razed. Furnishings and art from some of the cottages had been sold to the Sea Island Company, to an Atlanta antiques dealer, and to individuals for bargain-basement prices soon after the state purchased Jekyll. Other items of value vanished during the years when the island and its buildings were vacant. There were persistent rumors that area residents and others, including antiques dealers, broke into the cottages to steal furniture, artworks, and smaller pieces, carrying them away under cover of darkness on private boats. Fish was determined to save anything historic that remained, whether on or off the island. She collected historic documents, paintings, furniture, sculptures, textiles, and other bits and pieces of Jekyll's past, turning many of the items into exhibits. She began archiving old photographs and documents. Although she focused on the high-profile club era, Fish gathered arrowheads and pottery sherds made by prehistoric Native Americans who had lived on Jekyll thousands of years earlier; coins and buttons from the colonial era; and china and crockery from the plantation period. She tracked down the location

of tables, chairs, glassware, menus from the club dining room, letters to and from club members, architectural drawings, antique maps, and a wealth of other memorabilia all over Georgia and beyond.

Her tiny budget did not permit her to buy back anything that had been sold or stolen, but she did persuade many people to donate historic Jekyll items to the new museum. She paid island children a penny or two to bring her sand dollars from Jekyll's beach, which she resold to help fund the museum. Fish also found creative ways to publicize the facility. She invented a story about an ornately carved chair that had once been part of the clubhouse furnishings, claiming the chair granted wishes to anyone who sat in it, as most museum visitors did. She made sure, however, that they first paid the museum's small admission fee. Fish had a knack for staging unusual exhibits. One featured a collection of chamber pots that had once cradled the bottoms of millionaire club members. Shabby-looking game animals and birds preserved years earlier by the club's resident taxidermist were featured in another exhibit. Fish also collected stories about earlier times on Jekyll. She met several former club members and, using her journalistic skills, milked them for memories of the island. One was Bert Jekyll, a relative of Sir Joseph Jekyll, for whom the island was named. He visited the state park, met Fish, and told her that Robert Louis Stevenson, who wrote *The Strange*

The restored Rockefeller cottage, named Indian Mound for the large prehistoric shell mound found on the property. It once housed Jekyll's museum, but now has been restored and opened to visitors.

A display of chamber pots that once cradled the bottoms of some of the world's wealthiest people—one of the creative and unusual exhibits staged by Tallu Fish at the island's first museum. (Courtesy of the Jekyll Island Museum Archives)

Exhibits on display at the Jekyll Island Museum. The artifacts span the history of the island.

An ornately carved remnant of the Jekyll Island Club. Tallu Fish, curator of the island's first museum, called it a wishing chair. To raise funds for the museum, Fish required anyone who sat in the chair to pay a modest fee.

Case of Dr. Jekyll and Mr. Hyde, had chosen the name for his mad scientist because Stevenson and a member of Sir Joseph's family were friends. The famous author liked the name "Jekyll" and asked to borrow it for one facet of his book's main character.

By the 1960s, Judge Hartley, the island's manager, and others were beginning to recognize the value of Jekyll's historic buildings. Hartley proposed making the area of the former millionaires' club into a historic tourist attraction along the lines of Colonial Williamsburg, in Virginia. The park authority allocated a budget of fifty thousand dollars for restoration of the entire village, an amount inadequate for such an ambitious enterprise. The authority hired a full-time preservationist, who tried to stabilize the buildings in order to prevent further deterioration. In the early years, most people referred to the historic buildings collectively as the Millionaires' Village. Later, after the buildings and the colonial-era Horton House were given National Historic Landmark status, the official name became the Jekyll Island Historic District.

From its inception as a state park, Jekyll was racially segregated like the rest of the Deep South. Although numbers of African Americans were employed on the island, they were banned from enjoying any of its natural resources or other amenities. They could not eat in island restaurants, stay in island motels, or ride the Ferris wheel or the miniature train at Peppermint Land Amusement Park. They were banned from walking on Jekyll beaches or swimming in the ocean, much less in island pools.

As early as 1950, black leaders from Brunswick and Savannah had begun lobbying the park authority to designate an island tract where people of color could enjoy Jekyll. They pointed out that taxes paid by black Georgians had helped pay for the park's purchase and for any other state-funded improvements on the island. The authority agreed to designate a small, remote area on the south end of Jekyll overlooking St. Andrews Sound for black visitors, but failed to improve the property until 1955. The state constructed a beach pavilion, seven years after the pavilion for white people opened on Jekyll. The new pavilion offered dressing rooms, a concession stand, and a covered picnic area. The two pavilions were known for years as the Negro Bath House and the White Bath House. With the opening of the Negro Bath House, Jekyll became the only place in Georgia, and one of the few places in the Deep South, where black vacationers had access to the beach and ocean, although island motels, restaurants, and Peppermint Park were still off-limits.

In 1960, when the national chapter of the NAACP announced plans to integrate all southern beaches, Georgia's attorney general, then a member of the park authority, asked Governor Griffin to declare martial law if any attempt were made to integrate

A stretch of beach on the south end of Jekyll Island that was one of the first in Georgia that state officials opened, albeit reluctantly, to black visitors. (Courtesy of the Jekyll Island Museum Archives)

the island. As the civil rights movement progressed, authority members tried to keep black and white facilities "separate but equal" on Jekyll by building a swimming pool at the St. Andrews compound. The new pool paled in comparison to the whites-only Aquarama in size and design. Since there was no place for black visitors to stay overnight on Jekyll, a group of black investors and civic leaders from all over Georgia formed a corporation and sold stock to finance the building of the Dolphin Club and Motor Hotel in the late 1950s. The motel featured about sixty rooms, a lounge and dance floor, and a restaurant. Forty residential lots nearby were offered for lease to black people who wanted to build houses on the island. The first two people to build houses in the St. Andrews subdivision had been employees of the Jekyll Island Club and had fallen in love with Jekyll then. Another former club employee, Earl Hill, who had caddied for the millionaires during the 1920s, organized the Southeastern Golf Tournament for black golfers in 1964. Hill often referred to the tournament as the "Classic." The Frontier Club, the organization that found sponsors for the tournament, hosted an Otis Redding concert at the St. Andrews Auditorium to fund the first tournament. A number of well-known golf professionals competed for money; in 1975, the first-place winner, Nate Starks, a PGA golfer, won $2,500.

Packed school buses began arriving at St. Andrews loaded with children from all over Georgia, many of whom had never seen the ocean. Many older black people still

From Integrated Canada to Segregated Georgia

IN 1958, while Marvin Griffin was still governor, a disaster in a Canadian coal mine linked the tiny Springhill community of Nova Scotia to Jekyll Island. An underground bump, or earthquake, collapsed thousands of feet of tunnels, released toxic gas, and killed seventy-four miners. One hundred others were trapped, some of them almost a mile underground. Rescuers worked in mine shafts blocked by tons of debris, running the risk of penetrating pockets of poisonous gas and triggering future collapses as they hacked through the rubble. Everyone in Springhill was connected to the mine, and the entire community turned out to comfort loved ones as the bodies of the victims were brought to the surface in airtight coffins. Friends and family members waited at the pithead, the mouth of the mine shaft, for word of those still unaccounted for.

The rescue effort, which continued for more than a week, captured the attention of the international press. A Canadian Broadcasting Company television crew later claimed to have aired the first live footage of a tragedy that made international news. One group of miners was trapped underground for almost nine days. When rescuers finally freed them, they emerged from stygian darkness into the limelight of international celebrity. Several were invited to tour New York City and appear on *The Ed Sullivan Show*. Maurice Ruddick, the only black miner, was lauded for being the last man out. The forty-six-year-old father of twelve insisted on staying behind until all his comrades had escaped. For his bravery, he was named Canada's Citizen of the Year. The Springhill mine was permanently closed, in part because some of the bodies could not be retrieved. When the mine shut down, so did the town. A fund established to help miners and their families rapidly grew to more than $1 million.

All the hype was noted in the Georgia governor's office. Griffin's top aide came up with an idea to refocus the spotlight on Jekyll. Griffin was hunting in Manitoba and out of touch, but the aide invited the miners and their families to spend a week on Jekyll Island, all expenses paid. When he issued the invitation, the aide was unaware that one of the miners was black. Griffin, who had campaigned for governor on a strong segregationist platform, was apoplectic when he learned that a black man and his family had been invited to vacation at a Georgia state park. Griffin amended the invitation. He announced that the Ruddicks could come, but because of segregation laws, they would have to be separated from the white miners. Ruddick's coworkers were incensed and wanted to decline the invitation, but Ruddick accepted so that everyone could enjoy a much-needed sea island vacation.

To accommodate the Ruddicks, Griffin had three new trailers hauled across the causeway and set up in the Negro Bath House parking lot, miles from the state park's whites-only facilities. The trailers were wired for electricity, connected to newly dug septic tanks, and stocked with food and provisions, including beach chairs. Workers carpeted the area around the trailers with squares of sod. The grass, laid in salty beach sand, would have lasted about as long as the miners' vacation. The Ruddicks, who brought their four youngest children to Jekyll, occupied one trailer, a maid and cook stayed in the second, and Dr. W. K. Payne, the president of Savannah State College and a community leader, and his wife were housed in the third. Griffin had invited the Paynes to keep the Ruddicks company. The fact that a Nova Scotian coal miner and a college president from the Deep South might have little in common except their race apparently never occurred to Griffin.

While the white miners and their families were doing the bunny hop at the Jekyll Island Hotel, the Ruddicks visited segregated clubs in Brunswick, where they danced to live jazz, blues, and rock and roll. At one of the clubs, Ruddick, who was reputed to have a good singing voice, was persuaded to perform. While the white miners and their families took a sightseeing trip around Jekyll on a shrimp boat, Ruddick went fishing with local black fishermen in small boats. Asked by a reporter how he felt about being segregated, Ruddick answered that he seemed to be enjoying himself just as much as the others.

Griffin wanted to be photographed while welcoming the white miners to Jekyll, but he did not want to be photographed shaking a black man's hand. The governor knew, however, that he would be attacked by the press if he excluded Ruddick from the greeting. Griffin traveled in secret to Jekyll early one morning to visit the Ruddick compound. Out of sight of reporters and cameras, Griffin welcomed the Ruddicks and even cradled their baby in his arms. His aide took a photograph of the governor posing with the family, but deliberately overexposed the film to make sure there was no visual record of the event. Griffin then went to the other end of Jekyll to greet the white miners. When reporters asked why Ruddick was not in attendance, Griffin explained that he had already welcomed the miner and his family. When the press questioned Ruddick later, he confirmed the governor's story.

The first motel on Jekyll designed to accommodate black visitors, opened by a consortium of black businessmen. (Courtesy of the Jekyll Island Museum Archives)

have fond feelings for Jekyll because it was where they first walked on an island beach and poked their toes in the Atlantic.

Not long after the Dolphin complex opened, it was sold to the park authority because of disagreements among the stockholders, who dissolved the corporation. A year later, the facilities were leased to Dave Jackson, a successful black farmer and banker from Adel who relied on family members to help him run the property until the island was fully integrated. During Jackson's tenure, the club's lounge was renowned for the quality of entertainment. Area musicians and top performers, including B. B. King and Percy Sledge, appeared at the Dolphin Club during the early days.

In 1963, the Reverend Julius Caesar Hope, a Brunswick minister and president of the local NAACP chapter, and noted historian W. W. Law, who presided over the NAACP in Savannah, crossed the causeway to Jekyll in a well-publicized attempt to integrate the whole island. They were turned away at golf courses, the Aquarama, Peppermint Land Amusement Park, and whites-only motels. In the following year, a federal judge ordered Georgia and other southern states to integrate public accommodations. The Dolphin Club and Motor Hotel closed in 1965. The buildings were first used as a youth center and camp, and in 1983, became a 4-H environmental education center operated by the University of Georgia's Cooperative Extension Service. The 4-H center was replaced in 2014 by the Children and Youth Convention Center, a $12 million facility run by the park authority.

The so-called Johnson Rocks, which attempt to hold back the Atlantic on Jekyll Island's northern shore. After Hurricane Dora eroded Golden Isles beaches when it brushed past in 1964, President Lyndon Johnson ordered the granite boulders trucked in from northern Georgia to help protect beachfront development. Scientists now say seawalls contribute to beach erosion.

Shortly after the segregation of Jekyll officially ended, the island weathered another storm. In September, Hurricane Dora struck Jekyll a glancing blow. Storm tides scoured the beach, exposing the roots of an ancient forest long buried under sand. Waves undercut and collapsed about a hundred feet of paved road, tossed heavy concrete picnic tables and benches around like children's toys, and blew down the Ferris wheel at Peppermint Land. President Lyndon Johnson, who was running for reelection, toured the ravaged Glynn County sea islands and offered federal funds for the construction of seawalls. The walls, constructed of loose granite boulders trucked to the coast from northern Georgia quarries, still line the beaches of Jekyll, St. Simons and Sea Island and are called, collectively, the Johnson Rocks. Experts now say that hard structures on beaches accelerate erosion by interfering with the natural sand-sharing system between dunes, beaches, and offshore sandbars. In addition, seawalls prevent endangered sea turtles from nesting. On the other hand, some locals are convinced that the seawalls have protected public and private property from washing away entirely.

Many Jekyll experts agree that the state park's modern era began in the mid-1980s, when two creative businessmen rescued one of the island's most historic and high-profile structures.

The Turnaround Begins

THE PRESERVATION OF historic buildings was not a priority during Jekyll's early years as a state park. After the millionaires' clubhouse was leased in 1955 to a state senator who planned to operate it as a hotel, the Jekyll Island State Park Authority attempted to improve the structure. In doing so, it destroyed some of building's most significant historic features, including an elegant five-story wooden staircase with hand-carved railings that had been the focal point of the main entry hall. The staircase was ripped out so that an elevator could be installed. Probably to satisfy fire codes, the park authority then installed concrete steps with plumbing-pipe handrails. The new stairs were housed in a tall, oddly shaped structure tacked onto the front of the hotel near the porte cochere, where carriages once discharged some of the world's wealthiest people. The boxy wooden building and the concrete stairs were eyesores, especially

A picturesque wooden bridge spanning Clam Creek near Jekyll's fishing pier on the island's north end.

A blue moon sailing over the turreted spire of the Jekyll Island Club, now a hotel.

compared to the graceful lines and fine detailing of the Queen Anne clubhouse.

The hotel operated sporadically until 1970, when it closed for lack of business. For more than a decade, the grand old building quietly deteriorated, inhabited mainly by mice and memories. In 1984, Larry Evans, an architect from Brunswick, and Vance Hughes, an attorney from Washington, DC, who grew up together in Calhoun, Georgia, came to the rescue. After attending a high school reunion together, Evans took Hughes to Atlanta's Virginia-Highland neighborhood to show him historic houses he had restored.

Hughes called Evans the following morning from his office in Washington. "You know that old hotel on Jekyll?" he asked.

The two men decided to come up with a restoration plan for the hotel, the annex, and Sans Souci. Evans quit his job to work full-time on the project. A month later, Hughes resigned from the law firm where he worked. Together they formed the Circle Development Company, spent about nine months on drawings and construction estimates, and then took their proposal to George Chambliss, the executive secretary to the park authority, who handled day-to-day management of Jekyll. Chambliss greeted the project with enthusiasm. "We're going to put this out for bids to *real* developers all over the country," Evans recalled Chambliss saying. Evans added ruefully, "Those were his exact words."

When the other bids came in, all were backed by

Some of the original furnishings of the Jekyll Island Club and cottages. Many pieces were sold to the Sea Island Co., to antiques dealers, and to individuals. Others disappeared during World War II and immediately after, before the state bought Jekyll in 1947.

cash financing. The authority liked Circle Development's plan best, but gave the partners only thirty days to find a way to fund the project. The partners found $10 million of the needed money in industrial development bonds, got a $2 million loan from the City of Brunswick via a federal grant, and found a New York bank that agreed to finance the remainder of the $20 million project. The bank's law firm sent a team of nine silk-stocking lawyers to Atlanta for the closing, all of whom stayed at the Ritz-Carlton Hotel and later billed Circle Development about $800,000 in closing costs, which almost blew the budget at the outset, Evans said. For the bank to earn the lucrative 25 percent historic restoration tax credits, which were due to expire in less than a year, the restoration had to be completed in ten months.

Evans said the buildings were in dreadful shape. Pigeons and bats were nesting in the attics, except in the three-story Sans Souci, which had no roof or attic. The floors inside had rotted away, allowing a clear view from the ground floor to the sky. The state had been spending $200,000 a year to keep a roof on the clubhouse, but the historic buildings had been otherwise neglected. While much of the original furniture remained in the hotel, chairs and tables in the dining room were in poor repair. When the partners proposed restoring them to use in the hotel's refurbished dining room, they were told that the pieces, if restored, would have to be placed in a roped-off area to meet historic preservation guidelines at the time. As a result, the dining room furnishings were moved to a concrete building on the island for storage, although the building was without heat or air-conditioning.

The partners relied on old photographs to help replicate original features, including the hotel's grand staircase. They found one detailed photograph of the staircase in the Jekyll Archives and hired a well-known craftsman from Minnesota to replicate it, down to the last turned spindle. The restored staircase now soars five stories from the basement to the top floor. Evans spent almost every day at the construction site, troubleshooting problems as they cropped up. On one visit, he noticed that a column in the dining room was missing, probably removed during the earlier renovation carried out by the park authority. When Evans investigated, he discovered that the missing column was an integral part of a unique support truss designed by the original clubhouse architect. Without the column, the entire floor above the dining room was in danger of collapsing. The missing column was replicated and replaced. Parlor rooms were named for club members and historic events.

As many as 350 workers labored on the restoration six days a week, ten hours a day, through a drought-plagued summer when temperatures on Jekyll soared regularly toward and above 100 degrees. Proud of the work, they brought their families to the island on Sundays to admire the project in progress.

The hotel complex, renamed the Jekyll Island Club Hotel, reopened in 1986. The buildings now look much as they did during the millionaires' era, although the partners took certain liberties to make them more appealing to modern visitors. Whereas the interiors were originally done in dark shades of brown, red, and green, they are now painted creamy white. Some of the guest rooms feature showers and Jacuzzi tubs. Because there was no room for a required second staircase in the Sans Souci condominium, the partners used, in lieu of sprinklers, a system designed to drench the structure with massive amounts of water in case of fire. The Jekyll Island Club Hotel is now a fitting centerpiece for the National Historic Landmark District. It has been featured in numerous articles and television shows and has been the recipient of state and national historic preservation awards. Probably more than any other project, the hotel's restoration ushered in Jekyll's modern era.

CHAPTER VIII Jekyll Then and Now

[1987–present]

JEKYLL ISLAND has made a long and difficult passage since becoming a Georgia state park in the late 1940s. During its early decades of state ownership, the park came close to being torpedoed by rival politicians, political corruption, and ignorance on the part of the governing authority about the fragile nature of sea islands and the value of historic structures and archaeological sites. Older locals and longtime visitors who watched Jekyll struggle through tough times are gratified by the many changes for the better. Today, the majority of the sea island remains natural, or at least as natural as an island inhabited by humans for thousands of years can be. Laws passed in 2014 guarantee that only seventy-eight more acres of Jekyll will ever be developed, ending decades of controversy over how much development should be allowed.

As public parks go, Jekyll is unique. There is not another state park in the country that features the variety of natural and man-made attractions, and the scope and depth of human history, that Jekyll does, even though it is one of the smallest sea islands on the Georgia coast. Some say Jekyll is the smallest, but this is true only if island groups such as Cumberland and Little Cumberland, and St. Simons, Sea Island, and Little

Elevated walkways through the marsh, inviting exploration of Jekyll's more natural side. State law requires about two-thirds of the island to be preserved in its native condition.

St. Simons, are counted as single islands. Jekyll, which stands alone against the Atlantic, is not part of a tight-knit group. If individual islands are measured against Jekyll, then several, including Tybee, Wolf, and Sea Island, are smaller.

Jekyll Island today is an amalgam of natural and developed areas. The island's natural features include freshwater wetlands and brackish ponds; winding tidal creeks; nine miles of beach fronting on the Atlantic Ocean; the wide sounds that separate Jekyll from its neighboring sea islands; a picturesque boneyard beach where erosion is undercutting a maritime forest; a strip of manmade and natural sand dunes along the eastern shore and a mile of natural dunes on the south end; little pockets and wide sweeps of salt marsh; small marsh islands called hammocks; maritime forests with canopies pruned smooth by salty sea winds; and a variety of terrestrial, aquatic, avian, and marine life, some of it rare, threatened, or endangered.

Jekyll's developed areas include quiet subdivisions where private houses sit on lots leased for ninety-nine years from the state; modern churches and a restored historic

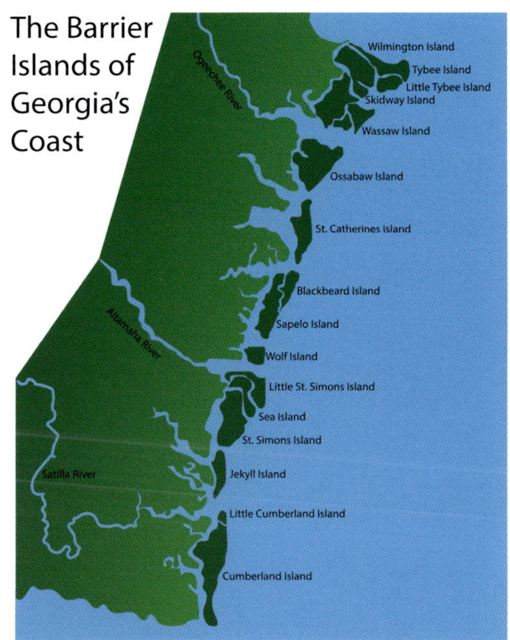

Jekyll's extensive bike paths, which provide an ideal way for locals and visitors to enjoy the island. Some of the paths wind through woodlands and high marshes.

chapel; new and refurbished beachfront motels; a large, unique, and mostly restored National Historic Landmark District; a new beachfront convention center; and cafes, restaurants, bars, shops, and stores, including some in a commercial beachside village now under phased construction. Jekyll's man-made recreation areas include four golf courses; a tennis complex; five soccer fields; a groomed croquet lawn; beachfront parks and picnic areas; a large fishing pier; a full-service boat marina on the Intracoastal Waterway; a historic wharf; twenty miles of bike trails; and a water park with giant slides, a lazy river, and a wave pool. Each summer, thousands of students from all over the South attend camps on Jekyll that focus on environmental education and include kayaking in tidal rivers and seining expeditions. Visitors can charter fishing boats at the Jekyll Marina and take dolphin-watching excursions around the island. Everybody enjoys fireworks exploding over the ocean on the Fourth of July and attending annual events such as the summer Beach Music Festival and the Shrimp and Grits Festival each fall. There are guided horseback rides through the woods and along the beach,

and twenty miles of bicycle paths. Jekyll boasts the only sea turtle rescue operation in the state, and one of the few in the world.

Jekyll's National Historic Landmark District, the majority of which is restored, features a historic hotel often described as Cinderella's castle, a cluster of mansion-sized cottages, and dozens of other structures built by the world's wealthiest people. The millionaires who formed the Jekyll Island Club wintered in "splendid solitude" on the island from 1888 until 1942, living, by their standards, simply. Their old clubhouse is now the elegant Jekyll Island Club Hotel. Millionaires' cottages and Sans Souci, one of the first condominium complexes in the country, provide additional overnight accommodations and fine dining. Several historic buildings have been repurposed for modern use: the Jekyll Museum is housed in the club stables; Jekyll Books is in the infirmary; the Goodyear Cottage is home to the Jekyll Island Arts Association; and the Georgia Sea Turtle Center is lodged in the power plant building. The historic district encompasses the tabby remains of one of the oldest two-story colonial houses in the state. The Horton tract also includes the site of Georgia's first brewery, although the wooden brew house has long since rotted away. Near the tabby house is a walled plantation-era cemetery where members of the du Bignon family are buried. The du Bignons owned Jekyll for almost a century. Many pre-Columbian Native American sites occupy the north end of the island, but most lie beneath more recent historic

structures, including those of the millionaires' compound. Shell middens, or garbage dumps, left by indigenous people dot the island. Many historic artifacts no doubt wait to be discovered under Jekyll's sandy soil and along its marshy riverbanks and sandy beaches, but it is illegal for anyone to collect artifacts from the state park without a special permit. Metal detectors are banned on the island.

Faculty from the University of Georgia and other institutions of higher learning, including Georgia Southern University, the Skidaway Institute of Oceanography, the University of West Georgia, Clemson University, and Armstrong Atlantic State University, direct a variety of research and educational projects on Jekyll. State and federal agencies regularly send representatives to the island to monitor beach erosion or survey nesting birds. The Jekyll Island Foundation, the park authority's fund-raising arm, seeks grants and donations for a variety of environmental causes, including a

The Georgia Sea Turtle Center

THE $3 MILLION Georgia Sea Turtle Center was established in 2007 with a $750,000 grant from the Robert W. Woodruff Foundation and contributions from sea turtle fans from the United States and other countries. The facility is the only one of its kind in the state and one of the few in the world. It is housed in the old brick power plant built in 1903 by the Jekyll Island Club to provide electricity for the millionaires. After toxic materials such as lead and asbestos were removed from the building, it was equipped to provide state-of-the-art care for sea turtles and other wildlife in distress, including diamondback terrapins, a tidal marsh species that is the only brackish-water terrapin in the United States. The saucer-sized terrapins, named for the diamond-shaped pattern on their carapaces, or top shells, are often injured or killed as they

The Georgia Sea Turtle Center, which, among other responsibilities, educates visitors about the importance of protecting the rare species. The center is housed in a refurbished building that once provided electrical power for the Jekyll Island Club.

cross coastal roads and causeways in late spring and early summer in search of higher ground to lay their eggs.

Jekyll has monitored loggerhead nesting on its beaches for more than forty years, making the state park's loggerhead program one of the oldest in the world. Most sea turtle programs are conducted on remote, sparsely populated islands such as Little Cumberland, St. Catherines, and Wassaw. The Georgia Sea Turtle Center provides researchers a unique opportunity to study the behavior of nesting turtles on a partly developed, heavily visited island. Center visitors get up-close views of loggerheads, Kemp's ridleys, greens, and other threatened sea turtle species as the animals paddle around in large rehabilitation tanks. When they are ready to return to the ocean, the public is invited to watch the releases, which are usually staged at Great Dunes Park.

On summer nights when sea turtles crawl ashore on Jekyll's beach to nest in dry, soft sand at the edge of the dunes, visitors are invited to walk along with center personnel to look for them. If lucky, they will witness a ritual that has taken place on sea island beaches since the time of the dinosaurs as a three-hundred-pound female lumbers out of the ocean to lay her eggs. Visitors can also ride along on all-terrain vehicles with the center's sea turtle patrol, which monitors nests and protects them until the silver-dollar-sized hatchlings bubble up from the sand and home in on the ocean's bright horizon. Workers from AmeriCorps, a national corporation that provides services to nonprofits, schools, and public agencies, are an essential part of the center's operations. They assist in the exhibit gallery, present educational programs, guide kayak and canoe trips through tidal waterways, help control invasive plants on the island, and clean debris from sensitive natural areas.

A recent effort by center personnel aims to educate the public about the harm done to sea turtles and other marine life by plastic grocery bags, balloons, fish hooks, monofilament fishing line, and other human garbage that winds up in the ocean. Loggerhead turtles feed on jellyfish and often mistake balloons and plastic bags for their favorite food. A small amount of such material can kill a giant loggerhead by blocking its digestive system. Through a cooperative effort between the center and the University of Georgia's Marine Debris Tracker, a cell phone app now allows people to track litter on land and in waterways so that it can be removed before it reaches the open sea.

spectacular education, research, and rehabilitation facility that opened on the island in 2007 in the historic district.

In the years before environmental protection and historic preservation were considered important, Jekyll's archaeological sites, historic buildings, and natural areas all suffered from uninformed management decisions. The Ben Fortson Parkway, which bisects the island's narrow waist between Jekyll Creek and the beach, cut off the flow of water to First Creek, a meandering tidal waterway that once flowed from freshwater ponds into a large brackish watershed now occupied by the Oleander golf course. Fortson Pond and the marshy area that surrounds it are screened by foliage from passing vehicles. For people walking or biking nearby, however, the smell of the stagnant pond is strong enough to make their eyes water, according to David Egan, a former university professor and longtime Jekyll resident. Egan and his wife, the psychologist Mindy Egan, founded the Initiative to Protect Jekyll Island in 2006 as a watchdog organization to keep tabs on the state park. Egan said islanders have nicknamed Fortson Pond "stinky pinky" because of its odor and the pink scum that coats its surface. On the positive side, the pond recently provided a natural—or unnatural—laboratory for scientific study. In 2014, Sharon E. Mozley-Standridge, a biology professor at Middle Georgia State College in Cochran, along with several colleagues and undergraduate volunteers, found magnetotactic bacteria in the pond. The researchers had been searching for live samples of the unusual bacteria along the Georgia coast for a year without success until someone suggested they try the pond on Jekyll. There they found the living bacteria, which have been described as tiny self-propelled compass needles or living lodestones, because they always align with the magnetic north; other bacteria move randomly. Magnetotactic bacteria concentrate metals such as magnetite, or lodestone, the mineral from which the first compasses were made, in their cell membranes and form them into chains of magnetic crystals. The bacteria live in low-oxygen conditions that would be deadly for many organisms, but higher levels of oxygen are toxic to them. When their muddy habitat is disturbed and gets an influx of oxygen, the bacteria find their way back to anaerobic safety by swimming north, or down, following the Earth's magnetic pull.

The unusual bacteria were discovered in 1975 when a scientist was examining a sample of marine marsh mud under a microscope and noticed fast-moving bacteria swimming across the slide, doggedly heading north. In the Southern Hemisphere, magnetotactic bacteria always align with the South Pole. In 1984, researchers found

The pond nicknamed Stinky Pinky for its smelly stagnant condition and sometimes-pink hue. It is home to unusual magnetotactic bacteria, tiny natural lodestones that always orient north. The Jekyll Island Authority plans to restore the natural hydrology of the area, eliminating the pond and its anaerobic bacterial inhabitants.

magnetic crystals in a meteorite that landed thousands of years ago in Antarctica; the crystals resembled those found in the bacteria on Jekyll. The meteorite had probably been knocked off the surface of Mars and then traveled through space for some sixteen million years before crash-landing on Earth. The presence of the crystals suggests that bacteria similar to those in Fortson Pond once lived on the red planet, although scientists are still debating that theory. In 2013, Jekyll received a $46,000 grant to conduct a two-year study aimed at restoring the First Creek watershed on a large scale, returning it to a more natural, well-oxygenated condition. At that point, Fortson Pond may be absorbed into the creek, and its magnetotectic bacteria will disappear.

The pond was named in honor of Ben Fortson, who served as Georgia's secretary of state for more than three decades and, by virtue of his office, was a member of Jekyll's governing authority for many years. Fortson, a colorful man who once shot Roman candles at flocks of starlings roosting in trees around the state capitol in Atlanta and befouling statues and sidewalks, liked nature neatened up. He considered the drifts

The north end of Jekyll, which is eroding badly. The south end is building. Sand sometimes overtakes mature woodlands, killing trees.

of brown marsh wrack—dead marsh grass—that washed up daily on Jekyll's beach unsightly, so he had workers rake the beach clean every morning.

Years ago, Jekyll's forty-foot-high sand dunes were bulldozed to give visitors a view of the ocean from Beachview Drive. In many areas, the dunes have since been rebuilt. They are smaller than the original sentinels of sand that once guarded the island's interior from the ocean, but they are far more appealing than the barren prerestoration seascape and unattractive concrete parking lot they replaced. Dune building continues, with help from man and nature. Wooden snow fences set at angles along the upper beach catch blowing sand. As new mounds form, the emerging dunes are planted with indigenous foliage such as railroad vine, beach pea, beach morning glory, Spanish bayonette, and sea oats (*Uniola paniculata*), the signature dune grass of the sea islands. Tall, slender sea oats thrust their deep roots below ground to form an effective sand-trapping matrix. When their oat-like clusters ripen to pale gold in late summer, people are tempted to pick the graceful stalks to dry and display at home, but they are protected by law in Georgia, as they are in most other coastal states. Without sea oats, Jekyll's dunes would be at greater risk of blowing away, and without dunes, the island would be more vulnerable to nor'easters, tropical storms, and hurricanes.

The natural erosion and building up of beaches. When storms strip sand from the beach and dunes, the bulk of the sand accumulates just offshore, ready to restore the beach in calmer weather. The so-called sand-sharing system is interrupted by hard structures like seawalls.

Some of the erosion on Jekyll's beach was probably caused or accelerated by destruction of the sand dunes. To protect the newly built and emerging dune fields, the park authority built a series of elevated wooden crossovers that allow pedestrians to access the beach without disturbing the dunes or the plants that colonize them. One crossover was constructed by the production company that made the 1989 movie *Glory*, a Civil War epic based on a true story and filmed in part on Jekyll's south beach. The moviemakers erected a sand fortress to represent Fort Wagner in South Carolina, which was stormed by a company of black Union soldiers led by a young white commander, Robert Gould Shaw, who died along with many of his men and was buried with them in a mass beach grave. The *Glory* boardwalk and other crossovers have become popular viewing platforms for bird and wildlife watchers. Deep swales behind the dunes collect fresh water and are thick with wax myrtle, red cedar, and other salt-tolerant plants. Birds, raccoons, snakes, voles, mice, and the

Great Dunes Pavilion, featuring sand dunes rebuilt in recent years to replace ones bulldozed during the early days of state ownership of the island.

occasional young alligator congregate in the swales to hide, hunt, feed, or nest. Jekyll is a wildlife sanctuary, which means that even species most people dislike or fear are protected, including rattlesnakes, water moccasins, and alligators. On Jekyll's golf courses, if a ball happens to land near an alligator, the golfer is permitted to drop another ball a safe distance away without taking a penalty stroke.

Another recent success story is Great Dunes Park, which covers almost twenty acres on the ocean side of the island adjacent to the new Jekyll Convention Center. In 2007, the acreage was part of a tract slated for upscale development, but public outcry and a recession prompted the developer to back out of the deal. With an open-air pavilion offering stunning waterfront views, Great Dunes Park has become a popular venue for major events and island-style weddings. Except at high tide, when the nearby beach is underwater, barefoot brides and grooms exchange vows on the damp sand, then dance, cut wedding cake, and sip champagne with friends and family at the pavilion.

The marina built in 1968 in a tidal marsh adjacent to Jekyll Creek had to be abandoned after repeated dredging was unable to keep its saltwater basin free of silt. The other basin, dredged to provide freshwater boat storage, is now an important feature of the 4-H Tidelands Nature Center, operated by the University of Georgia's Cooperative

The Tidelands Nature Center, whose activities focus on the nature of a small sea island.

Extension Service. Several acres of adjacent marsh were filled with dredged spoil during marina construction, and the land was slated to become the marina's parking lot. Unwelcome foreign plants invaded the area after the spoil killed many native species. For several decades, the Summer Waves Water Park has occupied the filled marshland; the park is a favorite with visiting children and teenagers. For a few years, a European company called Ski Rixen installed an overhead cable to pull water-skiers and wakeboarders around and around the freshwater basin.

To restore the saltwater basin, silt was pumped in; the area is reverting, albeit slowly, to marsh. The freshwater basin was opened via culverts to Jekyll Creek to allow salt water to mix with fresh and create a more natural, brackish environment. The Tidelands Nature Center, with its dock and outdoor bleachers, overlooks the pond, which provides a sheltered area for young visitors to canoe, paddleboat, and study nature. Exhibits at the center feature snakes, alligators, rare turtles and tortoises, and a touch tank. Summer day camps offer seining expeditions in which participants learn to drag a long net through the shallows to catch shrimp, fish, blue crabs, jellyfish, whelks, and a variety of other marine life. Campers are invited to feed center animals at a mid-morning brunch, gaze through telescopes at stars and planets on astronomy nights, and join a "belly biology" class in which campers lie stomach-down on a dock with dip nets, scooping up whatever happens to pass by. Sessions include a muddy slog through a salt marsh, where campers nibble on salty succulents called glasswort that early settlers used to make pickles. They watch macho male fiddler crabs waving their big

Canoes available for visitors to the Tidelands Nature Center to use in a pond built years ago as part of a marina on Jekyll Creek. The marina was dredged in a marsh that continued to fill with sediment. After making repeated and expensive attempts at sediment removal, members of the Jekyll Island Authority abandoned the project and let nature reclaim the land. The Tidelands pond now has outlets opening to the marsh and the creek.

claws around to attract mates and scare off rivals. Other programs at the center include beachcombing for shells and sea treasures, studies of fossils found on the island, and an art class that features coating the enamel-tipped scales of small sharks with paint to make *gyotaku* fish prints. Although Japanese artists use live fish for *gyotaku*, then clean and return them, unharmed, to the water, the sharks used for Jekyll fish prints are dead. Otherwise, campers might sacrifice a finger or two for art's sake, since even small sharks have razor-sharp teeth.

Some environmental problems on Jekyll today have nothing to do with mistakes made by state overseers in years past. Recently, Jekyll lost a large number of the red bays that represent one of its most ubiquitous understory plants. The small, shrubby trees died of laurel wilt disease, a fungus transmitted by the redbay ambrosia beetle, which was discovered in 2002 in the United States at the Port of Savannah. The beetles were first spotted on Jekyll in 2006. Just four years after the initial island sighting, almost all of Jekyll's red bays had succumbed to laurel wilt. Nobody knows how the beetles got to the island from the mainland. Larvae or adult beetles from infected areas may have hitchhiked over on vehicles or been brought over in logs of red bay wood, now widely marketed for burning in fireplaces and outdoor grills. With its spicy leaves, red bay is often used as a seasoning ingredient in the Deep South. It is a cousin of the better-known *Laurus nobilis*, the Mediterranean species of bay. Researchers do not yet understand the long-term implications of the loss of Jekyll's red bays, although painted buntings, swallowtail butterflies, and other wildlife will miss them. The absence of red

From François André Michaux's *The North American Sylva* (1819)

bays could also clear the way for unwelcome exotic species to move in and fill the void left by the shrubby trees.

Another common sea island species is under attack on Jekyll. The cactus moth ravaging the island's prickly pears is a South American invader that turned up in Florida in 1989. Prickly pears, with their large pad-like stems, bright yellow flowers, and plum-shaped red or purple pears, are decorative as well as edible. Most people avoid the plant; its sharp spines and small, penetrating bristles are so formidable that early Americans planted prickly pear hedges around their forts to deter invaders. Prickly pear pads, or *nopales*, are a popular ingredient in Mexican food, as are the pears, known as *tuna* in Spanish. The fruit is rich in vitamin C and was once used to prevent or cure scurvy.

Feral pigs became a problem on the island in the early 1900s, when golf replaced hunting as the Jekyll Island Club's most popular sport. As people stopped killing pigs, the porcine population soared. When the animals began rooting up the millionaires'

Blooms and fruit of the prickly pear cactus, edible to those who know how to avoid the plant's sharp spines. (Courtesy of Stan Shebs, Wikimedia Commons)

carefully tended golf course, the club superintendent declared war on feral pigs, without much success. Feral pigs were finally eradicated after the state's purchase of Jekyll, but because the animals live on the nearby mainland and islands and range through the marsh, they could easily invade Jekyll again. On sea islands, feral pigs destroy native plants, dig up sea turtle nests, and disturb ground-nesting birds in addition to rooting up golf course fairways and greens.

Since 2010, the park authority has participated in a trap-and-release program to control feral cats, thought to endanger the island's wild birds. John and Shelley Allison, Jekyll residents who led efforts to deal with the problem, estimated that about five hundred homeless felines once roamed the island, many abandoned by renters who left their pets behind when they moved away. The Allisons are the founders of Suzie's Friends Animal Sanctuary, a no-kill shelter for cats and dogs in Homerville, Georgia, and they own Envirospec, Inc., a company that makes environmentally friendly cleaning products. The Allisons donate all profits from the company's Chemical and Equipment Division to animal charities such as Suzie's Friends, the Humane Society of

the United States, the ASPCA, and to a number of local and regional facilities that aid animals. Now, feral cats are caught on Jekyll in humane traps. Area veterinarians check them for viruses and then neuter, spay, vaccinate, and microchip them. If possible, good homes are found for the cats. Studies continue to determine the impact of feral cats on wildlife populations.

There is disagreement whether the island is overpopulated with native white-tailed deer. In the wild, nature deals with overpopulation harshly: animals starve to death or die of diseases related to malnutrition, and females stop producing young when food is scarce. A study committee organized by the park authority found evidence that deer are overgrazing new forest growth, to the detriment of the island. They also say that deer on Jekyll tend to be undernourished and sickly because of overpopulation. As in many other parts of the country where deer are considered a problem, the question of what to do about them is contentious. The authority announced in 2014 that it would prefer to hire professional hunters or to stage-manage hunts to thin the herd, but that proposal has not been well received, especially by island residents. Experimental contraception methods and surgical sterilization are prohibitively expensive, time consuming, and sometimes ineffective. Ben Carswell, Jekyll's conservation director, favored reintroducing native bobcats to Jekyll to help control the deer population. Bobcats, which prey on foals and sick, elderly deer, were released on the sparsely populated Cumberland Island National Seashore and the heavily populated Kiawah Island, South Carolina, some years ago and have been effective at reducing deer populations on both islands. But committee members expressed concern that bobcats would prey on desirable Jekyll species too, including domestic pets, and might transmit diseases. The island's native bobcats were probably hunted to extinction during the club era or earlier.

There is no doubt that deer are present on Jekyll. They are easy to spot as they graze in the early mornings or late afternoons at sites around the island. Several white-tailed families favor the old amphitheater's overgrown parking lot. Other small groups browse in the historic district, where they enjoy the lush carpet of St. Augustine grass under the giant live oak trees. At the Soccer Complex, the deer have their choice of five fields' worth of groomed grass. If the park authority selects controlled wintertime hunts as the best method of population control, the deer would be donated as food for predators such as endangered Florida panthers at the White Oak wildlife conservation reservation in Yulee, Florida, which

Summer Waves Water Park: all about water.

provides habitat for species of concern, or to programs that provide food for needy people.

Since the restoration of the Jekyll Island Club Hotel in 1987, the state has made great strides in restoring many of the island's other historic buildings, bringing grand old cottages and more modest structures from the millionaires' era back to life. Restorations include Moss Cottage, built in 1896 by the Philadelphian William Strothers, who made his fortune in marble. The cottage was later occupied by George Henry Macy of Hudson, New York, the president of Union Pacific Tea, which later became the A&P supermarket chain. Mistletoe Cottage, built in the Dutch Colonial Revival style in 1900, was first owned by U.S. senator Henry Kirke Porter of Pittsburgh, who manufactured small locomotives. John Clafin, a Brooklyn merchant and financier, was Mistletoe's second owner. The cottage built for Gordon McKay, which dates to the early 1890s, is best known as the winter retreat of William Rockefeller, who named the cottage Indian Mound because of the large shell pile in the front yard, which represents the remains of meals eaten by prehistoric people on the island thousands of years ago. The Crane Cottage, the largest and most expensive vacation cottage built by any of the club members, was once rented out for teenage

house parties that were hard on the old Spanish-style structure. Now, the restored Crane Cottage, along with the Sans Souci condominium complex, is included in the Jekyll Island Club Hotel's lodging options. The hotel corporation also plans to open beachfront lodging in the future. Crane Cottage, with its sunken formal garden, is a popular venue for island weddings.

Faith Chapel in the historic district, also a popular place for couples to get married, was completed in 1904. It replaced a less impressive structure known as Union Chapel, which was afterward dedicated to the use of the club's black employees. Charlotte Maurice, whose husband was the wealthy bridge engineer Charles Stewart Maurice, served as the guiding spirit for religious affairs on the island. An Episcopalian, Charlotte invited members of many faiths to preach at both Union and Faith chapels. Charlotte Maurice and some of her family members attended services at Union Chapel when a black minister from Brunswick preached there, in defiance of segregationist practices at the time. Catholic missionaries, Episcopal bishops, and other visiting clergymen conducted services on Jekyll during the millionaires' era.

Faith Chapel's large stained-glass window, designed by Louis Comfort Tiffany, is titled "David Set Singers Before the Lord." The window was installed in 1921 and dedicated to Frederick Gilbert Bourne, the club member who founded the Singer Manufacturing Company. The window's theme honored both the name of Bourne's company and his enthusiasm for singing in church choirs. When the state bought Jekyll, club members voted to donate Faith Chapel's furnishings to the new owner, except for the articles of communion and the altar cloth, which went to St. Mark's Episcopal Church in Brunswick.

Several modern churches on Jekyll now serve visitors and island residents. The number of people who live full-time on Jekyll has

Faith Chapel, formerly a place of worship for millionaire members of the Jekyll Island Club, now a popular venue for island weddings.

dwindled in recent years. The 1980 census recorded 1,400 year-round residents; by 2010 that number had dropped to 805, more than a 40 percent decrease. Nobody really knows why. Some homeowners may prefer to make money by renting their island properties; in addition, no residential lots have been available for lease since the 1970s for construction of new houses. Many of the existing houses on Jekyll were built during the 1960s and 1970s and reflect the low-slung ranch style popular at the time. Developers have proposed opening new subdivisions on the island; an Atlanta developer wanted to build ninety houses at starting prices of $750,000.

Nowadays, there are only about a dozen school-age children on the island. Since there are no schools on Jekyll, students ride buses to mainland schools in Brunswick. A one-way trip from the causeway bridge to the closest school takes about twenty minutes; trips for most students are longer.

Most of Jekyll's year-round residents are retirees of accomplishment: university professors, medical doctors, inventors, psychologists, artists, high-ranking military officers, and former business executives. Collectively, they serve as canaries in the coal mine. They attend park authority meetings to keep abreast of island business and plans. They volunteer. They form organizations such as the Jekyll Island Citizens Association, the Friends of Historic Jekyll Island, the Initiative to Protect Jekyll Island, the Jekyll Island Garden Club, and the Jekyll Island Arts Association. Because so many islanders are retired and well educated, they have the time and expertise to wade through reams of paperwork, analyze proposals, interpret financial statements, and act en masse as island ombudspersons. Because Jekyll today is a varied combination of state park, commercial resort, natural area, residential enclave, educational campus, research area, and National Historic Landmark District, many island watchers say that the authority should be restructured to include experts in such fields as outdoor recreation, park management, historic preservation, archaeology, coastal geology, hotel-motel-restaurant operations, and others whose training and experience would be helpful on a board that makes vital decisions about a small and fragile sea island.

In 2014, the authority agreed to limit the height of new commercial buildings on the island to forty-five feet, to match the Glynn County limit. On heavily developed Tybee Island, east of Savannah, building height is limited to thirty-five feet. The Jekyll decision came after the new Westin Hotel went up adjacent to the beachfront convention center. The Westin is seventy-two feet high, the same height as the Jekyll Island Club Hotel, which nestles in a grove of giant live oaks, pines, and magnolias on the western

How Much, How Many

FOR MANY YEARS, one of the chief recurring controversies on Jekyll has been the question of how much of the island could be developed and in what fashion. The park authority has generally wanted to develop more of Jekyll in order to generate revenue; residents, conservationists, and visitors generally favor a more natural approach. For decades, the island operated under the so-called 65/35 law, which required the bulk of the island above mean high tide to be kept in its natural state. During the drafting of the most recent management plan, a conflict arose over how much of the island had already been developed. When members of an advisory committee declared that the 35 percent development limit had already been exceeded, the authority sought an opinion from the state attorney general, whose ruling allowed certain marshes to be counted as land lying above mean high tide, thus expanding the amount of Jekyll available for development to more than three hundred acres. After a contentious battle between the authority, island residents, conservation organizations, and others, a compromise was reached. In April 2014, Governor Nathan Deal signed legislation that limits any new development on the island to seventy-eight acres. Twelve of the acres will be used to expand the old Cherokee Campground on Jekyll's north end. Forty-six acres will be dedicated to projects involving public health, safety, or recreation. The remaining twenty acres will be available for "unrestricted uses." The new law took effect on July 1, 2014.

With the development controversy settled, island watchdogs are now focusing on other matters, including the island's carrying capacity. Nobody knows how many visitors the small island can host before its beaches, bike paths, and other areas are overwhelmed. There is also the issue of affordability. The original legislation creating the state park requires it to remain within the price range of average-income Georgians. In recent years, authority members have favored more upscale development, claiming it is needed to fund island operations. In 2007, a company with strong ties to state

A magnet for thousands of visitors annually: musical events and other large attractions on Jekyll.

Cherokee Campground on Jekyll's north end, which offers a lower-budget option for visitors.

and national Republicans, including Georgia's then governor, presented a proposal to build a beachfront complex on Jekyll that would have included condominiums priced at almost $1 million, well out of reach of ordinary Georgians. The project would have occupied the state's last significant stretch of undeveloped beachfront accessible by car. It would have disturbed a maritime forest and freshwater wetlands that are home to rare species of plants and animals. Outcry from more than 10,000 people and a series of lawsuits halted the project, but there are still complaints that rooms are too pricey at new and planned motels.

The law requiring the island to support itself—unlike any other state park in Georgia—was amended in 1972, during Jimmy Carter's term as governor. Now the legislature funds capital improvements on Jekyll, including the $50 million convention center and Great Dunes Park, which were financed with state-backed revenue bonds. The lion's share of funds for restoration of the historic district has come from legislative appropriations, not from authority revenues.

The new Westin Hotel adjoins the new Jekyll Convention Center.

side of the island. The five-story Westin towers above anything else in its beachfront setting. Although all new construction on Jekyll will have to conform to the new height limit, many of the older two-story motels are being replaced or refurbished into three- or four-story structures that will increase the number of available rooms and the number of people on the island, which now hosts about 1.5 million visitors a year.

Among the authority's long-term goals for Jekyll are plans for waste reduction and water and energy conservation. The new convention center has large cisterns that collect rainwater, which is used for irrigation; the Holiday Inn uses rainwater to flush the motel's toilets. Because of continuing erosion on the north end and a rapidly degrading rock seawall, the authority hopes to explore new and better methods of protecting the island from the ocean. Scientists say the task will become even more difficult as sea-level rises accelerate because of global warming. Other authority goals include ongoing restoration of the historic district, refurbishing the amphitheater, improving the Clam Creek and St. Andrews picnic areas, expanding programs about the island's African American history, and a host of additional projects.

As long as Jekyll is state owned, politics will continue to play a leading role in the island's future. Citizen activists and organizations can continue to keep watch and raise alarms if policy makers seem to be steering the state park in the wrong direction. Jekyll's fate will ultimately be decided by the people who own the island: the citizens of Georgia.

A solitary bagpiper inspired by gorgeous island sunset.

Afterword

The Ghosts of a Golden Isle

There is a legend on the southern sea islands. It claims that once a visitor gets sea island beach sand in his or her shoes, that person will always return to the islands. On Jekyll, that prediction extends even to the dead. Several members of the Jekyll Island Club, billed as the most exclusive club in the world from 1888 until 1942, are reported to turn up at their favorite haunts on the island from time to time, according to employees and guests who claim close encounters with the island's spirit world.

One of the best-known ghosts is that of the wealthy banker and financier J. Pierpont Morgan, who owned one of the six units in Sans Souci. Morgan favored a particular brand of cigars with a distinctive aroma. Although it has been a century since the living Morgan set foot on Jekyll, and his condominium has been redone many times since then, guests often report smelling cigar smoke in the rooms he once occupied—and perhaps still does in spirit.

General Lloyd Aspinwall, a founding member of the Jekyll Island Club, was elected its first president. He was excited about spending winters on the island with other wealthy captains of industry but died suddenly at age fifty-one on September 4, 1886, more than a year before the club officially opened. Some club members later reported seeing Aspinwall's distinct figure, hands clasped behind his back, striding up and down the clubhouse verandah every year on the date of his death. When the clubhouse was restored as the Jekyll Island Club Hotel, part of the verandah was enclosed in glass as a sunroom and named the Aspinwall Room in the general's honor.

Most of the cottages in Jekyll's National Historic Landmark District have been restored in recent decades. One of the loveliest and most unusual, Hollybourne

Cottage, remains in more or less its original condition. It was built as the winter home for Charles Stewart Maurice, his wife, Charlotte, and their eight children. Maurice designed the cottage structure in the same way that he designed his bridges, with brick support piers in the basement and attic trusses. He built the place of tabby, a durable and historic coastal masonry made of oyster-shell lime, whole oyster shells, salt-free sand, and fresh water. Charlie Hill, the local man who worked for the Maurices for many years as a butler and carriage driver, said Charles Maurice was an easygoing man but expected people who accompanied him on his afternoon carriage rides around Jekyll to be punctual. "The wheels roll at four," Maurice would call out, letting everyone at Hollybourne know to be waiting on the porch when Hill arrived to pick them up. Latecomers were always left behind.

Hollybourne today is closed to visitors. There is a story that contractors who came to restore the cottage in recent years had their tools disappear when they stored them overnight in the locked building. Some speculate that Maurice's ghost stole the tools because he built the cottage to last and wants to prove it will stand the test of time. Hollybourne has become known as Jekyll's haunted house. Island employees and others who toured the interior have reported overhearing scraps of conversations and chamber music coming from unoccupied rooms, walking through spots of extreme cold, seeing objects fly through the air, and having powdery white footprints appear on their clothing, says Greg Lowery of Rentz, who has written about the island.

Not all of Jekyll's ghosts were wealthy in their former lives. One of the island's most famous apparitions is the ghost of a bellhop who wears a 1920s-style uniform with striped trousers and a pillbox cap. Island employees report seeing the bellhop at the Jekyll Island Club Hotel. He is most often seen bringing freshly pressed suits to bridegrooms in advance of their weddings. Visitors have also reported opening their hotel doors to a bellhop dressed in old-fashioned clothes who hands them their laundry and then quickly departs without saying a word—or even waiting for a tip, which makes their stories a bit harder to believe.

Ghost tours are offered by a private vendor on Jekyll who takes visitors through the historic district on trolley rides that usually begin around sundown and continue until after dark. The tours include a visit to the historic du Bignon cemetery, whose graves date back to the early 1800s. There is a rumor that bodies are missing from some of the graves, washed away on an eroding creek bank. An island expert said that isn't the case.

She said that some of the remains have deteriorated over the centuries, but the original bricks are still in place.

Ghosts are one more facet of Jekyll Island's rich and varied history. No doubt the spirits feel right at home among the island's Victorian-era buildings, its Spanish moss–shrouded live oak trees, and its shadowy woods filled with the cries of strange creatures. The spirits are evidence that the Jekyll Island State Park today welcomes everyone.

Selected Bibliography

Bagwell, Tyler E. *The Jekyll Island Club*. Charleston: Arcadia, 2001.

———. *Jekyll Island: A State Park*. Charleston: Arcadia, 2001.

Bordo, Michael D., and William Roberds, eds. *The Origins, History, and Future of the Federal Reserve*. New York: Cambridge University Press, 2013.

Brooker, Colin. "The William Horton House, Jekyll Island, Georgia: Analysis, Care, and Display; A Report Submitted to the Friends of Historic Jekyll Island." Beaufort, S.C.: Brooker Preservation Design Consultants, Jan. 2001.

Brown, Kate. *It Is a Wonderfully Lovely Place: Jekyll Island as Seen through Kate Brown's Fresh Eyes: The Letters of Kate Brown, February–March 1917*. Edited by Nanette M. Bahlinge. Jekyll Island, Ga.: Jekyll Island Museum, 1992.

Bullard, Mary R. *Cumberland Island: A History*. Athens: University of Georgia Press, 2005.

Cate, Margaret Davis. *Early Days of Coastal Georgia*. St. Simons Island, Ga.: Fort Frederica Association, 1955.

Chowns, Timothy M., Bryan S. Schultz, and James R. Griffin. "Relocation of Brunswick River and Other Estuaries on the Georgia, USA Coast as a Consequence of Holocene Transgression." *Southeastern Geology* 45, no. 3 (Apr. 2008): 143–89.

Colonius, Erik. *The Wanderer: The Last American Slave Ship and the Conspiracy That Set Her Sails*. New York: St. Martin's, 2006.

Davidson, Cannon. Interview by Tyler E. Bagwell, July 1998. Jekyll Archives. As a teenager, Davidson came to Jekyll with a friend whose father guarded prisoners at the state park in 1948.

de la Cova, Antonio Rafael. "Fernandina Filibuster Fiasco: Birth of the 1895 Cuban War of Independence." *Florida Historical Quarterly* 82, no. 1 (Summer 2003): 16–42.

Du Bois, W. E. B. *The Suppression of the African Slave Trade to the United States, 1638–1870*. Baton Rouge: Louisiana State University Press, 1965. Orig. pub. 1896.

Faber, Cat. "Living Lodestones: Magnetotactic Bacteria." *Strange Horizons*, July 2, 2001. Accessed June 23, 2014. www.strangehorizons.com/2001/20010702/living_lodestones.shtml

Gandhi, Lakshmi. "The Extraordinary Story of Why a 'Cakewalk' Wasn't Always Easy." NPR.org, December 23, 2013. www.npr.org/blogs/codeswitch/2013/12/23/256566647/the-extraordinary-story-of-why-a-cakewalk-wasnt-always-easy.

Greene, Melissa Fay. *Last Man Out: The Story of the Springhill Mine Disaster*. New York: Harcourt, 2003.

Griffin, G. Edward. *The Creature from Jekyll Island: A Second Look at the Federal Reserve*. New York: American Media, 2002.

Harris, Thaddeus Mason. *Biographical Memorials of James Oglethorpe, Founder of the Colony of Georgia in North America*. Boston, 1841. Accessed Apr. 13, 2013. https://archive.org/details/biographicalmemo01harr.

Hoffman, Paul E. *A New Andalucia and a Way to the Orient: The American Southeast during the Sixteenth Century*. Baton Rouge: Louisiana State University Press, 1990.

Hurston, Zora Neale. "The Last Slave Ship." *American Mercury*, March 1944, 351–58. Accessed Dec. 12, 2013. www.unz.org/Pub/AmMercury-1944mar-00351.

Hutto, Richard J. *The Gilded Cage: The Jekyll Island Club Members*. Macon, Ga.: Indigo Custom Publishing, 2005.

Irwin, Neil. *The Alchemists: Three Central Bankers and a World on Fire*. New York: Penguin, 2013.

———. "The Federal Reserve Was Created 100 Years Ago." *Washington Post*, Dec. 13, 2013. Accessed Apr. 16, 2014. www.washingtonpost.com/blogs/wonkblog/wp/2013/12/21/the-federal-reserve-was-created-100-years-ago-this-is-how-it-happened/

Jekyll Island Club. *Meet Me on Jekyll Island*. Nashville: Southwestern Publishing Group, 2012.

Johnson, James Weldon. *The Autobiography of an Ex-Colored Man*. Boston: Sherman, French, 1912. Accessed Mar. 22, 2014.

Keber, Martha L. *Seas of Gold, Seas of Cotton: Christophe Poulain DuBignon of Jekyll Island*. Athens: University of Georgia Press, 2002.

Knetsch, Joe, and Nick Wynne. *Florida in the Spanish-American War*. Charleston: Arcadia, 2011.

Martin, Anthony J. *Life Traces of the Georgia Coast: Revealing the Unseen Lives of Plants and Animals*. Bloomington: Indiana University Press, 2012.

McCash, June Hall. *The Jekyll Island Cottage Colony*. Athens: University of Georgia Press, 1998.

———. *Jekyll Island's Early Years: From Prehistory through Reconstruction*. Athens: University of Georgia Press, 2005.

McCash, William Barton, and June Hall McCash. *The Jekyll Island Club: Southern Haven for America's Millionaires*. Athens: University of Georgia Press, 1989.

McDonald, Babs. *Remember Jekyll Island*. Minneapolis: Langdon Street, 2010.

Olmstead, Marty. *Hidden Georgia: Including Atlanta, Savannah, Jekyll Island, and the Okefenokee*. Berkeley, Calif.: Ulysses, 2005.

Reese, Trevor R. *Colonial Georgia: A Study in British Imperial Policy in the Eighteenth Century*. Athens: University of Georgia Press, 1963.

Rickenbach, Richard V. "Filibustering with the *Dauntless*." *Florida Historical Quarterly* 28, no. 4 (Apr. 1950): 231–53.

Sandrik, Al, and Brian Jarvinen. "A Re-evaluation of the Georgia and Northeast Florida Tropical Cyclone of 2 October 1898." In *Preprints of the 23rd Conference on Hurricanes and Tropical Meteorology*, 475–78. Boston: American Meteorological Society. Accessed Dec. 22, 2013. www.srh.noaa.gov/jax/?n=cyclone_1898.

Schoettle, Taylor. *A Guide to a Georgia Barrier Island: Featuring Jekyll Island with St. Simons and Sapelo Islands*. H. E. Taylor Schoettle, 1996.

Snow, Tony. "The Night Britain Burned Down the White House and Stole the President's Clothes." *Daily Mail*, Sept. 6, 2013. Accessed Mar. 13, 2014. www.dailymail.co.uk/news/article-2414528/War-1812-Special-relationship-Britain-burned-White-House-stole-Presidents-clothes.html.

Stephens, William. *Stephens' Journal, 1737–1740. The Colonial Records of the State of Georgia*, vol. 4. Edited by Allen D. Candler. Atlanta: Franklin, 1906.

Vanstory, Bernette. *Georgia's Land of the Golden Isles*. Athens: University of Georgia Press, 1981. Orig. pub. 1956.

Verne, Violette. *Glynn County, Georgia: Including Its History, the Jekyll Island Museum, the Fort Frederica National Monument, and More*. Earth Eyes Travel Guides, 2012.

Wells, Tom Henderson. *The Slave Ship "Wanderer."* Athens: University of Georgia Press, 1967.

Wilkes, Elizabeth Geiger. *Jekyll Island: A Visual Tour*. Fernandina, Ga.: Wilkes Helicopter Services, 2007.

Wood, Virginia Steele, and Mary R. Bullard, eds. *The Journal of a Visit to the Georgia Islands of St. Catherines, Green, Ossabaw, Sapelo, St. Simons, Jekyll and Cumberland with Comments on the Florida Islands of Amelia, Talbot, and St. George in 1753*. Macon, Ga.: Mercer University Press, 1996.

Wylly, Charles Spalding. *Memories and Annals*. Brunswick, Ga: Glover Brothers, [1916?]. Available in the Digital Library of Georgia, University of Georgia Libraries. Accessed Sept. 27, 2013. http://dlg.galileo.usg.edu/meta/html/dlg/zlgb/meta_dlg_zlgb_gb0394.html?Welcome

Index